DCR   HIS   3/24   £3
EURO.

D1345835

Chasing Shadows

HUGO GRYN

with NAOMI GRYN

VIKING

VIKING

Published by the Penguin Group
Penguin Books Ltd, 27 Wrights Lane, London w8 5tz, England
Penguin Putnam Inc., 375 Hudson Street, New York, New York 10014, USA
Penguin Books Australia Ltd, Ringwood, Victoria, Australia
Penguin Books Canada Ltd, 10 Alcorn Avenue, Toronto, Ontario, Canada m4v 3b2
Penguin Books (NZ) Ltd, Private Bag 102902, NSMC, Auckland, New Zealand

Penguin Books Ltd, Registered Offices: Harmondsworth, Middlesex, England

First published 2000
First published in Great Britain by Viking 2000
3 5 7 9 10 8 6 4 2

Copyright © The Estate of Hugo Gryn, 2000
Introduction copyright © Naomi Gryn, 2000

The moral right of the author has been asserted

All rights reserved
Without limiting the rights under copyright
reserved above, no part of this publication may be
reproduced, stored in or introduced into a retrieval system,
or transmitted, in any form or by any means (electronic, mechanical,
photocopying, recording or otherwise), without the prior
written permission of both the copyright owner and
the above publisher of this book

Set in 11.25/15pt Monotype Trump Medieval
Typeset by Rowland Phototypesetting Ltd,
Bury St Edmunds, Suffolk
Printed in England by Clays Ltd, St Ives, plc

A CIP catalogue record for this book is available from the British Library

ISBN 0-670-88793-5

Do not mistake shadows for reality and waste your life chasing after trivial things which cannot really help you.

Maimonides
(1135–1204)

The whole world is a narrow bridge; the important thing is not to be afraid.

Rabbi Nachman of Bratslav
(1772–1810)

Contents

Acknowledgements

With grateful appreciation to Mara Vishniac Kohn for allowing me to use her father Roman Vishniac's photographs of Carpathian Jews and to Magdalena Ignáczy for the use of her father Géza Ignáczy's photographs of Berehovo. Other illustrations were provided by Vera Gotesman, the Katz family, Imre Klein, Max Lebowitz, Erwin Leiser, the Lieberose Archive, Magyar Munkásmozgalmi Múzeum, the Wiener Library and Yad Vashem.

Preparation of the text for publication was made possible by a grant from the Memorial Foundation for Jewish Culture. Anton Gill and Melanie Phillips gave permission to use their quotations. Jud Fisher gave permission to reproduce his grandfather Major Cameron Coffman's 1945 news release about the liberation of Gunskirchen which I found on John Mooney's website (http://www.remember.org).

Andreas Weigelt in Lieberose and Natasha Arapova in Berehovo diligently responded to my endless queries and were both extremely accommodating and helpful. The copyediting was painstakingly executed by Martin Bryant. Rachelle Gryn Brettler, Shula Chalif, David Gryn, Jacqueline Gryn, József Katz, Juliet Landau-Pope, Gabrielle Massey and Agnes Whyte checked proofs and offered many welcome suggestions and improvements, as did Sir Martin Gilbert who also contributed invaluable advice on maps and railways.

Krishan Arora, Benjamin Kuras, Susie Halter and Gőngyi Moskovic generously shared their linguistic skills. Professor Chimen Abramsky, Professor David Cesarani, Eva Geddis, Dr Jerry

Hochbaum, Anna Kobryn, Rosemarie Nief, Maria Pont, Edward Roberts, David Seidel, Dr Alice Shalvi, Eugene Shvedkov, Kay Thomson, Anne Webber and Paula Weiman-Kelman contributed expertise, inspiration and other acts of kindness.

Grief is a great big onion and I am especially grateful to Dr Michael Harding, Rabbi Na'amah Kelman, Dr Derry Macdiarmid and Paul Tucker who, with heroic patience and compassion, helped mop up my tears. Thanks also to Bob Towler who commissioned our film for Channel 4 and to Juliet Gardiner who nearly convinced my father to finish this book in 1990.

Above all, I am indebted to Tony Lacey at Viking and to my – and my late father's – agent Peter Robinson for their unfailing enthusiasm and encouragement, and to Jeremy Ettinghausen and Camilla Hornby for not losing their sense of humour, even when I turned into a fire-breathing dragon, which sometimes happens when you spend too much time thinking about dead dads and the Holocaust.

I remember my father's words on the day that Adam Massey – his first grandson – was born: 'If you had told me when I was fourteen years old that I would not only survive the war, but that one day I would become a grandfather, I would have rolled over and died laughing.' This book is dedicated to Adam, Clio, Isaac, Joseph and to all of Hugo's descendants because they will carry into the future not just his story, but also his spirit of hope and indomitability. May his memory be a blessing.

N.S.G.

List of Illustrations

Maps

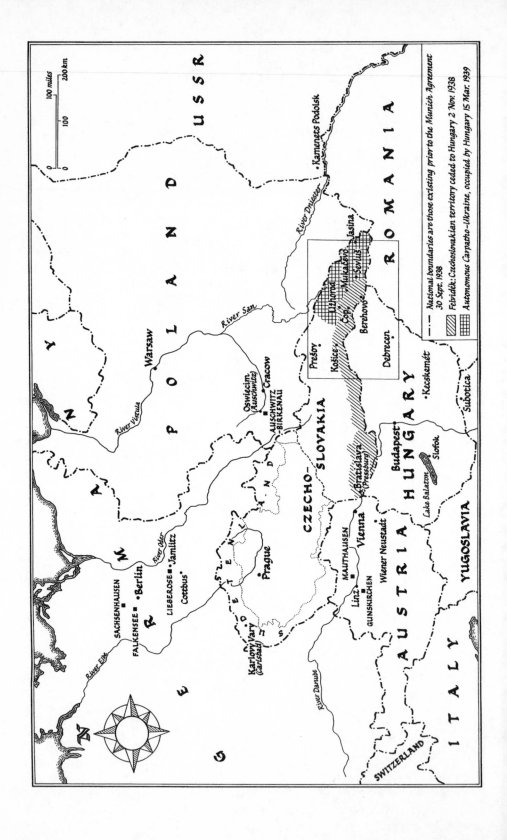

100 miles
100
200 km

U S S R

P O L A N D

· Kamenets Podolsk

R O M A N I A

River Dniester

Jasina

Uzhorod · Mukačevo · Sevluš

Prešov · Cop · Berehovo

Košice · Debrecen

National boundaries are those existing prior to the Munich Agreement 30 Sept. 1938

Felvidék: Czechoslovakian territory ceded to Hungary 2 Nov. 1938

Autonomous Carpatho–Ukraine, occupied by Hungary 15 Mar. 1939

River San

Warsaw

River Vistula

Oświęcim (Auschwitz)
Cracow

AUSCHWITZ-BIRKENAU

· Kecskemét

CZECHO-SLOVAKIA

H U N G A R Y

Budapest

· Subotica

S U D E T E N L A N D

Prague

Bratislava (Pressburg)

Lake Balaton
· Siófok

G E R M A N Y

SACHSENHAUSEN
· Berlin
FALKENSEE ■
LIEBEROSE · Jamlitz
Cottbus ·

River Oder

River Elbe

Karlovy Vary (Carlsbad)

MAUTHAUSEN ■
Linz ■ Vienna
GUNSKIRCHEN
Wiener Neustadt

A U S T R I A

River Danube

SWITZERLAND

I T A L Y

Y U G O S L A V I A

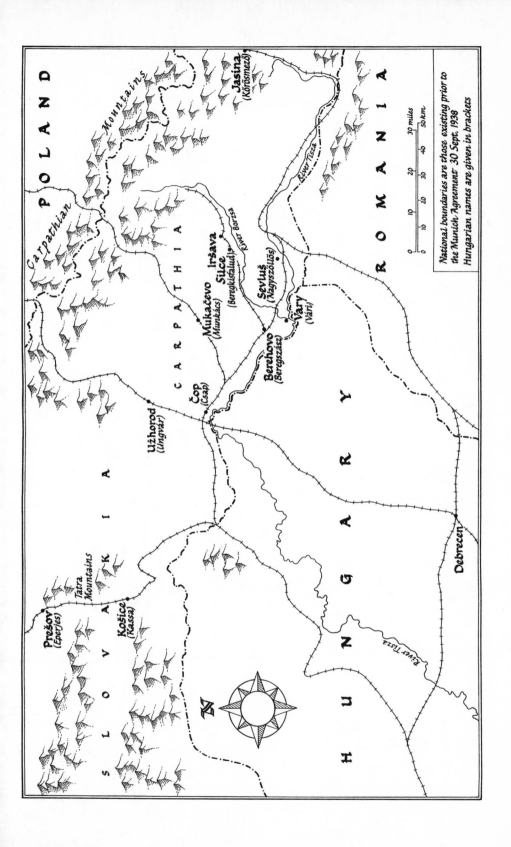

POLAND

Carpathian

Mountains

Jasina
(Kőrösmező)

CARPATHIA

River Borzsa

Iršava
(Bregkisfalud)

Mukačevo
(Munkács)

Silce

Sevluš
(Nagyszőllős)

Berehovo
(Beregszász)

Čop
(Csap)

Vary
(Vári)

River Tisza

Užhorod
(Ungvár)

S L O V A K I A

Prešov
(Eperjes)

Tatra Mountains

Košice
(Kassa)

H U N G A R Y

Debrecen

River Tisza

R O M A N I A

National boundaries are those existing prior to
the Munich Agreement 30 Sept. 1938
Hungarian names are given in brackets

30 miles

50 km

0   10   20   30   40

0   10   20   30

Introduction

A STRANGE LEGACY

In the days that followed the shattering news of my father's final illness, he appointed me to keep him entertained during whatever remained of his ordeal. It was a gruesome challenge, but one I could not refuse. I was helpless to prevent my father being devoured by his cancer, and then diabetes and pneumonia – complications of the drugs that the doctors insisted were keeping him alive – but I made it my mission to find ways to distract him.

I returned from our local library with a selection of videos. My father loved comedies and I had tried to find a film that would lift his sombre mood. *Funny Bones*, starring Jerry Lewis, sounded like a good fit. We sat together on the sofa in my parents' living room and I watched with horror as the black comedy, which mostly took place in the morgue of an out-of-season seaside town, unfurled its morbid and wholly unsuitable tale. But my father was engaged with it and besides he had seen all the other videos in my pile. There was a musical theme running through the film and my father recognized it, but he could not quite recall its name. Suddenly he blurted out: 'I know! It's "Caravan". It was a hit song in Lieberose!' Well done, Nao! I had managed to pick out a film that reminded him of the miserable camp where he and his father, Géza, had spent several months as slave labourers during the Second World War.

But that is how it was in our house. The shadow of those

awful times hovered above our heads like a cloud of sadness, while we made the most of all the sunny days. And now I too know what it is to be robbed of someone you love very much, to watch them die in front of you, just as my father watched his father fade in front of him a few days after they had been liberated by the Americans in May 1945.

The public response to my father's death was quite overwhelming. Obituaries blared out from every direction and there were many wonderful tributes. Volunteers had to be recruited to help open thousands of letters of condolence. He was mourned and celebrated as a national hero.

In the *Observer* (25 August 1996), Melanie Phillips wrote:

What was it about him that touched a chord in so many people? At root, it was surely that in an age searching with increasing desperation for moral guidance, he didn't preach moral authority – he embodied it. As a teenager in Auschwitz, he had witnessed people performing the greatest, and to us unimaginable, evil upon their fellow human beings and he had risen above the whole experience, transmuted the horror into a life-affirming generosity and sweetness of spirit which only looked forwards, never backwards.

He was not merely a survivor of the Holocaust which had claimed his father, brother and grandparents. He turned that incomprehensible experience into a source of humanity and hopefulness. He emerged from it with no bitterness or hatred. Not that he ever minimized what had happened by an inappropriate forgiveness; his profound sense of justice meant he neither forgave nor forgot. Anger, after all, is a moral response. But he accepted what had passed and embraced life, devoting his own not to dwelling on what had happened, but to preventing such things from ever happening again . . . he always fought by seeking to heal, to reconcile, never to blame and thus divide.

It was a fantastic send-off but I was not yet ready to hear references to my father in the past tense. As soon as I could, I left for Israel to hide under a rock until my grief had subsided a little. It took many months to conjure enough courage to return to London and begin work on the other job he had entrusted to me – to take care of his extensive collection of books and papers which crammed the elegant 1930s office at the West London Synagogue where he had been Rabbi for thirty-two years. As I started to catalogue and box up his books and belongings, I surveyed the vast breadth of my father's knowledge and interests and it quite took my breath away. And I understood how, through this priceless legacy of radio scripts, sermons, letters and talks, even after his death I could continue to enjoy – and share with others – something of my father's unique humour and magnificent intellect.

Buried in a drawer beneath a pile of ancient bank statements and cheque-book stubs, I found a worn orange foolscap folder. Inside was the handwritten manuscript of a book my father had begun in October 1951. Immediately I understood that this was my father's first attempt to record the tale of his family's descent into the Nazi inferno. At first, I could not bring myself to read it, fearing that it might be more dreadful than anything I could have imagined, but my father's charm pervades even the retelling of this most awful episode, written in recently acquired English when he was just twenty-one, when the images were still so fresh in his mind.

My father refers to himself in these chapters as Hugo Green. He used to tell the story of how, when he first arrived in Britain in February 1946, the immigration officer had asked him for his name. In those days he spoke no English at all, but understood the sentiment. 'Gryn,' he said. G-R-E-E-N, wrote the official. 'Nem,' said my father, 'ipsilon', and pointed vigorously at this unfamiliar spelling of his family name. Ipsilon. Hungarian for 'y'. Bemused, the official led him by the hand and showed him to the toilet. 'Green' was the spelling he sported proudly until the mid-1950s when he was naturalized as an American citizen and began to feel more confident about his exotic roots. He reverted officially to 'Gryn' (rather than the more Teutonic alternative 'Grün'), and at the same time he took as his middle name that of his murdered brother, Gabriel.

He has chosen English equivalents for many of the names and there are certain anomalies, such as the 'reincarnation' of a younger brother, Clem (Kálmán), who had actually died in infancy. As my father puts it: '. . . little exaggerations ought to be excused, but this is a personal account'.

He writes in the voice of a thirteen-year-old trying to make sense of the drama unfolding around him, as the fragile mask of civilization begins to crumble. He details the gradual process of dehumanization and describes his feelings of frustration and humiliation as well as his shock when he discovers the truth about Auschwitz. His narrative finishes abruptly in the middle of the third chapter, soon after his arrival at Lieberose, which means 'lovely rose', but which was actually a very nasty *Arbeitslager*, or labour camp, in Upper Silesia. Perhaps the next months were too terrible for him to revisit. Or perhaps he was distracted by matters more pressing, such as his studies at Hebrew Union College in Cincinnati, where he was preparing to become a rabbi. But along with his text and a hand-drawn map of Lieberose, I found three pages of notes highlighting the other episodes he had intended to relate, and I used these as the basis of the final chapters in which I have pieced together some of his missing tale.

Some weeks after he died, while I was still in Jerusalem clinging to seclusion like a barnacle, I heard that Jan (Yossi) Czuker, a childhood friend of my father, was also in town. They were in the *lagers** together until the end of the war

* From *Konzentrationslager*, concentration camp.

and it was a legend in our family how once, when Jan had an epileptic fit during a forced march, my father had heroically put down his blanket and carried Jan instead for the rest of the day.

In May 1996, only three months before my father's death, Jan convinced my parents to join him and his wife, Susanne, in accepting an invitation from Andreas Weigelt in Lieberose, to visit the camp in which they had once been prisoners. My father had always been adamant that he had no desire ever to set foot again in Germany, but Jan was persuasive and my father finally agreed. To his great surprise, he found the trip both enjoyable and curiously healing. He was tickled pink to discover that the little museum where Andreas was curator had included a special exhibit on the Gryn family.

Jan and I met and reminisced. He told me how, after their liberation from Gunskirchen in Austria, they had shared a barracks. One day, Jan had gone outside and was told that there was room for him on a lorry which was about to leave for a hospital. He was given no time to say goodbye but, not wanting to miss such an opportunity, he had jumped on board. That was how they lost contact with each other – and why my father had assumed that Jan had died – until an exciting reunion in 1988.

Jan then remarked that, as far as he knew, it was extremely rare in the *lagers* for a father and son to survive together as Hugo and Géza had done. I was struck by the profundity of this observation – how, throughout all their horrific months in captivity, my father had been shielded by his own father's love – and it became crystal clear where my father had learnt his skills as Super Dad.

He had an instinctive commitment to protect the weak and the vulnerable, and his capacity for responsibility was unlimited. Gentle, caring, funny, inspiring, generous to a fault and extraordinarily wise. And the sweetest, most loving father to my brother, my sisters and me. I savour my memories of the marvellous years we shared, each of which I unwrap like priceless gemstones.

As a child, I developed a chronic antipathy towards Bar Mitzvah parties, which I attributed to an intense dislike of the ubiquitous snare drum. Quite a disability for a rabbi's daughter. So my father took me to a performance of Ravel's *Bolero* at the Albert Hall and I was cured. Every moment we spent together was a joyful journey of discovery, and through his eyes the world was full of wonder, an ever-unfolding mystery, scripted and stage-managed by Hugo's Big Buddy, God.

My father could make me laugh at even my greatest misfortunes – the pain of a broken leg would pale into insignificance under the spell of his charm. 'You have two Jewish mothers!' he would declare to justify his overzealous parental concern. Certainly he was very protective, but always encouraged my unquenchable thirst for adventure and often found space in his hectic schedule to drive me to Victoria Station or Heathrow when I was setting off on one of my jaunts.

He loved jazz, klezmer,* Mozart, *M.A.S.H.,* the Marx Brothers, Mel Brooks, Humphrey Bogart and Lauren Bacall, Westerns, Woody Allen, Dave Allen, Phil Silvers (everyone remarked how they looked just like brothers), the *Nine O'Clock News*; anything starring cherished congregants Felicity Kendal and Maureen Lipman, natural redheads, Kafka, crummy thrillers, fresh figs and breakfast in bed.

My father's lust for life was indisputable, yet he remained a creature of habit and modest taste. When we went out to eat, it was invariably for tandoori chicken or to Pizza Express, where he would always ask to see the menu but never failed to order an American Hot with a bottle of Peroni beer.

He taught me about justice and equality, respect for good wine and single malt whisky, and never to fear the unknown.

---

* Jewish soul music.

He instilled in me an insatiable curiosity about our shared Jewish heritage, which spilled into much of my own work. As did my father, who, as a victim of several of my film-making enterprises, dubbed me his 'director with the iron whim'.

Whenever I could, on Friday evenings I would join my father at his synagogue. If he was leading the service, he would catch my eye as soon as I entered and we would bow towards each other, beaming with silent appreciation. I hung on to every word of his sermons, as I did his lectures and broadcasts. It made me swell with pride to see how he could win the hearts and rapt attention of any audience with his tobacco-stained, chocolate-brown voice and his animated hand gestures which spoke in a language of their own. If he was sitting in the congregation, I would find a place next to him and we would pray and sometimes play together, singing with great confidence, but often shamelessly off-key. Afterwards, I would hover while he greeted his congregants and put away his robes. Then we would walk home, arm in arm, along Bryanston Square, discussing Spinoza, Freud, Maimonides, dramatic happenings in Anglo-Jewry. Or else I would harangue him with Interesting Thoughts prompted by his sermon, and by the time we reached my parents' flat in Marylebone the tensions of the working week would have faded into history. For me, anyway.

Shabbat and Jewish holidays were always magical occasions, as were all our family celebrations. Friends thought it strange that I never tired of my family's company, but the atmosphere around our dinner table, usually alive with visitors from far and wide, had a powerful allure. Relaxed after a shot of whisky or a large slivovitz poured ice-cold straight from the freezer, my father would sit at the head of the table and welcome everyone with a specially tailored announcement about each of our latest triumphs or disasters. Then he would raise a glass of well-chosen wine and toast 'l'chaim', to life. He was the ultimate host. His seemingly endless store of jokes and anecdotes, improved and embellished with every new telling, was matched only by my mother's bottomless pot of perfect chicken soup and a repertoire of hearty Hungarian dishes which would evoke for my father fond memories of his distant childhood home.

I grew up on stories that my father told me about his wondrous childhood in the town of Berehovo. Once upon a time, in a faraway fairy-tale land beneath the Carpathian mountains, where children drank wine instead of water, and uncles played violin with the Gypsies under a moon that was always full . . . Of course I always knew that there was no happy ending and that something unimaginably awful had happened to him and his family, that everyone he loved had vanished into a place where they threw live babies into ovens. My mother never cooked boiled cabbage because the smell reminded him of burning flesh and gave him bad dreams, while we – my two sisters Gaby and Rachelle, and my brother David – never asked for the end of the story because we did not want to add to his pain. Nor did he want to burden us with his grief, or with the guilt that is peculiar to survivors, and between us lay a void of silence.

I was thirteen when my father brought me to Israel to celebrate my Bat Mitzvah. He showed me the land of our ancestors, from the Sinai in the south to the orange groves of Galilee. And we came to Yad Vashem, the memorial in Jerusalem to the martyrs of the *Shoah*.* Stopping at a model of Auschwitz-Birkenau, he pointed to one of the barracks and said: 'That is where I spent a few weeks with my father when I was your age.' It was the beginning of his nightmare tale, the one that until then I had not been ready to hear.

Many years later, having survived an inevitable explosion of teenage rebellion without getting pregnant or developing any major drug addiction, my childhood habit of documenting

---

* Hebrew term for the Holocaust, meaning 'catastrophe'.

daily life with a pocket Instamatic camera had blossomed into a career as a documentary film maker. I had my own production company and one day suggested to my father that we make a film that would follow his first return to Berehovo – then part of the Soviet Union – since 1945.

We have become so accustomed to seeing the same monochrome images of mounds of rotting corpses being shovelled into mass graves, of the emaciated survivors of the Nazi death camps, naked or dressed in filthy rags, exhausted by sickness, starvation and incomprehensible suffering, that they have become almost worn-out and clichéd. Sometimes the response is indifference; more grotesquely, it sometimes verges on the pornographic. My father and I wanted to give our audience a microcosmic peep into *what* was destroyed in the *Shoah*, the life and the culture that had disappeared for ever when the thick curtain of night and fog was drawn across the stage of European Jewry. We decided to make a very intimate portrait of the world of his childhood, through which people might be able to identify more closely with the pain of its annihilation, and not to delve beyond May 1944, when his family, together with all the other Jews of Berehovo, were deported to Auschwitz.

When we hit on the title *Chasing Shadows*, it held great resonance for us both. My mission was to give shape to the swirling shadows of my father's past, which are part of my shadow also. The making of the film afforded me two years' hunting through the archives in London, Prague, Budapest, Israel, and the United States, and I was able to bring together a magnificent collection of photographs and archive film: of raftsmen and farmers, Gypsies, Ruthenians and Jews; newsreel of the day the Hungarians entered Berehovo; and a documentary showing the very sawmill and vineyard my grandfather once part-owned. I even managed to obtain a photograph of my great-great-grandmother Roizi from a distant relative in the United States. I built up a vivid image of a world where, despite poverty and isolation, the land was bountiful and many communities lived together in harmony.

I saw for the first time a book known as the *Auschwitz Album*, which shows the only known photographs of the arrival and selection of Jews at Auschwitz, taken by SS photographers. Incredibly, I learned from the foreword that the only identified faces were of Jews who had gone through the Berehovo ghetto. My father and I pored over the pictures, looking for the faces of his own family – perhaps his own – but the only face he thought he recognized was that of his former *cheder** teacher, Mr Jakubovics.

I spent the summer of 1988 in Israel, scouring libraries and archives and meeting former citizens of Berehovo. Of its pre-war Jewish population of 10,000, about 800 survived, and most seem to live in the seaside town of Netanya where the coffee shops echo with tales from the Old Country and lousy Hungarian jokes. They showered me with welcome and I had the feeling that the history they shared with my father gave them all the roles of honorary uncles and aunts.

Also for the first time, I met my father's cousin, Patyu, a.k.a. József Katz, who had also been with my father and grandfather in the camps. Like my father, Patyu had returned to Carpathia after liberation, to see who else might come home, but that is where Patyu stayed and he only managed to leave the Soviet Union for Israel in 1975. I visited him often that summer in his framing shop on Bograshov Street, near the beach in Tel Aviv, as I still like to do whenever I can. His wife, Joli, offered me coffee and cakes while I interrogated Patyu about great-uncles and aunts, grandparents and great-grandparents and about life in Carpathia under the hammer and sickle. He said he would give anything to come with us to Berehovo, although at that time it was still unheard of for Jews who had left the Soviet Union to return as tourists.

* Traditional Jewish elementary school.

Our nails were bitten down to the quick waiting for permission for Patyu's visit. It was granted only a week before
we set off, but true to style, he managed to reach Berehovo
the day before we did.

The filming itself, in May 1989, was an unforgettable experience. We were a veritable circus. My loving, ever-dependable
sister, Rachelle, as production assistant, Michael Darlow – a
most supportive executive producer who came to protect
me from the unwanted scrutiny of the representative of the
Novosti press agency assigned to our project – and a crew
hand-picked in the hope that they would be able to withstand
the emotional aspects of such a pilgrimage. They were all
vastly overqualified for such a modest television documentary, but *glasnost* was then still a new addition to our
vocabulary and we were each keen to explore this recently
opened corner of the Soviet Empire.

Our entourage included Agnes Whyte (née Kálmán), also
from Berehovo (who so wanted to see her home town again
that she offered to be our 'runner' and proved to be an elegant
and exceptionally useful addition to the team), my father's
cousin Simcha Neufeld, a.k.a. József Horvat, whom I had met
on a research trip to Budapest, and several other amiable
hangers-on. We had forty-three boxes of equipment with us
– enough to fill the coach we hired in Slovakia – and we
reached the Soviet border in the middle of the night. The
customs official checked every item and it was nearly dawn
when we arrived.

The town was exactly as my father had described it, and a
perfect location for a fairy-tale. It was as if time had stood
still. The streets were still cobbled, milk churns left outside
to be refilled when the milkman turned up with his horse
and cart. In Berehovo's three restaurants, the musicians had
swapped violins and accordions for electric guitars and key-
boards, but the melodies they played were not so very different
from the tunes of my father's youth, and they all still had in

their repertoire one Yiddish song that seemed so pertinent, *Mein Stetl Belz*, 'My Little Town Belz'.

My father was in a kind of fog. For him the town was filled with shadows and every street corner littered with ghosts. It was frightening to see him looking so vulnerable, and I was hugely relieved that he had some company with whom he could talk about the old days and look up long-lost friends and acquaintances. People came from miles around when they heard that Patyu was back in town. He organized our roubles and our laundry collection and shared a bedroom with my father, since there was a shortage of accommodation in what was the only hotel in Berehovo. The town's sewage system was in bad need of repair and there was an appalling stench in the bathroom, but when my father remarked on this, Patyu replied: 'Ah, Hugo, the last time we shared a room it was much worse!'

There were many technical problems to contend with and so little electrical power available that we had to link up every house in the street in order to light a single interior. But we were welcomed everywhere with open arms and plenty of vodka, and when it turned out that Berehovo's Secretary-General was related to us by marriage, nothing was too much trouble. He even arranged matters so that when we returned to Slovakia we were given an official escort and the border guards received us like visiting dignitaries. 'The best ten days in the history of the Gryn family!' said Patyu, with tears in his eyes when it was over.

We asked everyone we met if they had any photographs taken before the deportations. Agnes struck gold when she discovered Magdalena Ignáczy, the daughter of Berehovo's official town photographer in the 1940s who lent me all her father's negatives to print up when I returned to London, but there was not much other response. Then, as we gathered outside the only synagogue still functioning in Berehovo for the Friday evening service, a woman handed me a picture of

Berehovo's Jewish Elementary School. It was the class of 1942–3. I passed the photograph to my father. The colour drained from his face. Pointing to one of the children, he gasped, 'That's Gabi in the back row.' It was as if his brother had found a way to say hello.

One day, we were filming in Vary, the village on the Hungarian border where Patyu and my grandfather's family had once lived. In a derelict Jewish cemetery, we were saying Kaddish, the Jewish prayer for the dead, at the grave of a revered great-great-grandmother, Esther. My father turned to me and said, 'Picture this, once there were hundreds of villages just like this all over Carpathia.' And I could. Calm, contented villages dotting the luscious countryside, where Jews had lived side by side with their non-Jewish neighbours for centuries. Tending the land and running the inns. Studying Torah and waiting for the Messiah. I could also picture my great-grandfather Jacob, with his white beard and hat. A pious farmer, best known for his cure for toothache. And just as easily, I could imagine my uncle Gabi, forever ten years old, with a cheeky grin. In that very same moment, I could see them outside the gas chambers of Auschwitz, getting undressed and walking hand in hand towards their senseless deaths.

In that cemetery, on that day, I somehow bridged the divide between the vanished world of my father's childhood and the monstrous hell that had consumed it. I cried from the depths of my soul and understood it less than ever.

The film, shown first on Channel 4 in 1991 and repeated after my father's death, was an enormous success, but in fifty-two minutes it could hardly do justice to his story. Wanting to encourage him to record more, my brother, sisters and I clubbed together to buy him a state-of-the-art Sony Walkman for his sixtieth birthday, on which we inscribed his name – Hugo Gabriel Gryn. In his desk, after all these years, I found the card which had accompanied our gift. On one side of the card was a tawny owl listening to a 1935 wireless and on the back we had written: 'For all your wise words . . .' Now I am using the same machine to transcribe the many hours of recollections he recorded into it, often while he and I sat together in his study at home, because he found it easier to talk to an audience and I was always his shadow puppet, his most eager muse.

Sadly, the book was never finished. His heavy workload and busy diary kept getting in the way. The tapes and transcripts sat in a box, waiting patiently for his retirement, but that, too, was never to be realized. My father did find time to edit the first few chapters and elsewhere scribbled notes indicating where he intended to expand on certain themes.

In compiling this book, I found it difficult to decide whether to make any changes to his text at all. I concluded that since, undoubtedly, I would have helped my father edit the book had he finished it himself, I should do so now, but with a light hand. I have tried to standardize his spellings and transliterations, and even though I have decimated his use of inverted commas, there are plenty left as evidence; the round brackets are mostly my father's, the square ones are mine. I have added footnotes for clarification, and where corrections were necessary I have tried to keep the tone as close as I could to my father's voice. Chapters 1 to 10 of what follows were written in 1990; chapters 11 to 13 were written in 1951; chapters 14 and 15 were compiled from various articles and broadcasts that he made, as well as occasional interviews that I had recorded with him myself.

My father often remarked that his recall of the camps, especially of names and faces, had become blurred over the years. I have attempted to verify facts wherever possible, but many of the dates and statistics documented are contradictory. Andreas Weigelt tells me that Lieberose was evacuated – and the prisoners who were too sick to march, massacred – on 2 February 1945; but intriguingly, in later years my father remembered this death march as having taken place in December 1944. He always celebrated the anniversary of his liberation on 5 May, while the Americans actually reached Gunskirchen one day earlier, on 4 May 1945. And he was deeply perplexed that he had forgotten the date of his father's death.

Once I asked my father whether he had ever lost his sanity in the camps. He told me how, at the end of their forced march from Lieberose to Sachsenhausen, they stopped first at Falkensee, near Berlin. There they were taken to be showered and deloused. When my father was standing naked and skinny under the shower, he became convinced that they were about to be gassed: 'We'd come through the selection at Auschwitz, all the miseries of Lieberose and a death march only to be killed now.' He told me how, at that moment, he was so scared that he temporarily lost his mind and even though hot water soon began to burst through the showerheads, it took quite a while before he could recover his equilibrium.

This is not the only story of significance that is missing from these texts. Whenever my family meets for dinner on Friday evenings, I watch my beautiful mother light the Shabbat candles and remember how my father would tell newcomers to our table how, even while they were being rounded up to be taken to the ghetto, this same pair of silver candlesticks had been buried in the garden by my grandmother Bella, together with my grandfather's silver *kiddush* cup, their *chanukiah* – the eight-branched candelabrum used during Chanukah – and my father's excellent school report of that year. They were still there when my grandmother returned home after the war and eventually she managed to smuggle them out to my father – evidently some time after he had written in 1951 his description of their deportation to Auschwitz. For my father, that these family treasures had survived the war was a powerful parable about the values that his mother cherished most: not her furs and jewellery, but the symbols of a Jewish home. Together with a handful of photographs, these precious heirlooms are the only tangible remnants of my father's past.

Nor does my father refer to what happened in 1954 when he was sent as a student rabbi to officiate at the High Holy Day services in Jasper, Alabama. How, when he met the president of the congregation, J. George Mitnick, it struck my father that his name was surprisingly familiar. Looking through his documents, my father discovered that in 1945 his liberation papers had been signed by the same J. George Mitnick, then an officer in the US Army. Cemented by such a historic bond, this first professional assignment was a great success. 'Hugo Green received from everyone the same prophecy: "This young man is going places, remember his name." Mitnick wrote to one of Hugo's teachers: 'His mesmeric charm had all our children throwing their arms around him and kissing him. All the kids vied with one another to sit next to him. We have never had such a tremendous upsurge of religious feeling and warmth in our community before. We like Hugo Green. We want him back once a month. Please exercise every effort to return him to us.'

We concluded our film *Chasing Shadows* with the dedication: 'For Bella, Géza, Gabi and the Jews of Berehovo and all the love, learning and laughter that is no more. *Zikronom l'vracha*. May their memory be a blessing.' I imagine that my father would have dedicated this book in a similar vein. Originally it was conceived as a kind of eulogy for his family and community, but it also charts the evolution of the ethical code which guided him for the rest of his life.

Amongst Jews, there is a tradition of spiritual legacies which stretches back as far as Moses and Jacob. In bygone times, rabbis used to impart final words of wisdom to their communities with instructions about the proper way to live a Jewish life. The impoverished Jews of Eastern Europe could not bequeath to their offspring wealth and property – for there was little to leave – instead they wrote an 'ethical will', their blueprint for how people ought to be. In 1995, I made a radio programme which I called *A Strange Legacy*, about how Jews are preserving the story of the *Shoah* for posterity. Recording an interview with my father, I asked how he would want this devastating chapter in our people's history passed on to his own descendants:

> I would like you to try and convey to those who'll come after you this very specific thing, that you come from a world that was a beautiful world, that was caring, that was God-fearing, that had a very high set of values. It was honest, it was hardworking, it prized learning, the gifts of the spirit and of the intellect. It was in fact civilized, and whatever you do, make sure that something of what makes for genuine civiliz-ation gets carried into the rising generations. That will be the finest way in which you will honour the memory of those who went before you. (BBC Radio 4, 1995)

Only a year later, still blissfully ignorant of the tumours already growing inside his noble head, but with macabre foresight, I asked him what he would like as his epitaph. Without hesitation, he quoted from the book of Micah: 'Do justice, love mercy and walk humbly with your God.' This was my father's creed. His genuine humility, his kindness and lack of pretentiousness endeared him to all. He reserved anger only for the petty and bigoted, the thoughtless and the inconsiderate, which included traffic wardens, reckless drivers, and anyone with bad body odour.

The cancer was diagnosed in June 1996, the day after my father married – so to speak – my brother, David, to Jane, his radiant bride. We had gathered in my parents' living room – my mother, Jackie; the newly-weds about to set off for their honeymoon; Gaby, visiting from New York for the wedding with her husband, David Massey, and their children, Adam and Clio; Rachelle and me. We should have been excitedly extolling the virtues of the previous day, but my father was already feeling deathly ill and we were all anxious, waiting for him to return from his appointment with a neurologist. When he finally arrived, I poured him a whisky. 'Kids,' he said, 'I'm afraid I've got some bad news.'

The next day was his sixty-sixth birthday, but no one felt much like celebrating. Within weeks, he had become emaciated and what was left of his hair had fallen out through the twin effects of steroids and radiotherapy. It was as if the *Shoah* had reclaimed him after all these years, as if his survival had been only a temporary loan. Pneumonia was filling his lungs, making every breath an effort of sheer willpower. I was trying to sell my dear, dying father my latest cosmic theory, that maybe bacteria and viruses feel that they have a right to this planet too.

'Yes, Naomi,' he whispered, 'but the thing is, we have to learn how to get on with each other.'

Naomi Gryn

There are so many doorways – and so many memories chasing in and out of them:

Of Uncle Dezső – director of the Jewish bank who came to his sisters' home every Shabbat and for whom they religiously saved the jellied carp's head.

Of Uncle Viktor – so meticulous – and how once returning from Prague we heard an angry exchange about the quality of cheese in the dining car – and my father whispering – 'Your uncle Viktor is on the train!' – and he was.

Of Uncle Marci – who used a very bad smelling depilatory because of the biblical prohibition against shaving with a razor – and me planning to visit my lovely cousin – Zvi Hirsh, of course – when it wasn't a 'shaving day'.

Of my best friend's house – Dénes – so bright and so much fun – and I am ashamed because I cannot recall his full name.

Of a garden gate where I waited for hours to catch a glimpse of Éva – whom I loved but hadn't the nerve ever to speak to her – and how I wish I had . . .

Of Gabi – such a splendid brother and I grieve because when it mattered – I could not protect him . . .

H.G.G.
16 April 1989

I

CHASING SHADOWS

My previous return to Berehovo was in the summer of 1945. It was just a few weeks after the war. I had barely recovered from typhoid and the effects of starvation. After many adventures on the journey from Austria heading east, I found myself on the train from Budapest to my home town. I was travelling alone, but convinced that if anyone else from our family had managed to survive then surely they, too, would return to Berehovo in the hope that there would be a reunion.

A man got on the train at Čop* – where you now left Hungary and entered the Soviet Union – who recognized me. He was delighted to tell me that my mother was waiting for the return of my father and me because she had heard that we were both liberated from Gunskirchen, a concentration camp in Austria. The news was wonderful and terrifying at the same time. The fact was that a few days after liberation, my father had died. Suddenly the prospect of the encounter with my mother filled me with great fear. How was I to tell her what had happened? What would be her reaction?

When the train finally pulled into Berehovo's station, I refused to get off. The man I had been speaking to and several other people tried to persuade and cajole me to get off the train. I protested. Let me get to the next station, which was

* Csap in Hungarian. Mostly Czech place names have been used, consistent with Hugo's own preference.

Ujlak. Let me think a little longer, then I shall return and I will find some way in which I can explain everything to her. The train was held up for at least twenty minutes and eventually I did get off and began to walk towards the house which she lived in at that time. It was on Széchényi Street, the home of my great-uncle József. She shared that house with our cousin Gabi, who had also survived. He had joined the Czech Army and later on the Russian Army, and was now actually the Chief of Police in the town.

It was a very sunny and hot afternoon. Every day, around the time when the train from Budapest was due to arrive, my mother would lean out of the window of this house and wait. The sight of my walking alone told her everything. When I came into the house we embraced, held each other for a long time; without a word she took a low stool and sat on it in the way that Jewish people sit *shiva*.* She sat on that stool for a full hour. We hardly spoke. When the hour was up, she got up. We embraced again and she said, 'Well, life has to go on and you and I will have to get on with our lives.'

Now forty-four years later I was back in Berehovo again. The return was not my idea at all. It was my daughter Naomi who had wanted to make a film that would pay tribute to a community which for me has a personal history that is both happy and tragic.

When I last left it, at the end of that summer in 1945, the town was half empty. Its Jewish population was devastated. A small handful of survivors, dispirited, most of them waiting in vain for the return of other members of their families, were still there. There was a sense of being unwanted, even resented by the non-Jewish population. The town had been ceded to the Soviet Union as soon as the war was over and I guessed

* Seven-day period of mourning that starts after the funeral. When somebody discovers too late that they have been bereaved, it is customary to sit *shiva* for just one hour.

that the new masters of the town had some major scores to settle with the predominantly Hungarian population. During the time that the town was part of fascist Hungary, they had given both sympathy and support to fascism and to the atrocities that were to come a little later. I concluded that to have any kind of creative life I had to be away from the traumatic reminders.

My mother was then still a young woman of thirty-seven. She was wounded by the loss of her husband, my younger brother Gabi, as well as the loss of her mother, brothers, sisters and their families. She too had some dreadful experiences in Auschwitz and in Stutthof, but she did not want to leave. Not yet. She wanted more time. I felt that she wanted to wait just in case anyone else did turn up, but she encouraged me to go and to resume my education.

During that summer I had spent a few weeks attached to a United Nations refugees and relief team which travelled deep into the Soviet Union. It gave me an opportunity not only to travel but also to see something of our new country. By the time I came back to Berehovo, I had no desire to continue living in that State at all. Despite the offer of a scholarship to a boarding school in Moscow, I decided that I wanted to head west.

The obvious place was Prague. For if we had any kind of pull to a nation, it was to Czechoslovakia. As it turned out, Prague just wasn't far enough. True, I resumed my schooling there, got a bursary and even managed to find a comfortable place to live. By the end of 1945, my mother had also left Berehovo and moved to Karlovy Vary. Two of her brothers also survived: Béla, who was liberated from Buchenwald but lost his entire family, and József, her youngest brother, who escaped from a forced labour battalion, managed to join up with the Czech Army in Russia and was now a beer distributor in this beautiful resort town.

Meanwhile, I was studying in Prague but in a half-hearted

fashion. Most of my time was spent working as a volunteer in the Jewish community, helping in a children's home, escorting Polish Jews from one railway station to another as they were fleeing Poland and who, paradoxically, could only find any kind of safe haven in the American and British zones in Germany.

From time to time there would be transports to Britain for children under the age of sixteen. Unexpectedly, by February 1946, I found myself busy milking cows in a farm school in Scotland and learning English as fast as I could. Before long, I managed to get a place at a university, spent some months in the summer of 1948 as a volunteer attached to the Israeli Army, a career cut short by a bout of jaundice. I returned to England, but instead of continuing with mathematics and biochemistry, I increasingly devoted my time to the study of Hebrew, Semitics and Philosophy. Eventually in 1951, I entered the Hebrew Union College in Cincinnati, became a rabbi, got married, lived and worked in India at first, then in New York. In 1964, my wife, Jackie, and I together with our four children returned to London where I became a rabbi at the West London Synagogue.

A few weeks before this move, my mother – who had remarried and for five years fought the dread disease of cancer with extraordinary courage and dignity – died and was buried in Karlovy Vary. Berehovo had become part of our family's history, at times nostalgic and happy and at times painful and distressing. The return in 1989 was due to the fact that I must have conveyed more of the happy memories to my family.

Naomi, our second daughter, who is the sole proprietor and chief asset of See More Productions,* got a commission to make a film. She recruited her sister Rachelle as production assistant and together with a crew of competent professionals

---

* See More Productions ceased trading in 1992 so that its sole proprietor could move on to other things.

we set off for Berehovo. It was a happy thought to invite my cousins – József Katz (better known as Patyu), who was the last of the family to leave Carpathia and now lives with his family in Israel, and Simcha Neufeld, who left for Budapest as a young apprentice and survived there as József Horvat.* They were not only good company, but also helped to recall people and events.

In the event, and perhaps predictably, we found very little left from the past. The Gryn homes in Vary, a village near Berehovo where my father was born, and where Patyu grew up, were destroyed in a violent flood soon after the war. The Neufeld homes and the oil mill in the village of Silce, where my mother was born and where Simcha had spent his childhood, fared not much better. Even the cemeteries were looted and many family tombstones had been taken to shore up stables and used to make pavements.

Our own home in Berehovo, the house where I was born, was still standing. It was a bit derelict, inhabited by a family who had clearly given up trying to keep it in good repair. Certainly they had long ago abandoned maintaining the beautiful garden that was once one of its glories. Indeed, wherever we went there was neglect. A kind of tiredness hung over the town. The elegance and energy which I remembered so well had gone. I had the sensation that much of it had been taken away when we were taken away. What we found instead was emptiness and ghosts, and that we were chasing shadows.

* Simcha died in Budapest in 1995.

2

BEREHOVO: A BRIEF HISTORY

A man from Berehovo arrives at the gates of heaven. 'Before you can enter,' says the guardian angel, 'you have to tell us the story of your life.' 'Well,' the man replies, 'I was born in the Austro-Hungarian Empire to decent and God-fearing parents, received my education in Czechoslovakia and started to work as an apprentice in Hungary. For a time I also worked in Germany, but I raised my own family and did most of my life's work in the Soviet Union.' The angel was impressed. 'You certainly travelled and moved about a great deal.' 'Oh, no,' the man protested, 'I never left Berehovo!'

Berehovo must be the historical map-maker's nightmare. Now in this country, now in that. Should it be called by its present name, Beregovo, or Berehovo when it was in Czechoslovakia? Or Beregszász which is its Hungarian name? For me it will always be Berehovo because that is what it was called when I was born there and while this was its name the town was at its loveliest. Full of energy, excitement and fun. When its name changed, towards the end of 1938, so did its fortune. Berehovo is the place which will haunt me to the last day of my life.

People have lived in the town for more than a thousand years. Local historians believe that its original name was Lampert's House. But some of these historians consider Lampert to have been the son of King Bela I and others argue that he was King Géza II's son. My preference is for King Géza only because my own father's name was Géza as well. Both schools agree that Lampert invited a group of Flemish settlers to develop his domain, but to the local people all foreigners were 'saxons' or '*szasz*', while '*bereg*' is a Slavonic term for 'riverside' or 'borderline'. Since the town sits comfortably on both sides of the River Verke, and regardless of the country in which it happened to be – there was always a border a few miles away – the name makes good sense.

There is, of course, a legend as well. About a simple shepherd called Szasz who, one day, was busy patching up a hole in the field where two bulls had just had a fight. When he looked into the hole, Szasz spotted a golden coin. Instead of filling, he began to dig deeper and deeper and to his surprise – but not to the surprise of those familiar with fairy-tales – he found a great hoard of treasure. The shepherd was a pious and good-hearted man and his first act was to commission the building of a church above the treasure hole. He also invited all and sundry to settle around the church and the grateful people insisted on calling their new and more civilized home – Beregszász.

The town nestles at the foothills of the Carpathian mountain range, third in size in the region that has been variously called Podkarpatska Rus (Czech), Kárpátalja (Hungarian), Zakarpatskaya Oblast (Russian) and Karpatoruthenen (German). Sub-Carpathian Ruthenia does fullest justice to it in English. Its capital is Užhorod (Ungvár in Hungarian), second is Mukačevo (Munkács).

There is evidence that human settlement in Carpathia – which is what I shall call it – goes back to the Stone and Bronze Ages. It has large areas of fertile land, minerals and hot springs, vast forests, vineyards and orchards as well as rivers and mountain streams with abundant fish. All of this accounts for the region's popularity and attraction to a succession of invading tribes, princes and kings. For most of its recorded history Carpathia was part of the Hungarian

Kingdom and later of the Austro-Hungarian Empire. After the First World War – from 1918 to 1938 – it was the eastern section of the Czechoslovak Republic and for just one day – from 14 to 15 March 1939 – it even declared its independence as Carpatho-Ukraine. But since 29 June 1945, less than two months after the Second World War, when there was 'a unanimous vote to reunite with the USSR' it has been part of the Soviet Union. Just how you can 'reunite' with a nation or an entity which you were never a part of was never explained. Indeed on 22 January 1946 the Presidium of the USSR Supreme Soviet formally incorporated Carpathia into the Ukrainian Socialist Soviet Republic and that is where it is likely to remain for some time to come!*

The population of Carpathia inevitably and naturally reflects this history. Hungarians or Magyars came to rub shoulders – and at times shovels, pickaxes and swords as well – with the Huculs who came with their Ukrainian dialect and Russian Orthodox religion and settled mostly in mountain villages. Germans came, mainly from Swabia in the Tyrol districts of Austria, and established colonies in the region. Their Roman Catholic churches were always surrounded with flowers and, because many of them were afflicted with goitres, I instinctively spoke German with everyone who had slightly popping eyes.

Most of the towns and larger villages had Gypsy camps on their outskirts. Many of the Gypsies were itinerant tinsmiths and seasonal labourers as well as musicians and acrobats.

---

* Only a year after this was written, on 24 August 1991, the Republic of the Ukraine declared its independence from the former Soviet Union. Berehovo is therefore now in the Zakarpathian Province of Ukraine. Today, everyone has the right to travel abroad, the right to choose a religion and the right to freedom of thought and speech, but despite the introduction of economic reforms, the region has the highest unemployment rate in the Ukraine and poverty is widespread.

Their migration from India must have been considerably more difficult and complicated than that of the Huns whose Magyar descendants treated them with such shameful hostility. There were also clusters of Romanians whose Roman legionnaire forebears only left them a language which set them apart. There were Turks in Carpathia as well as Bulgarians – remnants of the Ottoman occupation which lasted over 170 years and ended in 1699. In Berehovo the ice cream was Turkish made and the finest vegetables were grown by the Bulgarians. There were Slovaks who had to make the shortest journey and, of course, the Czechs who came as administrators, teachers, engineers and soldiers as soon as Carpathia – or PKR – became part of Czechoslovakia – or CSR.

But what of my people, the Jews?

As I was growing up there was a sense that Jews had lived in the region for ever. As if we had come there straight from the ruins of Jerusalem after its destruction by Rome in the year 70. Or directly from Babylonia a few centuries later. The truth is neither that romantic nor so deep in history. Early historical records are so sparse that it is simply not possible to say exactly when, or how, or even from whence did the Jews arrive. In the few archives and original manuscripts which survived periodic floods and fires, as well as changes of government and borders – not to speak of wars – there are documents dated 1357 and 1420 which describe *sidomezen* and *zydohawasa* meaning 'Jewish fields'. There are also official lists from the 1570s which included many *sidó** serfs. It is therefore reasonable to assume that there were early Jewish settlements.§

There was an unexpected arrival of Jews alongside the

---

* Jewish.

§ See *Deep-Rooted Yet Alien: Some Aspects of the History of the Jews in Subcarpathian Ruthenia* by Livia Rothkirchen, Yad Vashem Studies, Vol. XII, Jerusalem 1977, pp. 156–7.

invasion of the Turks. Užhorod, the capital of Carpathia, had an organized Sephardi congregation in the seventeenth century. These Jews had fled from Spain and Portugal in the wake of Ferdinand and Isabella's decree of 1492 to expel all Jews and Muslims refusing to convert to Christianity. Turkey was glad to receive a large proportion of these refugees who, in return, threw themselves wholeheartedly into the commercial and intellectual life of their new country. There are no records of the number of Jews who settled in the region, nor of those who returned with the defeated Ottoman legions and administrators. It is nevertheless a curious fact that the style of prayer in Berehovo was Sephardi, and that even in my childhood we were often called a 'Sephardi Community'. This may have had more to do with a liturgical preference by the Hassidic rabbis who came to have a dominating role in Carpathia than actual descent from Spanish Jewry. One of my own great-grandmothers was a Ladino or medieval Spanish-speaking Sephardi, but she was 'imported' from today's Yugoslavia,* as was the wife of one of my uncles.

There were two great waves of immigration into Carpathia which are well-documented and account for the arrival of the majority of Jews in Berehovo and the scores of its neighbouring villages. The first took place in the wake of the unspeakably brutal pogroms led by the Cossack General Bogdan Chmielnicki in 1648. Originally a revolt against the Polish nobility in Galicia and the Ukraine, it soon turned into an unprecedented and wholesale attack on Jews. Chmielnicki's followers were joined by Polish peasants who pillaged, raped and eventually murdered over 100,000 Jews. By the time these pogroms ended, some eight years later, entire Jewish communities were destroyed. Some of those who managed to survive found their way to Bohemia, Germany, Holland and the Balkans. One of the very few possible escape routes were the mountain

* Now the former Yugoslavia.

passes from the Ukraine to Carpathia and the relative tranquillity which greeted them, coupled with large but under-
populated and reasonably fertile areas tempted many Jews to
stay and rebuild their shattered lives and families.

When I revisited Berehovo in 1989 to film *Chasing
Shadows*, it was with a mixture of personal anger and historic
irony that I saw how the Bocskay Street of my childhood –
where at least half the houses were Jewish homes – was
renamed Bogdan Chmielnicki Street! It seemed to me then,
as it still does, that neither the Nazi experience nor the
Stalinist period, which took a sizeable toll of non-Jewish life
and liberty in Berehovo, had altered the local leadership's
fascination and admiration for violent heroes.

A second large-scale migration followed the partition of
Poland in 1772. Galicia was annexed to the Austro-Hungarian
Empire, then ruled by Maria Theresa. The authorities encouraged this movement of their newly acquired Jewish subjects
for economic as well as political reasons. Any minority that
would reduce, and thus lessen, the Hungarian element in
the population was welcome. Especially if they could speak
German. Since Yiddish, a virtually unchanged medieval German (or *Mittelhochdeutsch* to give it its philological title),
was the popular language of the Jews they served this purpose
very well. Local officials and the hereditary owners of great
estates were equally glad to greet the Jewish artisans. Their
needs were modest, their willingness to work hard was great,
and their habits of sobriety, religious piety and family loyalty
made them ideal immigrants.

Berehovo was the seat of Bereg County, one of the four
counties which occupied Carpathia. The other three were
Ung, Ugocsa and Máramaros. Bereg County itself was part of
the Hungarian Rakóczy family estate in the period of the
Chmielnicki disaster, but in 1711 the Hapsburg king, Leopold
I, expropriated it from the Rakóczys and gave it to Bishop
Friedrich Luther Schoenborn. He was a German nobleman

who had served the Hapsburgs well and, in one way or another, his family had a controlling presence right up to the middle of the twentieth century. The Bishop himself was no friend of the Jews, calling them 'parasites' and worse, but his descendants and those in charge of administrating the estates took a more practical and indeed, helpful view.

When, for example, the leaders of the community in Mukačevo, the somewhat larger town no more than a few miles from Berehovo, asked for permission to build a new synagogue in 1768, the Count Schoenborn of the day readily agreed. The only stipulation he made was that the builders of this synagogue urge their fellow-Jews from Galicia to come and settle on his estate!*

Initially, the Jews leased farming lands and vineyards and they ran the inns that catered to the local population and the growing number of travellers coming from Vienna, Budapest and other parts of the Austrian Empire to exploit the forests and mineral resources of the area. They were also expected to market the produce of the many and widely scattered farms. Above all, the Jews had to pay taxes, to which there seemed to be no end. There was a head tax as well as a land tax and animal tax. Even a *Toleranz* or toleration tax. For the Jews who groaned under the burden of their landlords' rapacity there may have been a measure of perspective and comfort in the observation of Rabbi Ezekiel Landau, the Chief Rabbi of Prague from 1755 until his death in 1793: 'Obviously, the tax we are paying is for the privilege of living in their countries, like a rent . . . for their permission to live in their midst.'

It was during his term of office that Emperor Joseph II attempted to introduce a series of reforms called *Toleranzpatent* which aimed to give equality to the Protestants of Austria, greater independence to the peasants from their feudal land-

---

* See *Piety and Perseverance: Jews from the Carpathian Mountains* by Herman Dicker, Sepher-Hermon Press, Inc. 1981, pp. 5–6.

lords and to make elementary education compulsory throughout the land. In this way he hoped to create conditions that
would stimulate economic growth, even in the backwaters of
his empire. Since Jews might also benefit from these reforms,
Joseph was quick to explain in a note dated October 1781: 'It
is by no means my intention to expand the Jewish nation in
the hereditary lands or to reintroduce them to areas where
they are not tolerated, but only to make them more useful to
the State in those places they already exist and to the extent
that they are already tolerated.'

In Berehovo itself, it is difficult to say just how the Jews
were to be 'more useful to the State'. The only document I
was able to find in Berehovo's well-guarded but ill-organized
archives is a list which bears the date of 1735 and speaks of
the presence of just under a hundred Jewish households. The
community's extensive records did not survive, though I cher-
ish the hope that among the batches of papers, thick with
dust, in the municipal archives there may still come to light
a bit more of our history.

By the second half of the eighteenth century the Jewish community was well-established. The population of the town
and surrounding villages was growing. Synagogues were built
together with *chedarim*, or schools, as were facilities for
kosher meat and poultry, the baking of *matzot*, or unleavened
bread for Passover, and a *mikveh* for ritual bathing.

The community's first 'official' rabbi was Yizchak Rochlitz
whose dates I have not been able to verify. In Berehovo's large
Jewish cemetery, his tombstone still stands but my attempts
to decipher the faded Hebrew letters at its base proved unsuc-
cessful. '*Morenu HaRav*' ('our master and teacher') and '*tsa-
dik*' ('righteous') still survive in the inscription and testify to
the great esteem in which he was held.

One of his successors was Rabbi Avraham Yehuda Leib
Aryeh Schwartz, who was appointed in 1861. He was a pupil

of Rabbi Moses Sofer (1762–1839), known as the Chatam
Sofer* and arguably the outstanding religious leader of East
European Jewry.§ Rabbi Sofer himself was born and educated
in Germany and was the spiritual leader of Bratislava, the
capital of Slovakia and head of its *yeshiva* or talmudic academy. He had immense authority and he was an uncompromis-
ing opponent of all assimilationist tendencies and many of
the expressions of modernity, especially the religious sort.
Rabbi Schwartz, born in the small Hungarian town of Mád,
must have arrived in Berehovo eager to further his own
teacher's ideas. I have more than passing sympathy with the
ideological conflict in which he was soon embroiled.

The Sofer tradition, 'Western' and laying great stress on
academic learning and rigorous intellectual standards, had to
come face to face with the Hassidic tradition founded by Israel
ben Eliezer (1700–1760), who came to be known as the Baal
Shem Tov, meaning 'Master of the Good Name'. He and his
rapidly growing disciples in Galicia and in many Carpathian
communities stressed the joyful observance of the commandments, laid great store by popular expressions of mysticism
and produced a series of charismatic leaders, or *rebbes*,¶ whose
words were commandments in themselves.

At first Rabbi Schwartz clearly resisted the Hassidic tempta-
tion. He attended a rabbinic conference at Mihalovce in Slovakia in 1866 which led to the formation of the Union of
Orthodox Rabbis in Carpathia and a formal declaration which
insisted that sermons may only be given in Yiddish. Three
years later he attended another gathering in Budapest which
was to decide the shape of a national Jewish community. It

---

* 'Seal of the Scribe'.

§ The Chatam Sofer's grave has been miraculously preserved in Bratislava
and to this day it remains a powerful place of pilgrimage, though it is
covered by a modern and constantly busy highway contructed during the
time of the Nazi puppet state of Slovakia.

¶ Rabbis.

opened on 14 December 1868 and the discussions and debates lasted until 23 February 1869! The Neolog, or reformist section, argued in favour of changes in religious practice and education, while the Orthodox delegation stood firmly on the side of Moses Sofer's insistence that nothing may alter in religious observance. When these issues were put to the vote and the Neologs had a majority, Rabbi Schwartz was among those who walked out of the Congress and the split was permanent.

But Rabbi Schwartz himself was increasingly drawn to the Hassidic camp. He was particularly captivated by the personal style and teaching of Rabbi Hayim Halberstam who held 'court' in the small Galician town of Zanz and it was a mark of the Berehovo rabbi's enthusiasm and devotion that for twenty-six successive [festivals of] Shavuot* he chose to celebrate not with his own community, but in Zanz!

While the Hassidic minority in Berehovo may have approved of the rabbi's preference, the more strait-laced majority clearly did not. Although I have not been able to discover the precise reasons or the exact nature of the controversy, the fact is that in 1880, just three years before his death, Rabbi Schwartz resigned his post in Berehovo. His one published work, Kol Aryeh ('The Voice of Aryeh'), a collection of responses and decisions given to questions sent to the Rabbi from far and wide, appeared posthumously in 1904 and is highly regarded by Orthodox authorities to this day.

Even before Rabbi Schwartz came to Berehovo, Mukačevo's Rabbi Ezriel Gruen or Gryn, who was appointed in 1829, had changed the style of prayers to the Sephardi and more kabbalistic ritual known as Nusach Ari whose chief advocate was Rabbi Isaac Luria, a mystic who lived in the sixteenth century in the small but influential town of Safed in Palestine,

---

* Jewish festival of Weeks, marking the season of the wheat harvest and the celebration of the giving of Torah on Mount Sinai.

and was filled with Messianic expectations. Whether it was a heritage of the Spanish Jews or just a preference for the mystical touches in this liturgy, the Hassidim had a clear preference for the *Nusach Ari* and Ezriel Gryn was glad to accommodate them. Perhaps my own inclination to say 'yes' whenever there is a theological alternative comes from him, as he was one of my illustrious great-great-uncles!

The momentous event of this period occurred in 1867 when the Austro-Hungarian government passed legislation which gave all its Jewish citizens full economic, social, personal and legal rights. Industries were established, businesses given new energy, land was bought and sold, vineyards and orchards planted and Berehovo began to resemble a beehive on a balmy summer day. Before long, Jews occupied the position of mayor of the town; the city and district engineers were Jewish, as were two High Court judges. Three large brick factories, two flour-mills and a modern sawmill quickly took shape and created hundreds of jobs. In addition to the railway which connected the town to all parts of Europe, a narrow-gauge railway leading into the timber-rich mountains was constructed with Berehovo as its terminus.

Rabbi Shlomo Sofer-Schreiber, a grandson of Moses Sofer, was elected as Berehovo's Chief Rabbi in 1883 – a position he was to hold until his death in 1930. His *yeshiva* attracted fine teachers as well as a succession of talented students who, in turn, became rabbis and teachers thus making sure that even the smallest communities had proper spiritual and educational leadership. Rabbi Schreiber regenerated the *Chevrah Kadisha*, literally 'the holy brotherhood', which was first established in 1795 and took responsibility for the needs of the dead and their bereaved families. Like all the larger towns in Carpathia, Berehovo also attracted many poor Jews who came from their mountain villages in search of work or charity.

Rabbi Schreiber saw to it that his community's more afflu-
ent members subscribed generously to the various funds
designed to cope with the chronic misery of the region and
that no child was left without education or winter clothes.
He also managed to leave two books for posterity, both written
in an elegant Hebrew. *Chut Hameshlash* ('The Threefold
Cord') is a powerful defence of traditionalism. Parts of it
develop one of his famous grandfather's sayings: 'There are
no quarrels without wounds', though there is scant regard in
it for the sensitivities and the progressive ideas of the Neologs!
This book was published in 1887 but even in my childhood
copies of it decorated many of the town's households. Visitors
from more distant parts were told: 'You know, this book was
written right here in Berehovo', but I suspected even then
that not too many of the proud owners actually read it.

His other work, *Igrot Soferim* ('Letters of the Sofer Family')
is an anthology of letters by his distinguished ancestors which
must have been a tremendous labour of love. It also includes
pictures of the writers but sadly none of Shlomo's own correspondence. I was moved and excited to find an ownerless copy
of it atop a dusty and worm-eaten pile of books in Berehovo's
only remaining and derelict synagogue. Indeed on several
occasions I too have shown it to visitors in our London home
and found myself saying: 'Look, such a fine Hebrew book and
it comes from my hometown!'

When Rabbi Schreiber died in 1930, the year I was born,
the community elected his son-in-law Solomon Hirsch as
their Chief Rabbi. By then the town had undergone changes
that my own direct ancestors who settled in the nearby villages of Vary and Silce, and in Feketeerdő and Sevluš – the
Neimans and the Neufelds, the Schönfelds and the Gryns –
could never have predicted. That following the First World
War Carpathia would become the Podkarpatska Rus province
in the newly created Czechoslovak Republic. That in this
Republic, Jewish rights would be respected to the point of

being able to claim Jewish nationality. That Berehovo's Jews would account for almost half of the town's population. That it would have six purpose-built synagogues and at least as many prayer houses. That the language of instruction in the Jewish elementary school would be Czech and modern Hebrew with each class sporting pictures of Tomáš Masaryk, the founding president of the Republic and of Theodor Herzl, the founder of the Zionist movement. Nor could they, or for that matter we who lived and prayed, grew and played, worked and built, and felt so secure in that town – none of us could have predicted that it would only last for twenty years.

3

OUR HOUSE

Our house on Rozsoskert 72 was built by my father. It was a tradition in the family that the men would have their own houses by the time they married. Well before 1929 – the year my parents married – my father had bought a plot which ran all the way to Széchényi Street. It was an exceedingly long garden. At the other end, his Uncle József had already built his house and had a growing family. Our house was certainly very modern by the standards of Berehovo. All the rooms interconnected and, with the exception of the kitchen, had parquet flooring, most of them covered with Persian carpets. In each room there was a large ceramic tile stove which only required one wooden fire to be lit in the morning; for the rest of the day and through the night these stoves gave out an even and gentle heat. The furniture was made to order and virtually designed by my father himself. The main living room was a covered veranda which overlooked an immaculate flower garden and beyond it a much longer orchard which was immensely productive. Its two far sides were lined with raspberry and gooseberry bushes, the central path was covered with trained vines forming a delightful tunnel. Their grapes were of a perfumed variety and especially reserved for the table. Between the path and the fences, there was a series of fruit trees. Cherries were always the first to come to fruit, followed soon by apricots and greengages. Then came apples and pears and peaches. But the majority of the trees were plum trees.

During the long summer months it was my job to collect, practically every day, the plums that had dropped off the trees. They were kept in a couple of large barrels discreetly placed at the top end of the garden. As the layers of rotting plums grew, handfuls of yeast were spread over them. By the end of the summer the barrels were filled, taken away by a team of strong men, only to return a few weeks later by way of a relative's distillery in the form of the most potent and delicious slivovitz, or plum brandy. The plums that managed to survive on the trees were eventually picked and a large copper cauldron over an open fire became the annual scene of producing vast quantities of *lekvar* or plum jam.

The ground between the trees was divided into sections where we grew, year by year, cucumbers, spinach, sorrel, beetroot, radishes, kohlrabi, onions, carrots and parsnips. There were long rows of runner beans, punctured with beds of strawberries and a particularly delicious variety of green peas that I was rarely asked to pick because I would always return with more empty shells than peas!

My father's greatest joy was to grow things and nothing gave him greater pleasure than the rose garden, with its bushes and trees carefully planted and tended. It was a riot of colour in the summer and a source of much anxiety during the cold winters. The carefully pruned branches were covered with sacking, and springtime was always marked by the arrival of the finest fertilizers to ensure another beautiful season.

A few steps from the kitchen there was a huge apricot tree and under it two massive logs on either side of a large wooden table for outdoor meals and entertaining. Beyond them stood a woodshed, a summer kitchen and an intriguing small shed for geese, for my mother had never quite left her own village behind. Goose was a great winter favourite. Its liver, baked or fried, was the delicacy of the week. But to get the liver as large as possible, the poor creature had to be force-fed with dry corn. From time to time I protested as my mother tucked the bird under her legs and held tight to its bill as the handful of corn was swallowed. Occasionally she would remind me that my protests would have greater authority if I was not the one who always asked for a second helping of the liver!

Our home had a telephone. The number was 169. Eventually, it also had an indoor bathroom which was sufficiently novel for all my friends to want to come and play at my house and they would disappear frequently to try out this convenience.

My first conscious memory of our family and home in Berehovo is the death of my younger brother, Kálmán. He was one of twins who were born when I was just a little over three. By all accounts the birth was difficult and complicated and his death, when he was only three days old, was a traumatic experience for everyone. I can still picture the tiny coffin being carried out of our home. Both my parents were sobbing uncontrollably and for some strange reason, I was sitting on a potty when this tragic scene was taking place. Gabi,* the other twin, survived. In time he became the most loving and loyal of brothers. A reliable ally in good times and bad. He had the most twinkling blue eyes, a quick intelligence and a delicious sense of humour. Unfortunately, my mother could not give him her own milk and it became necessary to engage a wet nurse as quickly as possible.

My second memory is, in fact, of this lady. She was very large and had already had six or seven children. In one arm she would hold Gabi at one of her immense breasts, with her own baby suckling at the other. Her husband was a somewhat impoverished tinsmith and such was my parents' appreciation and gratitude that before Gabi was one year old, they had built for this family a house on a plot adjacent to our own

---

* His Hebrew name was Gabriel; Gábor was the Hungarian equivalent.

home. It was bought originally by my father so that his children could live nearby when we grew up. Instead we grew up as neighbours of this large and noisy family who had a special place in all our hearts.

Some years later I discovered that many of our other neighbours, in our supposedly better district of the town, were less than pleased to have a tinsmith periodically hammering away in his workshop. But I know that my parents never had any regrets about their spontaneous act of generosity.

It is often in my mind that I have yet to meet two people more generous and kind-hearted than my parents. Our home was literally open day and night, mostly to family who popped in for a short visit and stayed for a meal. There was also a seemingly endless succession of *schnorrers* who made their way to our door. They were professional alms-seekers, mostly men from the poorer villages, but sometimes haggard-looking women as well. In the culture of our community they were considered to have a legitimate claim for *tzedakah*, or charity on those who were better off. First-timers were often armed with a letter from their own community explaining their circumstances and needs by way of introduction. There was another succession of men who came to collect gifts of money for institutions of learning, orphanages and homes for the aged. They came from other towns in Czechoslovakia and from Poland and Romania as well as from Palestine. I enjoyed listening to their stories, heart-rending as they always were, of distant communities and customs, and can still picture a drawer in the living room, filled with the receipts they left behind. Friends and acquaintances knew full well that my mother's snacks could not be improved upon anywhere. I cannot recall anyone who was ever disappointed either in the hospitality or in the response that they received to their requests.

I particularly remember one occasion when I accompanied my mother on one of her more massive shopping trips to the market. She was a very attractive woman. Relatively tall and slim, always neat and methodical. She loved to laugh and sing – especially the hit songs from Viennese operettas. She was well-educated and had it not been for her marriage when she was twenty-one, she would have completed her medical studies. But I suspect that as I was growing up, I read more of her various textbooks than she did. She was also very easily moved to tears. Tear-stained novels dotted the house and she was probably the easiest pushover for the sad stories of the *schnorrers*. Her name, Bella, and her Hebrew name Bracha, which means 'blessing', suited her perfectly.

At the time of this excursion, I was old enough and strong enough to carry a basket in each hand. Near the marketplace, between the synagogue and the Royal Hotel, there was a cab rank. On one side there were horse-drawn fiacres, and on the other, two or three motor taxis. Generally, your choice of transport depended on the urgency of your trip as much as on your budget. As we came near the hotel, the heavens opened and the prospect of walking home became very unpleasant. As my mother began to head for one of the waiting fiacres I protested that a taxi would be quicker and drier. By this time she already had a foot on the carriage and her explanation was simple: 'The taxi driver's wife is not in the hospital, but this man's is.'

A more serious episode in the life of our family taught me that my mother was truly an exceptional woman. My parents had engaged a Fräulein when I was still a baby who combined the role of governess and mother's help. One of her functions was to make sure that my German, and later on my brother Gabi's, was of a high standard. Over the years she came to be considered a part of the family. She joined in all the family and festival celebrations. She was a thin, attractive woman. She had brown hair and was generally very quiet. Her name was Klára, but she was always referred to as 'the Fräulein'. We never met her own family, who lived in the Sudeten part of Czechoslovakia. When I was about seven, she showed me a photograph of a young soldier in Austrian or German uniform and told me that one day she hoped to marry him.

It must have been very painful to my mother when the Fräulein suddenly announced a short time before we were 'liberated' by the Hungarians that she herself was an ardent supporter of the Nazi ideology and that she could no longer work for Jews and was certainly unwilling to live with them. Within hours of this declaration, she was gone. I still remember my sense of having been deeply betrayed. We had no idea where she moved to or what happened to her, until we got a message from the Mukačevo hospital that she was a patient in the isolation ward, suffering with typhoid, very ill and lonely. It was in the winter and by chance I was at home on holiday from my boarding school. By this time my initial sadness had turned into anger and I began to argue with my mother who was already busy filling a basket with cakes and fruits and some of the Fräulein's favourite dishes. My protests were of no avail. 'She is a sick woman, perhaps dying,' said my mother, 'and for a long time she was good to you and Gabi.'

I did not want my mother to go alone so I swallowed my pride and went with her on the bus to Mukačevo. It was a pathetic meeting. We were only allowed to stand in the doorway of her room in the hospital. A nurse took out and arranged all the presents we had brought with us on a small bedside table. My mother cried, and so did the Fräulein. I know that my mother continued to visit her until she recovered and was discharged from the hospital, but I never saw her again.

My own ventures into the complicated field of *tzedakah* – that remarkable Hebrew term which combines the notion of social justice, righteousness and charity – began when I was about six years old. Towards the end of every summer, the same man came to our home for a few days to chop a large pile of logs – with mathematical precision – into firewood for the winter. By the time he had finished, the woodshed was completely filled. He was a very strong and gentle man. He had a straggly grey beard and long *peyot* or sidelocks which proclaimed that he was a pious Jew. His *tsizit* – the woollen fringes which are attached to the four corners of a special garment, ordained in the Book of Numbers as a reminder of God's commandments – were always hanging out of his shirt. Whenever he took a break from his work he pulled out a much-worn little book of Psalms from his pocket and recited them with great devotion.

It was about this time that I had first heard the story of the *lamed vav tsadikim*. This legend insists that at any given time there are thirty-six perfectly righteous men in the world. It is because of them, and only because of them, that the world can actually exist. They know who they are, but they are not allowed to tell anyone else about it. It was not long before I convinced myself, beyond any shadow of doubt, that our woodcutter was one of these thirty-six people. Naturally I questioned him about this, at first with indirect subtlety, and the more he smiled and modestly denied any such distinction, the more convinced I became that I was right. Whatever delicacies I could think of and find in our home, I would take to him and was delighted that he invariably accepted them. As I never had any pocket money – because there was no such custom in our family – I could not share this with him as well, though I would have wanted to. My benefactions finally came to an end when it was discovered that I had given him one of my father's sweaters which was not only brand new but it had taken one of his sisters many months to knit! My father managed to convince me that if he was one of the *lamed vav tsadikim*, then he also had the right to privacy and to perform his tasks on earth without constant interference from me.

Home life and religious life were inseparable. The

mezuzah* fixed to our front door and the *mizrach*§ tablet depicting Rachel's tomb just outside Jerusalem were among the early imports from Palestine. The *mizrach* had a place of honour on our veranda wall which faced east and served as a reminder, especially to visitors, as to the direction we were to face when reciting certain prayers. Prayer books, elegant editions of Bibles as well as well-thumbed ones dotted the shelves in our home. One of my earliest literary activities was to cut open the pages of the religious books to which we had endless subscriptions. Set prayers were recited three times a day. Although my father considered himself an emancipated man, he would never fail to put on his *tefillin* – the leather phylacteries – while reciting the morning prayers before breakfast. Gabi and I usually joined him, each with our own prayer books. During the winter months we joined him in reciting the evening service before supper as well.

As far as I know, virtually every Jewish home in Berehovo observed a high level of *kashrut*.¶ Only ritually slaughtered meat and poultry were eaten – and great care was taken to remove every possible trace of blood. Meat and dairy dishes were strictly separated and it would never have occurred to anyone that any of the biblically forbidden foods were even tempting! Before baking bread or *challot*, the special plaited loaves for Shabbat, my mother would take a small ball of dough and throw it into an open fire in memory of the Temple in Jerusalem.

I cannot recall actually learning, but only knowing the blessings before eating and after meals, or before tasting fruits or cakes. I came to recite the special blessings instinctively

---

* Oblong container in which is kept a parchment inscribed with the words of the *Shema*, the watchword of Jewish faith (Deut 6:4), which includes the commandment that the *Shema* itself must be written on the *mezuzot*, or doorposts of Jewish homes.

§ Hebrew for east.

¶ Jewish dietary laws.

on seeing lightning, hearing thunder and looking at a rainbow. There was a special blessing when wearing new clothes for the first time. On one occasion, Gabi insisted that I ask my teacher whether he, too, had to recite such a blessing when he started to wear my hand-me-down clothes. After each visit to the toilet, we had to wash our hands and recite the appropriate blessing and in one of my more pious phases I actually kept a list to make sure that in the course of any given day I recited the recommended one hundred benedictions. There was a blessing on waking up and to this day I cannot drop off to sleep before invoking the archangels Michael on my right, Gabriel on the left, Uriel ahead of me and Raphael behind and the *Shechinah*, or the presence of God, always above my head, and always ending with the line 'Stand in awe and do not sin, commune with your own heart on your bed and be still, *selah!*'

4

JEWISH LIFE

In every town and village in Carpathia the synagogue was very much the centre of its Jewish life. Berehovo was no exception. We had six purpose-built synagogues and at least as many smaller and more informal *shtieblach* – largish rooms or halls in various neighbourhoods which were used for study during the day, but mornings and evenings, and especially on Sabbaths and festivals, they became places of communal prayer.

In the centre of the town there was a huge courtyard with the Great Synagogue, its elegant long windows facing the main square of the town. This was the synagogue where my father had his own seat. There was a box in front of him which had its own lock and key and where he kept his *tallit*, his prayer shawl, with its beautiful hand-worked silver decoration. In our community such prayer shawls were only worn by married men and this one was a wedding present from his father-in-law. We also kept a set of prayer books for Shabbat and the festivals in that box together with a little jar of smelling salts which I sniffed proudly and piously once I was old enough to begin fasting on Yom Kippur.

Our seat was located between the reading desk in the centre of the synagogue and the magnificently curtained ark for the Torah scroll, built into its eastern wall. Next to the ark was the Rabbi's special seat, but as often as not he had his own *minyan* – a group of people who worshipped in one of the

large rooms that was part of his home. The first part of
the Shabbat and festival services was usually conducted by
different members of the congregation. But the main sections
of the service were the special preserve of the Chazan,* whose
silvery beard was matched by an exceptionally high and silvery voice. To illustrate the line from the Psalm: 'Out of the
depths I cry to you, O Lord,' the Chazan's place was slightly
to the right of the Ark, facing the Ark itself and he stepped
down into it.

Most of his melodies and chants were traditional, but every
now and then, especially on happy occasions, knowing nods
and smiles greeted the recognition of well-known tunes from
the Viennese operettas which he set to the words of the
prayers. I was told that in the late 1920s, he emigrated to
the United States of America in response to a call from a
community of former Berehovo families who had set up their
own congregation in New York, but the call of his large family
proved stronger in the end, and he returned to the great joy
of the community.

Our rabbi, Solomon Hirsch, had one part of the liturgy
reserved specially for him. It was a prayer chanted with extraordinary feeling and dignity on the Shabbat preceding the new
moon. I can still hear the supplication to God that 'the new
moon bring us a life of fulfilment and peace, a life of goodness
and blessing, a life filled with awe of God and fear of sin, a
life without self-reproach and shame, a life that is marked by
love of God's teaching, when the desires of our hearts may
be fulfilled for good'.

Although there were many people in our community who
had *semicha* – rabbinic ordination – Rabbi Hirsch alone was
the official and salaried spiritual leader of Berehovo. He was
responsible for running the Beth Din, the religious court of
the district, which clarified religious laws, gave rulings on

* Cantor.

ritual matters, adjudicated in matters of inheritance, marriage settlements and divorce, the licensing of those who supplied kosher food and wine as well as resolving business and family disputes. He was also in charge of the *yeshiva*, a Talmud academy famous throughout the land, which had over a hundred full-time students who came from villages and towns near and far to study with him and a group of distinguished teachers whom he recruited from other parts of Czechoslovakia, as well as from Hungary, Poland and Yugoslavia. He not only had to find salaries for his colleagues, but also bursaries for the students, make board and lodging arrangements for them and quite often find a subsidy for the families of the students whose task as breadwinners was delayed.

Rabbi Hirsch only preached twice a year; on Shabbat Haggadol, the Great Shabbat before Passover, and on Shabbat Shuva, the Shabbat of Repentance, between Rosh Hashana and Yom Kippur. They were great and splendid occasions, always in the afternoon, a special lectern placed in front of the Ark in the Great Synagogue.

The sermons themselves were two- or even three-hour-long discourses delivered to packed congregations. Lunch on those occasions was a hurried affair and many people from the outlying districts missed it altogether. Everyone wanted to make sure of a good seat in the synagogue and there were always scores of people who had to stand crowded in the back of the synagogue and in the aisles. Rabbi Hirsch had a very dignified presence with a large, square beard and a deep resonating voice. I cannot claim that I still remember the actual content of these sermons, but I can still picture the rapt attention of all his hearers and can hear clearly the enthusiastic shouts of 'Sh'koach!', or 'Well done!', as he concluded his discourse.

For over twenty-five years I have served my present congregation in London and as its senior rabbi I have to preach at least once a week. Not surprisingly, I often think of Solomon

Hirsch and there are times when nostalgia is tinged not only with admiration, but also with envy.

In between these great state occasions, Berehovo would be visited by travelling *maggidim* – itinerant preachers who, more than anything else, were exceptionally talented story-tellers. They had the gift of weaving stories out of Bible stories and bringing famous characters to life. They could give relevance to ancient teachings and the smaller congregations which would come to hear them later on Shabbat afternoon welcomed them as much for their learning as for their great power to entertain.

Many of the institutions that were important and necessary for the Jewish life of the community were located around the Great Synagogue.* Interestingly enough, the term for the synagogue was the 'Temple'. In the huge courtyard behind this elegant and imposing building, there was another and somewhat smaller synagogue, as well as the Kloiz, which was an even more informal and smaller prayer house, but it had the distinction of being the oldest religious building in the town. It had very thick walls and small windows, a stone floor and quaintly gabled roof. Just beyond the Kloiz, there was another courtyard which housed the community's leaders.

The general religious standards and orientation of the com-munity were orthodox. However, during the First World War groups of Jews from Galicia and other parts of Carpathia arrived in Berehovo; many of these people were adherents of various Hassidic sects who wanted stricter – indeed the strictest possible – observance. Whatever the causes and reasons of their unhappiness, by the mid-1920s they had organized themselves into a separate group who were anxious to have their own *shechita*, or ritual slaughter facilities, their own Beth Din and their own schools for their children.

To achieve this, and to obtain a measure of State support,

---

* *Nagy Templom* in Hungarian.

they required a special Act of Parliament. The sitting Member of the day was ready to help and I have been told on several occasions the story of how a delegation went to see him in Prague and were delighted with the courteous reception he extended to them. What they did not realize was that this Member of Parliament, himself a Jew, was clearly an adherent or, at the very least, a sympathizer of the Neolog, or reformed community, who stood pretty well for everything that the Hassidim opposed with conviction and vehemence.

In no time at all the proposed Act was drafted, but the breakaway community had to have its own title and when the Member of Parliament suggested, perhaps as a joke or possibly as a missionary gesture on his part, that they should call it the 'Neolog' community, the Hassidim – unaware of the implications of this term – readily agreed. A short time later the bill received Parliamentary approval and soon after that, a sign went over the gate of that courtyard proclaiming it to be the Berehovo Neolog Community. It was an anomaly which our townspeople soon got used to and the shock and surprise of visitors to our town generally gave way to knowing smiles.

On this latest visit, it was with a mixture of sadness, shock and anger that I saw what had happened to the synagogue and its surroundings. The Great Synagogue itself is now completely encased in concrete and turned into a cultural centre. It seems that the authorities originally wanted to efface it, but the Jewish symbols which dotted its exterior proved more stubborn than the state-authorized vandals' chisels. I was told stories of workmen who fell off the scaffolding – one of them to his death and the other to permanent injuries. That, and what may have remained of a public sensitivity, must have influenced the decision to wrap it in its ugly cement coat.

As for the Kloiz – one of the few truly historic buildings in the town – it was completely demolished to give way to a dull little garden, and in the centre in front of the Temple

there stands the larger than life statue of Lenin, with his
thumb hooked in his waistcoat, and his back to what was not
very long ago one of the glories of the town.

Sitting on the marble steps of this statue, this time with
my back to Lenin, I could still picture the streams of men
and boys and some women, going in and out of the synagogue
on Shabbat and festivals, always dressed in their finest clothes
and, during the week to the many communal offices beyond
the synagogue as well as the home of the Rabbi or that of the
Chazan.

Beyond the synagogue, on the town's Main Street,* there
was a row of shops which belonged to the congregation, as
did two arcades built in a modernistic style where kosher
meat and poultry, as well as fish and Passover supplies were
sold. The last communal building facing Main Street was
built in 1911 and housed the communal *mikveh*. Inside there
was a long row of cubicles, each of which contained a bath-tub
followed by a few steps that led to two large ritual pools.

Thursdays were invariably reserved for women, all of whom
would have a bath by way of preparing for the Sabbath, and
those women who had just completed their menstruation
would make their way to the pools for a ritual immersion as
well. Until I was judged to be too old, my mother often took
me along with her for these Thursday evening outings. Of
course I could only go as far as her cubicle, generally unwilling
to have a bath there myself, since I considered the bathroom
in our home superior to that in the *mikveh*, but I watched
with great curiosity and with a touch of mystery as woman
after woman, draped only in large white sheets, seemed to
glide towards the pool, and then return, occasionally shaking
their wet hair in my direction.

Whether it was necessary for my mother to go to the *mikveh*
that particular week or not, we also went there every Thursday

* 'Fő Utca' in Hungarian.

night in order to buy fish for Shabbat. It was a point of almost obsessive pride with my mother that she never cooked and served fish that was not alive when she bought it. I always found some excuse to look at something else in the street as the fishmonger pulled a carp or cod out of the tank and, with a wooden mallet, made it fit for our consumption.

From time to time, I went into the *mikveh* myself before the service in the synagogue. On Shabbat mornings, men would immerse themselves into warm water, and despite my father's protestations – who agreed that ours was one of the best indoor baths in the whole of Berehovo – I enjoyed the experience and did my best to ignore the powerful smell of sweat which hung in the air.

There were several *yeshivot* in the community which attracted students from towns and villages throughout Carpathia. Generally boys, especially from poorer families, were expected to go to work or into apprenticeship within days or weeks of the Bar Mitzvah which marked their thirteenth birthday. But if a boy was intellectually gifted, his family and community would make every effort to get him into a *yeshiva* which provided an opportunity for talmudic education, and many exceptionally gifted or highly motivated young men continued until their rabbinic ordination. Although relatively few such people actually became professional rabbis, having *semicha* (ordination) was a mark of distinction as well as achievement.

The Berehovo community was conscious of its obligation to the students who came from out of town and they not only provided communal dormitory facilities, but also assigned the students to take their meals with different families on specific days of the week. Virtually every family who could afford to extend this kind of hospitality was allocated two or three students and our family was no exception. Our students – or *yeshiva bochers* – came from the Yeshiva Bet Asher, which had over a hundred intense and always black-hatted boys, whose description of their study programme made me feel like a parasite.

That they had exceptionally retentive memories was brought home to me on a *sherut* – or shared taxi ride – from Tel Aviv to Jerusalem in the late 1970s. When a man sitting next to me discovered that I was from Berehovo, as well as my name, he reminded me of our address and of the fact that in our home on Thursdays lunch consisted of bean soup followed by slices of roast goose liver and purée of beans. And that in the summer it was a cold green bean soup, with cottage cheese and noodles as the main course. When we reached Jerusalem, he insisted on treating me to coffee and cakes by way of partial repayment and his invitation to his home for a Shabbat was both genuine and touching.

Halfway down the communal courtyard was a small abattoir where chickens, ducks and geese were ritually slaughtered, and in a side room a group of women were constantly busy plucking the freshly killed poultry. It was presided over by the Shochet.* He was a small man with a bright red beard and one of the gentlest people I knew. As my school was only a few steps away from this abattoir, and because the Shochet had a great fund of fascinating and amusing stories which he was very glad to share with me, I was a frequent visitor. It always puzzled me how such a gentle man should have such a seemingly cruel occupation. As time went on I came to admire the skill and patience with which he held his *chalef*, his gleaming stainless steel blade, and he went to great lengths to explain that getting his instrument to be as sharp and as smooth as possible would reduce the pain that he had to inflict on his victims. He also taught me the special blessing he recited before beginning his day's work and there was no question in his mind, nor eventually in mine, that his was a truly holy occupation.

* Ritual slaughterer.

Nearby there was a large bakery which had a special section for the preparation of *matzot* and was therefore busiest in the weeks leading up to the festival of Passover. I enjoyed watching the amazing speed with which flour and water were mixed, the swiftness of the kneading and the stretching of the dough into perfectly round even shapes. They were then perforated and, with trained ease, put into the oven. The entire process had to be completed in less than eighteen minutes – a time limit that made certain that the *matzot* were truly unleavened bread.

The main part of the bakery was used for bread and *barches*, the special twisted loaves that decorated every Sabbath table in Berehovo, and it was also the weekly scene that I came to believe to be nothing short of a miracle. It concerned what is still one of my favourite dishes, the *cholent*.

Early on Friday afternoons, my mother put into a special red pot kidney beans which had already soaked overnight, together with a handful of barley, some onions, a marrow bone and seasoning, as well as a few raw eggs in their shells. As my mother and the maid, together with the Fraülein, were generally busy making the house spick and span, I was often sent with the pot to the bakery and patiently instructed to add water to a spot marked inside the pot once I reached the bakery itself. Scores of children on similar errands were streaming towards the same destination. We each gave the baker a few coins and watched him place the pots inside the heated oven where they would cook slowly and evenly overnight. In this way, a hot dish was guaranteed for Shabbat without actually having to build a fire and cook in the home.

As the Shabbat morning services ended in the synagogues, an assortment of children and maids made their way to the bakery again, and as the baker lined up literally hundreds of pots on the stone floor in front of the oven, most of them the same shape and colour, using a special cloth handle, unerringly we picked and carried home our own *cholent* pot. The miracle was that I do not recall ever making a mistake and I came to believe that my own hands were truly guided by a universal hand.

Berehovo had more schools than most towns of that size and population. This was due to the composition of its nationalities and languages. There were Hungarian and Ruthenian elementary and secondary schools, an academic *gimnázium* with Czech and Hungarian strands as well as a commercial high school. The sole university in Carpathia was in Užhorod. The only elementary school where Czech was the language of instruction was the Jewish school.

I often think that while most people in the Czechoslovak Republic were either Czechs, Slovaks, Hungarians or Germans, it was mainly the Jews who were Czechoslovaks. As my father was a great enthusiast for the Republic, it was natural that my brother and I were sent to this school. Unusually it was also a school where modern, spoken Hebrew was taught as well.

My first teacher there was a Mr Václav. A tall, pale man, not much given to jokes or to laughter, but willing to spend extra time with me to improve my grammar and Czech spelling. He was always appreciative of the odd basket of grapes I would pick especially for him in our garden or vineyard. He was not Jewish himself and I considered it an honour to be asked for explanations of our festivals. Fortunately for me, he remained my teacher for the first three years of my schooling and for many months I carried in my pocket his final report, stating that I could read, write and speak Czech like a native.

Perhaps only someone born in a town like Berehovo could have the sort of embarrassing experience that happened to me many years later, while undergoing training analysis in Cincinnati in the United States. One day, my analyst wanted to know in which language I dreamt.

'English,' was my prompt reply. 'Are you sure?' he pressed. Of course I was. And I counted in English as well.

'Which then is your mother tongue?' he asked. Suddenly I wasn't sure and I was made to feel that I was covering up some dark secret.

We dropped the subject for the time being, but a few months later I visited my mother in Karlovy Vary, and as we were walking along its graceful colonnade, sipping mineral-rich hot water, I asked her, as I felt it was my right to do, what was my mother tongue. She stopped. I could swear she blushed. 'I'm not sure,' she said. 'But you are my mother, can you not remember?' 'Well,' she explained, 'it depended who else was in the house. With the family we spoke mostly Hungarian, but when cousins visited from certain villages it was Yiddish and then again when the Fräulein was around it had to be German. And when we had neighbours in, it was polite to converse in Czech. But you hardly knew any Ruthenian. That' – she smiled – 'was my advantage over you and your father because I was from Silce.'

There was also Hebrew, biblical and rabbinic, which came to me in *cheder*, with an Ashkenazi – or East European – pronunciation, and the more modern Sephardi accents we had to learn in school. Because I had a good ear, I made it a point to speak, or try to speak all of them with the right intonation. One of Tomáš Garrigue Masaryk's mottoes for education in the country was '*kolik reči umiš, tolikrát jsi člověkem*' – that as many times as you speak another language, so many times you are another person – had a real life illustration in me. Even if it confused my helpful analyst in Cincinnati, it served me very well in later life.

Elementary school was mornings only. For six days a week the afternoons were spent in the *cheder* classes. There were dozens of *cheder* schools in Berehovo. Each more or less owned and managed by the teacher in charge. I was enrolled in the Jakubovics' *cheder*.

Mr Jakubovics was lame, kindly and strict, and a heavy
smoker who was incessantly filling ready-made cigarette
shells with the help of a thin tube and mounds of finely cut
tobacco. I cannot recall actually learning the *alef bet** and
Hebrew reading; it must have happened at home, or perhaps
in the home of my grandparents when I was still younger.
What I do recall is my first day, just after Passover and a
couple of months before my fourth birthday and, having been
told over and over again that I was now a big boy, I arrived
dressed in my still new Passover suit. There was a small group
of us new children and our first lesson was to lick a generous
portion of acacia honey spread over the opening verses of the
Book of Leviticus. It was to teach us that the words of Torah
were sweet and that to study Torah was a joyous experience.
When we actually had to grapple with the text of this most
difficult of biblical books and to translate the Hebrew words
into an equally incomprehensible Yiddish, I had other and far
less sweet thoughts. But Mr Jakubovics was patient, his wife's
occasional snacks delicious, and his motto 'torah is di beste
s'choyra' – that Torah is the finest merchandise – which he
repeated over and over again, in time became my motto as
well.

* The Hebrew alphabet.

5

LIFEMANSHIP

There is a Yiddish saying which originally referred to Máramaros, and which expresses painfully and clearly the condition
of this area during much of its history. 'Ten measures of
poverty were given to the world. Nine were taken by Carpathia.'

Indeed, what united Jews, Ruthenians and Gypsies over
many generations, and across the mountains and the valleys,
was a relentless struggle for food, housing and clothing. For
most of its history, Carpathia was an economic backwater
where disease, especially tuberculosis, and illiteracy went
hand in hand with long stretches of worklessness and mount-
ing debts to landlords and shopkeepers.

It was a common sight in the villages that children going
to school and men on their way to work carried their shoes
on their shoulders to save leather. In Berehovo itself, pros-
perity was certainly not universal. At certain seasons, especially during planting and harvest time, hundreds of men
huddled at the edge of the market place long before dawn,
waiting for a day's work and wages, hoping with a solemn
desperation to be selected by arbitrary and capricious foremen
on the way to vineyards or the fields.

Yet the overall impression of Berehovo was that it was a
prosperous town. Its two market places, the Little Market
and the Big Market, separated by a long row of quite elegant
shops, were teeming with stalls. They were busiest always

on Mondays and Thursdays and on Sundays as well. On Saturday, because it was Shabbat, the area was deserted. Many of the stalls were occupied by farmers or their wives from the neighbouring villages, their produce was always seasonal and the poultry invariably alive. There were stalls with ribbons, toiletries and toys and many featured cheap or second-hand clothing.

In Berehovo, as far as I could tell, no one ever threw anything away. Even used pots and pans found willing buyers from tinsmiths who could plug almost any hole and guaranteed their work for life. Bargaining was part of the way of life and the purchase of even the smallest of items was preceded by lengthy and sociable discussions, often turning into noisy and profitable contests of wills. There were scores of regular shops which fringed the markets and each of them had a special atmosphere.

Quite a few of them belonged to relatives and I visited either those where I liked the smells, or where I knew I would be offered some home-made cakes, or where I was sent on one of my mother's many errands. At that time, relatively few people had telephones, so that if any news was to be given or gleaned, sending a child was the quickest way to achieve this.

My favourites included Rosner's, an elegant men's clothing shop where I was often given buttons that could be ground to a thinness that was just right for one of our games. My great-uncle Samuel had a textile shop, which had a wonderfully deep quiet about it coupled with a riot of colours.

Immediately next door was my great-uncle József, who was an exceptionally talented shoemaker. Although he sold a wide range of ready-made shoes and boots, our own footwear was always the custom-made work of Uncle József's hands. They too were guaranteed for life, or until my feet grew bigger.

I enjoyed the smell of the leather and various glues in his shop. His wife, my Aunt Julia, not only shared her always excellent snacks with me, but also taught me most of the social graces I possessed: how to remove dirt from under my fingernails, even how to cut them, and that nail parings must never be thrown away, but burnt, because after you die you have to come back to find and collect all your thoughtless rubbish. She taught me how to tie a double bow in my shoe-strings so that they did not come apart, how to comb my hair with a parting, even how to fart as quietly as possible. It was lifemanship imparted with love and a great deal of patient humour, and the habits she taught me in that shop are with me to this day.

My most favourite shop was the bookstore. It was filled with new and second-hand books. They were treasures, the very sight of which was a source of deep satisfaction. I was a voracious and totally non-discriminating reader. By the time I was six or seven it was well known in the family that any presents due to me, whether for birthdays or for Chanukah, should be in the form of money deposited in my account in the bookstore.

This arrangement had the added advantage of giving me a favoured-customer treatment by the owners. I was allowed to browse to my heart's content, trade in second-hand books as long as they were in reasonably good condition, and because I spent so much time in that shop, I was often called on to act as an adviser to adults who had no idea what could please their children.

I also made extensive use of Berehovo's one and only public library. It was not unusual for me, especially during school holidays, to take out two or three books in the morning and to return them the next day. On one occasion, the librarian challenged me, indeed virtually accused me, that I could not possibly have read three books so quickly. I felt sufficiently confident to ask her in turn to quiz me on the contents of the books. This she did with a measure of ferociousness, but after this experience I never had any trouble again.

My all-time favourites included the fantastic adventure stories of Jules Verne. Nor did I ever tire of Chinese fables which were stocked in our library both in Czech and Hungarian translations. There was endless pleasure in reading the plays of Shakespeare; Richard, as well as the various Henrys, together with Romeo and even Hamlet became almost personal friends. I found that the German translations were best for the English Bard, and I am still conscious of my regret that I knew no English, nor were there any opportunities to learn it.

There was great enjoyment from the short stories of Gogol and I made several attempts at reading Dostoevsky and Tolstoy. I must have borrowed *War and Peace* at least half-a-dozen times, but it was not until after my Bar Mitzvah that I managed to read it from beginning to end. Among my favourite Hungarian writers was Jókai Mór, whose stories and novels painted such vivid scenes of the world that was still known to my grandparents, but my all-time favourite was Karinthy Frigyes, hilarious and profound at the same time.

On many a winter evening, I would sit in the narrow space between the warm, tiled stove and the wall in our veranda. My aunts and uncles would be busy chatting with my parents around the table in the middle, or during Chanukah, playing cards – invariably 'Twenty-one' – while I, in my cosy nook, was so engrossed in a book that I would sometimes sob, and more often than not laugh out loud, quite oblivious to the looks and comments such as 'The child is really peculiar.'

I also enjoyed the stories of Yehuda Leib Peretz and Sholom Aleichem. My Yiddish was not quite good enough to read them in their original and I had to make do with Hungarian translations.

There was a period when I was determined to research for myself something of the modern history of our region. The few books and pamphlets I found in the library were very big on Garibaldi and Kossuth, as if a Golden Age beckoned in

1848. As best as I could understand, there was then a brief and intense revolt, inspired by the great Hungarian nationalist leader, Lajos Kossuth, and I was particularly interested in the fact that the Jews of the day supported him with tremendous enthusiasm. They fought in the revolution and when it failed, they paid a heavy price for their defeat.

I read of the attempt to modernize, indeed to Westernize, what was then the Hapsburg Empire, and to take account of the many economic and political grievances. Even as a child I could understand and sympathize with them.

For weeks the Jewish Lexicon was my bedside reading, and I was able to follow the rush that took place at the end of the nineteenth century on the part of Jews into professions and industry. Education was the main road which led to an outburst of initiative and energy that poured mainly towards Vienna and Budapest and some of the other real Hungarian cities.

I could see that Carpathia had somehow remained a stagnant backwater of the Empire, even in those heady days. Its timber and a few salt mines were useful enough, and so were some of the other mineral riches buried in the Carpathian mountains. But its wine and mineral waters were unable to travel too well or far enough. Another pamphlet described how many Jews, as well as Ruthenians, took a realistic look and decided that their future was as bleak as their past. They then joined the long lines at Ellis Island, beyond which was the more or less welcoming and opportunity promising life of America.

Indeed, soon after the turn of the century, two of my grandmother's brothers, Nathan and Bertie Neiman, emigrated to Pennsylvania and around that time, too, members of my mother's Neufeld family moved to nearby Ohio.

But the fact is that from my perspective as a child, Berehovo felt safe and secure, as well as prosperous and progressive.

Its three big churches, Roman Catholic, Protestant and

Russian Orthodox, had gleaming spires and meticulously kept gardens surrounding them. Just past the big Catholic church was Berehovo's one and only hospital, a modern and equally gleaming set of buildings, and said to be one of the finest hospitals in the district. I can still smell the powerful odour of iodine that seemed to envelop it.

Beyond the hospital a series of roads led to one of the town's great industries. A series of wine cellars at the foot of the hills and, further up, the vineyards themselves. By the time I was of school age my father was successful enough and certainly enthusiastic enough to have acquired both our own wine cellar as well as a vineyard on Rose Hill. From our wine cellar it was possible to see the grounds of the Berehovo football and tennis club, BFTC, which had its own semi-professional football team and whose players were both Jewish and Christian. During the football season, our Shabbat afternoon walks took us as far as our wine cellar and from its second-storey balcony, Gabi and I would follow the match in progress as best we could. There was great pride in our local team and we could generally tell whether they were winning or losing from the noise of the crowd, even more than from the distant scene of running figures.

The large entrance hall of the wine cellar housed the various presses, most of them still manual, but one was already mechanized. And beyond the presses stretched a five-hundred-metre-long tunnel, painstakingly cut into the rocky hillside, lined on either side with rows of oak barrels filled with an assortment of wines by the end of each autumn, and hopefully more or less empty by the following summer.

During the weeks of fermentation, the wine cellar was out of bounds because the fumes that filled it were lethal, but once that process was over, there came the all-important time of mixing and blending, which was the job of an expert.

Mr Samuel was one of the best wine masters in Berehovo, and my father employed him every year for this task. He was short and very bowlegged and when I was about seven I was allowed to spend a day mixing and blending the wine with him in the cellar. Dutifully I followed him from barrel to barrel and as he tasted the various red and white wines with the aid of a long glass funnel, I did the same with the help of a shorter one. The difference was that while Mr Samuel tasted the wine and then spat it out, I tasted and swallowed. By the time my father's younger brother Hershi joined us in the afternoon to see how we were getting on, he found me literally rolling among the barrels. For the first and one of the few times in my life I was well and truly drunk.

Hershi took one look, picked me up, bundled me into a waiting fiacre and took me home. My mother, whose one great fear was that of drunkenness, had no difficulty in diagnosing my condition, and also for the first time I received a merciless spanking on my bottom. With a bravado that was born of inebriation, I turned my head to her, saying, 'Go ahead, I can't feel a thing anyway!'

Not very far above the wine cellar was our vineyard. It too had a house and long rows of vines planted on a gentle slope. In springtime the carefully protected base of the plants was uncovered, the space between them hoed regularly. Wooden spades were repaired and weather-beaten ones replaced. As the vines grew they were made safe with raffia. From time to time they were sprayed with a solution of copper sulphate which Gabi and I learned to mix, to the delight of our father and the consternation of our mother, who could not remove the blue stains it left on our clothes.

By July, some of the more perfumed table grapes were ripe. But it was during the intermediate days of the festival of Succot, or Tabernacles, that the full grape harvest took place. Thirty to forty men were hired at dawn every day, because there were only three or four days for the harvest to be completed. All of us made our way to the vineyard, and by the time the sun came up, shears were busy clipping, *puttonys* –

large wooden containers – strapped to the strong backs of the labourers were filled and then taken down to be emptied into large vats. The vats themselves were on horse-drawn carriages and several times a day these were driven to the wine cellar. There the grapes were first put through a rough grinder and then put into one of the presses until only virtually dry husks were left. All the time, fresh juice flowed, and trickled into huge barrels. Then fermentation could begin. A selection of grapes remained on the vines until the first frostbite, and were quickly harvested by a much smaller group of men, and it was from this late crop that we produced some justly famous Aszu-type wine for our own consumption and some of it also for sale.

Other grapes were hung cluster by cluster on raffia from the ceiling of one of the large rooms in the house in the vineyard. Before sealing that room, sticks of sulphur were lit and, remarkably, through this process we had a supply of fresh grapes on our table at home right until Passover. Before the snow arrived, the base of the vines was covered with earth again and for months afterwards only a white stillness covered Rose Hill.

The other main industries of Berehovo included three large brick factories, which employed five hundred workers full-time and a great many others during certain seasons of the year. They were owned by the Vári, Kont and Winkler families who, like all those responsible for Berehovo's industries, were leading members of the Jewish community. There were two large barrel factories run by the Reisman and Neufeld families, who were distant relatives of my mother. There were three flour-mills, which belonged to the Kroh and Neuwelt families, as well as a stone quarry which belonged to the Fehér brothers and a kaolin mine operated by the Stern family.

Between them, they guaranteed full-time employment for two thousand workers, and many more on a seasonal basis. Berehovo also had insurance companies and four banks, which included the Jewish bank established soon after the First World War by the American Jewish Joint Distribution Committee and whose director was my mother's oldest brother, David (Desző).

Very near the railway station was the town's large sawmill complex, parts of which belonged to the Pritsch and Mermelstein families, and in time a part of it belonged to my father. In fact, many of my father's main business activities centred on the sawmill. Much of the timber developed by him in assorted parts of the Carpathian region was brought to this sawmill and turned into boards for furniture, railway sleepers, telegraph poles and pit props. I relished the noise of the blades, and even the smell of the sawdust had a pleasant excitement about it. My brother Gabi and I often volunteered to hammer the initials 'GG' on the side of thick pine, oak or walnut boards, announcing to all the world that these were the property of Géza Gryn, and took childish pride in the sight of growing piles neatly arranged next to the railway line, which was specially brought into the sawmill for easier loading into freight cars.

From time to time I was allowed to accompany my father to the forests where it all started. And when he was old enough, Gabi joined us on these expeditions as well. It took hours and sometimes most of a day to reach the beautiful sources of our livelihood. When a section of a forest was being developed, a rough road was readied for access. A few temporary timber huts were also constructed for a canteen and sleeping accommodation. They all smelled of fresh pine wood and strong pipe tobacco in roughly equal mixtures. There was also a shed where a variety of axes and chainsaws were kept. Gabi was a mathematical genius. Simply by looking at a tree, whether it was standing or felled, he could estimate how much timber it would eventually yield. He was seldom wrong and there was never any question about which of us would follow into that part of the family business.

It was in one of those forests that I learned my first lesson in ecology. The trees had been felled, their trunks already floating down a nearby river, tied to each other to form rafts. The roots had been dug out and the ground made even and smooth. 'On to the next project,' I exclaimed, surveying empty land. 'Oh no,' my father explained, 'not until we have replanted with saplings is this project done. It is only in that way that there is a future for the trees and for us.'

6

BELLA'S FAMILY

There has always been a certain amount of ambiguity about our family name, or rather about the correct spelling of that name. It may well be that it was a side-effect of the modernization that took place in Carpathia in the nineteenth century. To make for a tidier and more reliable public administration, it was decided that everyone in the region should have a surname. It was a splendid Napoleonic idea that was realized by a horde of census-taking Austro-Hungarian officials who descended on all the towns and villages of Carpathia at some point in the 1870s.

On one of our Shabbat afternoon walks, my grandfather Jacob told me this story of how this mass-naming enterprise came into being. He was a young boy himself when the officials came into his hometown of Sevluš,* a pretty Carpathian town near the Romanian border. It was in the autumn, and for several days before the town crier went around with his drum – a mode of communication that was still prevalent in my own childhood – and after a burst on the drum, which was meant to attract the people of every neighbourhood, he read out a proclamation. This stated that on a particular designated day, no one was to leave his or her home until the officials had visited their house, counted the heads who inhabited it and given each family their very own surname.

* Nagyszőllős in Hungarian; Vynohradiv in Ukrainian.

And so it was. But the day selected happened to be the eve of Yom Kippur. There was a particularly large number of Jewish families who lived at one end of the town. As the day wore on, they became increasingly impatient, but everyone waited as instructed. As the afternoon wore on, the men got ready for the synagogue by putting on the traditional white shroud or *kittel*. It was probably this sight that was responsible for the fact that by the time they got to the synagogue they discovered that they had all been called 'Weiss' ['White'].

We were never quite sure about our 'Gryn'. There were those in the family who claimed that it came with an ancestor via Holland and that it was originally 'Grijn' and then the 'ij' became a 'y', and sometimes I think that it may have been no more than a flower arrangement on the table with too much greenery in it, or perhaps a pre-Yom Kippur dish of spinach, because on most official documents – but surprisingly not on my birth certificate – our surname was spelt 'Grün', the German equivalent of what is still my favourite colour.*

It was our Jewish names that really mattered and how we lacked imagination! Or was it just an expression of being firmly rooted in the generations? In every third or at the most fourth generation the same names appear over and over again. My own name is Zvi-Hirsh – a 'deer' in Hebrew and Yiddish – and it was taken from my maternal great-grandfather, Reb Zvi-Hirsh Neufeld, who died just a few days before I was born in June 1930.§

He lived in Silce, a village not very far from Berehovo. He was the head of the Jewish community, which accounted for more than half of the population, and the owner of a great deal of its farming land, as well as a flour-mill and an oil

---

* See Chapter 7 for more about the Gryns of Vary.

§ Bella was reading Victor Hugo's *Les Misérables* at the time, which is why he was given Hugó as his Hungarian name.

mill that processed sunflower seeds. But some of his other grandchildren, including my uncles Béla and Marci, and my aunts Sara and Eta, as well as some of their cousins, also had boy children born not very long after me, and the result was that for many years afterwards, whenever there was a large family gathering, and a shout of 'Hershu!' or 'Hershele!' went up, six or seven children began to run.

Throughout my childhood it was a family tradition to visit Silce every four or five weeks, and much to the delight of Gabi and me, we always travelled by train. It was always on the first train on Sunday mornings. My parents, quite often joined by another aunt or uncle and their family, and my brother and me, made our way to the small station, which was the starting point for the narrow-gauge railway to Silce and beyond. Sometimes we arrived too early or occasionally the train was delayed, and then we waited in the warm and always busy inn, which was run by a Neufeld relative. Often the ticketing agent, or the conductor himself, would come into the doorway of the inn, calling: 'Let's go everybody! The train is ready' and within minutes we would be off.

It was understood that the front half of the train's two carriages was reserved for the *minyan*, that minimum of ten males over the age of Bar Mitzvah who constitute a worshipping congregation. Once the luggage was stowed away, the men and the boys would make their way to the front. Those over the age of thirteen would put their *tefillin* on their arms and heads, and the married men would don their *tallit* over their shoulders. And by the time the train pulled out of the station, the chant of the morning prayers drowned the clattering rhythms of the train.

Most of the members of this travelling congregation were salesmen, pedlars, or connected in one way or another with the timber industry. Many of them had come home to Berehovo on Friday in order to spend the Shabbat with their families and now it was time to return to work. By the time we reached Silce, after stopping at four or five other villages, the service was generally over. Many bottles of schnapps were being passed around, a perfect antidote to any germs, it was said.

Silce, or Beregkisfalud, was a typical Carpathian village. Its population was divided between Jews and Ruthenians and virtually everyone spoke both Yiddish and Malorus, or Little Russian, including the non-Jews. Indeed my mother often told me that she and her sisters were taught their first Hebrew blessings and prayers by their Russian Orthodox maid, who also made absolutely certain that her father's inn was strictly kosher.

The Neufeld family had lived here for more generations than anyone could remember. By the time of our family visits my great-grandfather Reb Hirsh had become part of the family's legend and a very powerful one at that. The oil mill was still functioning fully and well. Farmers would bring their crops of sunflower and other oil-bearing seeds to the mill by the sackful, and in time return to collect huge jars and tins filled with fresh oil of every sort of yellowish hue. His widow, my great-grandmother Roizi,* was very old, but still immensely energetic and she actually supervised the mill single-handed. The flour mill had already seen better days. It was never fully modernized or mechanized, and I suspect that she kept it going mainly because that was less complicated than to close it down.

The fields which began just behind her house, next to the railway station, stretched to well beyond the limits of the village. Many sections were planted with sunflowers and rape, as well as with corn and maize. Only two of her sons – my grandfather Abraham and my great-uncle Shmelke – chose to remain in the village. In addition to cultivating the fields, they also owned and ran the two inns of the village. In turn,

---

* Hebrew name, Rachel.

one of Abraham's sons, Uncle Alexander, had charge of the general store, and if there were any other businesses in Silce, I was not aware of them.

The village itself consisted of a single road with low houses lining both sides. A wide, but mostly shallow, river ran parallel with the road which was either dusty or thick with mud. The two most prominent buildings were the small Pravoslav, or Russian Orthodox church, and the synagogue, which was always beautifully whitewashed.

Because I was the first to be named after Reb Hirsh, I was Roizi's favourite. She was convinced that the soul of her husband had transmigrated into me. The fact that I had a number of somewhat younger cousins also called Hirsh, with varying equivalents of Hugo, Herman, and Hershu, made no difference. My memory is of a small woman, exuding nervous energy, always wearing a long black dress and an unchanging brown *sheitl* (wig). Because her house and the oil mill were next to the station, it was always our first port of call. Her opening greeting never varied: 'And when are you going back?' The answer never varied either. It was to be the last train returning to Berehovo.

She could be quite sharp, but because of my privileged status, uniquely in the family, I was above any chiding or criticism. I was even allowed to search through her sewing-machine box, which was crammed full with wonderful and mysterious objects and I could fill my pockets with roasted sunflower seeds with impunity.

Nor is it surprising that I quite often think about Reb Hirsh himself. Unfortunately none of his books or papers survived, and both the house and the oil mill have been demolished without a trace. Only the concrete floor of the ruined flour mill remains, perching precariously over the river.

From everything that I have been able to piece together, Reb Hirsh was a remarkable man indeed. He had the reputation of having been an *iluy*, a Hebrew term that describes young people whose phenomenal memory enables them to master the text of the Talmud virtually by heart. When he was still in his teens, he obtained *semicha* at the famous *yeshiva* of Bratislava which taught in the intellectual and spiritual tradition of the Chatam Sofer. He was therefore the unsalaried rabbi of Silce and because of his learning, as well as his family connections, people came from far and wide to consult him, and some stayed for quite long stretches of time to study with him as well.

The family relished the story of how Reb Hirsh nearly became the *rebbe* of the Satmar Hassidim. I have since discovered that the claim was more of a legend than historical fact. The charismatic leaders of this Hassidic sect were members of the Teitelbaum family, one of whom, Joel, or Reb Yoilish as we knew him, moved to Iršava in 1911, a small town next to Silce. There he led the community, and his learning as well as his strictness made him both famous and feared. His older brother, Chaim Zvi, had inherited the crown when their father died in 1904, but Chaim Zvi himself, who was both communal rabbi of Sziget, and the leader of the sect, died at the age of forty-six and his death was followed by a bitter struggle for his succession. There were those who wanted Chaim Zvi's fourteen-year-old son, Yekutiel Yehuda, to be the new *rebbe* and there were those who believed Reb Yoilish to be the right person.

It is possible that my great-grandfather may have been suggested as a compromise candidate, but despite the many conversations I overheard as a child, I doubt it. Reb Hirsh was not only his neighbour, but also a close associate of Reb Yoilish, and it was unlikely that he would have agreed to the role of competitor. But in this great dispute, which divided families as well as entire communities throughout Carpathia, he was in the perfect position to act as a power-broker. It is much more likely that he put his weight, not to mention his influence and considerable financial support, behind Reb

Yoilish. In the event, there was a surprising compromise. The fourteen-year-old Yekutiel was named communal rabbi of Sziget and Reb Yoilish became in time the undisputed leader of the Satmar Hassidim.

Throughout his long life he was, and remained, a vehement opponent of Zionism as well as of any reforms in Judaism itself. As a Reform rabbi who is also a Zionist, I sometimes think how different my own life might have been had Reb Hirsh been a serious contender. As a rule, such spiritual leadership is hereditary and the loyalty of the Satmar Hassidim is famous for its unquestioning fierceness. For reasons theological and temperamental, I am grateful that I only inherited Reb Hirsh's name; though if the oil mill and some of the fields had come with it, I would not have quibbled.

Of Reb Hirsh's many children, one daughter married into the Lebovics family in Feketeerdő and a few years later left with her family for America. Two daughters married and lived in Budapest, and another married into the Grosz family in Sevluš. Another son, Samuel, moved to Berehovo and ran a successful drapery business.

My grandfather Abraham was better known as Adolf, a fine enough name in the Austro-Hungarian monarchy, but a greatly despised one after 1933. On completing his *yeshiva* education, he travelled, made contact with his family members in Budapest and Prague, as well as in Silesia and the Balkans, but eventually returned and settled in Silce to work with his father.

His marriage to my grandmother is a questionably romantic story. Miriam Schönfeld, known as Mary or Mariska, was an attractive, intelligent and emancipated woman. In many ways she was considerably ahead of her time. Her family in Feketeerdő was even more extensive and prominent than the Neufelds. Young men came courting her from all parts of Carpathia, but as she had received some of her education in Budapest and Vienna, she made it abundantly clear that

anyone unfamiliar with German literature and general secular
culture had no chance with her at all.

When Adolf began to call on her family, he had the habit
of leaving Goethe's *Faust* or the collected works of Schiller,
or German translations of Shakespeare, Voltaire and Tolstoy
casually lying around. He also managed to quote a few lines
from Petőfi, the national poet of Hungary, and could whistle
the melodies of the latest Viennese operettas. There were no
psychological flies on Grandfather Adolf.

It was only after their wedding and the move to Silce,
which was totally barren of any secular culture, that Mariska
discovered that the pages in Adolf's German books were not
even cut. Before long, there came a succession of children –
David or Dezső, Rózsi, Alexander, Béla, Sara, my own mother
Bella, then twins – of whom only one, Eta, survived – and the
youngest son József. I was often told the story that when she
was pregnant with the last child and in the ninth month at
that, Mariska had no more than a mild stomach-ache and
only her dexterity saved József from being dropped into the
depths of the outhouse.

It was many years later, in the course of a conversation
with some of my older cousins, that I learned something of
Mariska's unhappiness and sense of isolation. Bright child
that I was, I never noticed that she had a problem with drink
but it explained why my own mother acted out of character
and so violently on the one occasion when I myself became
drunk. I can only guess at the depth of Mariska's misery,
which on one occasion drove her to attempt suicide, an
unheard-of and unspeakable act in Jewish life. She threw
herself into the river that flowed past their garden, but not
deep enough to do more than bruise herself.*

* *Entry from Hugo's journal, 24/25 December 1980*: 'More discoveries
about family . . . my grandmother, Mariska, DRANK! I was quite shocked
. . . It was very much the family secret – and it worked! She had run of the
family inn. Seems she rolled her tongue and that was the signal. Once she

The Neufeld family in Silce had its fair share of memorable, even eccentric characters. Great-uncle Shmelke was terrified of storms, and especially of lightning and thunder. During one of our visits, while I was walking off a heavy lunch, a sudden summer downpour sent me running for shelter into his house which, like my own grandfather's, was combined with a large inn. All the rooms were empty but I heard the sound of movement from a large wardrobe in one of the bedrooms. Thinking that a chicken or baby goat might be trapped in there, I opened the door only to find Uncle Shmelke hiding in it. I was no more than seven or eight at the time, yet I tried to explain to him everything I knew about electric charges, lightning conductors and the protective power of the blessing Jews recite on seeing lightning or hearing thunder, indeed praising God as the Author of the work of creation. It was all to no avail, and while he was alive I kept my promise not to tell anyone of our awkward encounter.

Another uncle had a glass eye. It was the result of a fishing accident and he was luckier than most people who had such accidents. Instead of using rods and hooks, or even nets, a popular method of getting a large and quick catch of carp or cod – the stuff of jellied *gefilte* fish – was to detonate a capsule of underwater dynamite and then simply pick up the temporarily stunned and floating fish. But quite often, a shift in current or a premature explosion would take the fisherman's arm or leg as well, and with that uncle it was an eye.

---

lay beside the river (which I recall running behind the house) and was all set to drown! Another time she fell, broke her shoulder, refused to go to the doctor and had pains, perhaps until she stepped into the gas chamber at Auschwitz! . . . At some stage my grandfather Abraham (Adolf) considered divorce or had it suggested to him and he took his wife to rabbi after rabbi, where she took solemn oaths that she would not drink again! But also she was "a lady" – and nonetheless greatly respected – and whenever she visited our home my mother would always offer her drinks from the tray and she always refused!'

1. Bella, Hugo, Gabi and Géza.

2. Bella and Géza on their engagement. In Hugo's eyes, no two people were more generous and kind-hearted than his parents.

3. Géza had piercing blue eyes and was always immaculately dressed.

4. Bella loved to laugh and sing, especially the hit songs from the Viennese operettas.

When Hugo returned to Berehovo in the summer of 1945, there was a mountain of papers belonging to the town's deported Jews piled outside the Great Synagogue. Uncannily, the handful he pulled out included some of these photographs of his own family.

1942.-43.

 elemi iskola אברהם הכהן קלעט מתנת עזר

5. Berehovo's Jewish Elementary School, 1942–3. Hugo's brother Gabi is standing in the back row, sixth from the left. One year later, all of these children would be selected for the gas chamber on their arrival at Auschwitz.

6. Lake Balaton, 1940. Gabi and Hugo with Géza's cousin, Boriska. While they were enjoying a family holiday, much of Europe was already at war.

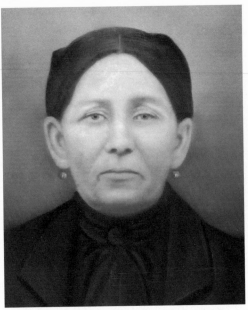

7. Bella's grandmother, Roizi. Her house was next to the railway station and on family visits to Silce, she was always the first port of call.

8. Hugo by the grave of his great-grandfather in Silce, 1989. Hugo's Hebrew name was Zvi, meaning 'a deer', after his illustrious great-grandfather, Reb Zvi-Hirsh Neufeld, who died just a few days before he was born. Roizi was convinced that her husband's soul had transmigrated into him. [*Naomi Gryn*]

9. Silce, 1989. Bella's family had lived in Silce for as long as anyone could remember. None of the original family homes or businesses is still standing. [*Naomi Gryn*]

10. Silce, 1989. Fifty years earlier Vasily had worked as a waiter in Hugo's grandfather's inn and still remembered some words of Yiddish. [*Naomi Gryn*]

11. Vary, 1936. In costume for a performance on New Year's Day.
Patyu is kneeling in the front row on the far right.

12. Vary, 1989. Everyone was thrilled to see Patyu back in town. [*Naomi Gryn*]

13. Géza's older brother, Lajos, survived the war serving in the Hungarian labour battalions. He emigrated to Israel in 1975 and died in 1986.

14. Géza's youngest brother, Icu. He died of tuberculosis as a young man.

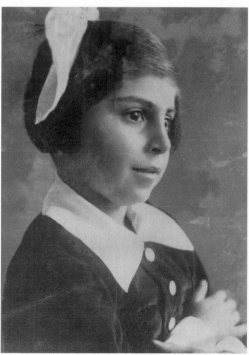

15. Lajos' daughter, Hédi, perished in Auschwitz when she was twelve years old.

16. Roman Vishniac's 16mm film of Carpathian
Jewish farmers from the 1930s briefly animates
the faces of these once beautiful lives.

By poignant coincidence, my great-grandmother Roizi and her son Abraham (Adolf) died within hours of each other – she of old age and he as a result of diabetes. My recollection of this sad chain of events is as clear as if it happened yesterday.

Grandfather was hospitalized in Mukačevo. Several times a week, my mother went by bus to visit him and quite often she took me along for company. Insulin treatment was still in its infancy and had not yet reached Carpathia. It was clear to everyone, especially to Grandfather himself, that he was dying.

He was a good-looking man. His white square-shaped beard was always meticulously groomed, but now his eyes were sunken and his conversation was whispered. It was his wish that two of his sons-in-law, my father and my aunt Rózsi's husband, Viktor Gelbman, should take him home as he wanted to die in his own bed in Silce. Perhaps because of my regular visits to him and the close bond that this forged between us, I was asked to accompany the two men, first from Berehovo to Mukačevo, where I waited in the large touring car until they led Abraham down the hospital steps. Then, on the way to Silce, I sat next to the driver and watched my father and uncle take off Grandfather's black suit and dress him in his *kittel*, the white shroud he wore in the synagogue during the High Holy Days and at the Passover Seder, and in which Jews are traditionally buried. It was done quietly and very gently and at Grandfather's own request. He wanted to meet his Maker in his own style.

To give him a little protection from the bumpy road that led to Silce, there were two large white cushions in the back of the car. It was a sad, yet very beautiful scene, and when he was finally able to rest, he asked me to lean towards him so that he could question me quite thoroughly about the Torah passage I was learning in my *cheder* class at that time. I knew that I must not cry and believed that I rose to the occasion by reciting quite long passages and could even quote some of the commentary of Rashi.* I was also aware of my father's appreciation. Some time later, he told me how glad he was that he let me join them.

On reaching Silce, I was allowed to visit my great-grandmother, but only after promising that I would say nothing about her son. Her own children and many of her grandchildren – including my mother – were already in the house, sitting around her large feather bed. By this time she was very small and frail and as I sat on the bed next to her she held my hand. I was often told afterwards that her last conversation was with me, but she believed that she was speaking with her husband. Within a couple of days, both of them were dead. It never ceased to puzzle me why the family decided that I was too young to attend their funerals.

On my last visit to Silce, not a single one of the original family homes or businesses were left. Some have disappeared altogether and grass is growing in their place, and some have been rebuilt in the dreary style of collective Russian villages. There was only one Jewish family – Yossel Blobstein and his wife – who were anxious to leave, as he said, 'before something awful happens to us again'. Yossel accompanied me on a walk through the small Jewish cemetery. It was overgrown with brambles and weeds and most of the family's tombstones were missing.

Only Roizi's stone was intact, and my daughter Naomi is quite convinced that her spirit was our guide and was responsible not only for the non-stop sunshine that facilitated our filming, but also for the breakdown of our equipment when I was about to sound off about some half-remembered unpleasantness in my childhood. We also met Vasily, who remembered me from the time he was a young waiter in my grandfather's inn. We spoke in Ruthenian about his troubles

* Rabbi Solomon ben Isaac (1040–1105), the great biblical commentator, who lived in France.

and angina, and about his nostalgia for the good old days. He wished me and my family – in a Yiddish that he had barely remembered after a lapse of fifty years – *mazel* and *bracha*, good luck and blessing, for the time ahead.

7

GÉZA'S FAMILY

One of the great joys of my childhood was visiting my paternal grandparents in Vary.* From about the age of seven or eight I was allowed to cycle on my own to them. It took me over two hours to get there, much of it spent climbing the one big hill on the outskirts of Berehovo, but after that it was pure pleasure to ride through a couple of villages, and on arrival to be greeted with a glass of fresh cold milk and a piece of brown bread stuffed with a large clove of garlic. It was my grandfather Jacob's firm conviction that living in the town was unhealthy – indeed unnatural – and that garlic was good for everything, especially the blood.

Vary itself was a sprawling village in a triangle between the rivers Borzsa and Tisza, bigger and more prosperous than Silce; Hungarian in language, culture and even in architecture. It was built on both sides of the Borzsa river, with a single bridge connecting two parts. A series of village greens dotted it, surrounded by triangular or square lines of low houses.

My association with Vary, peculiarly enough, is with the cows whose number seemed to exceed that of the humans living there. Or to be more precise, it is with the sound of cow bells tinkling evenly and mostly out of tune early in the morning and late in the afternoon. It would begin as the cows emerged in twos and threes or fives and sixes from the many

* Vári in Hungarian.

gateways and gradually joined up with each other, barely in need of the herdsman's prodding; soon they became a large herd and were taken for a day's grazing outside the village. Not unlike children going to school, but much more willingly and purposefully. The same chorus of bells was repeated as they returned at sunset with bulging udders, ready to yield their warm, foamy milk in the many small sheds behind the houses.

About a third of the population of Vary was Jewish, but there are no records of when Jews first came to settle there. Many of them knew Yiddish, but all of them spoke Hungarian in and out of the home. My father was born there and so was his mother, Hannah, who was known only as Hani, and it was her family, the Neimans, who in the course of the generations came to own several very large parcels of farmland including acres of meadows where most of the herds of cows went grazing, a vineyard of some repute, as well as an orchard of apples and pears. My grandparents also built a shop which was in the nature of a general store next to their long house. It faced the village green, and at the back, beyond the tall barn and an equally long cowshed, there was a steep drop to the Borzsa.

My great-grandfather, who died long before I was born, had a reputation of being a hard man. He was successful both as a farmer and a dealer in feed stuffs, and no one ever got the better of him in business. During the various kinds of harvest he had the habit of appearing in person and at the precise moment when lunch breaks were meant to be finished, to make sure that no one working for him would be able to slack off. He had learning as well, and the beautifully whitewashed synagogue was built largely through his initiative and with his financial backing.

My great-grandmother Esther was an entirely different personality. I know that she died in 1926 because the only memento I have of that family is a touching letter that was sent to her sons, Nathan and Bertie, in America, by my grandfather. In it, he gives them the sad news and reminds them in a beautifully written Hebrew postscript that the anniversary of her death, or *yarzheit* – when they were to recite Kaddish in her memory – is on Lag b'Omer, the thirty-third day after Passover.

Esther was by all accounts a saintly woman. Her generosity was proverbial and her particular speciality was to find husbands for poor or orphaned girls, as well as dowries to make them that much more attractive and desirable. That this is more than just family legend is proved by the fact that to this day her grave is a place of pilgrimage, mostly for women who come from considerable distances, especially if they have difficulties with their marriage. It may be, of course, that her reputation was enhanced by comparison with her husband, but I like to think that her goodness was just that: uncomplicated and spontaneous.

Certainly that was the great characteristic of her daughter, Hani, whose betrothal and marriage was an arranged one which I suspect was the work of the richly experienced Esther. The betrothal – as I have been told – took place in the early 1890s, when Jacob was imported from Sevluš. When Jacob arrived, Hani was playing with other young teenagers on the green. One of her brothers was sent to call her into the house. She was introduced to Jacob and then asked to go and change. While in her room, her parents joined her and asked her if she liked the young man. Not suspecting anything, she said that she did. 'That is just as well then,' they said, 'because he is going to be your husband', and that was that.

In the event, and from everything that I could observe, it was a very good marriage indeed. Their first child, Lajos, was born whilst Hani was still in her teens, and was soon followed by the birth of my father, Géza, in 1900. Then came three girls, Szerén, Rózsi and Gizi, and then two more boys, Hershi and Ignác, who was known as Icu.

Farming, shopkeeping, community tending and rearing the family kept Jacob busy. As a child, I was filled with awe at his versatility. A small room adjoining the barn was a shoe repair shop. Another room next to it was a carpentry workshop and yet another gleaming whitewashed room had churns for making butter and cheese. They were always tidy. The tools had a pleasing geometry and each had a unique and still-remembered smell of glue, wood shavings and milk. There was also the smell of oils for fuel and for lamps, because Vary did not yet have electricity, and they were stored in a shed which adjoined the corner shop. In the shop itself I relished the mixture of aromas of cigarettes, dried pulses, small open barrels of pickles and salted herrings.

It always amazed me that in whatever part of this varied estate Jacob was busy or at work, it was as if that and chiefly that was his lifelong speciality. He was also Vary's completely untrained, but informal and highly effective dentist. His cure for a toothache was to put some of the concentrated and still moist tobacco from his pipe on the aching spot, and to my surprise, and to the delight of his patients, the cure almost invariably worked.

During the First World War, Jacob was drafted into the Austro-Hungarian army, and at the age of fourteen the running of all the family's holdings fell on the shoulders of my father. It was a lasting source of pride in our family that when Jacob returned at the end of the war, he found everything in perfect order. The only regret was that my father never completed his schooling, but such was his intelligence – or perhaps it was his power of persuasion – that a year later he made his way to Germany, got a place in a technical college which specialized in forestry, and on qualifying, returned not to Vary but to Berehovo and began his own and separate career.

As a rule, when I visited Vary, I would spend a night, and sometimes two, with my grandparents. By this time Lajos had his own house and family in Vary. Before he married, there was a plan that he, too, should emigrate to America and join his two uncles who were already well-established there. He was given sufficient money by his father and mine for his travel expenses and a bit of capital to start a suitable enterprise once he got there, but in the event he only managed to get as far as Paris. His love of cards became his undoing, and for reasons that were never fully explained to me it became my father's brotherly responsibility to go to Paris himself, bail out Lajos and return with him to Vary.

In the intervening years, I have sometimes thought how different our life might have been had Lajos been able to complete his trip, made something of a success of his life there, and in that way set a pattern for the rest of his brothers and sisters. Eventually he married a quiet and very delightful woman from Subotice in Yugoslavia, and their elder daughter, Hédi, who was my age, pretty and funny, also became a trusted friend. She and I liked to look at the storks' nests built next to the chimneys on roof after roof, and we used to spend endless hours imagining and talking about their winter homes in Egypt. She and I also became adept at climbing some of the huge mulberry and chestnut trees which were abundant in Vary.*

My favourite companion was my cousin József, who was and still is known only as Patyu, and who is a few years older than me. His mother, Szerén, died when he was two; his father returned to his own family in Romania and Patyu was brought up by our grandparents. He was about my size, but much stronger, more daring and very skilled in milking, fishing and handling every kind of farm machinery. With my bits

---

* Hédi, together with her six-year old sister, Ági, and their mother, Klári, were gassed on arrival at Auschwitz. Lajos survived the war, serving in the Hungarian labour battalions. He remarried, had another child, and came to Israel at the same time as Patyu in 1975. Lajos lived in Be'ersheva until his death in 1986.

of biblical knowledge, I often thought that it was a case of Jacob's hands being passed down to Joseph. He also had a great advantage over me. Whereas I would get punished for making a mess or for neglecting chores, Patyu could come and go as he pleased and do as he liked, and if I ever questioned the unfairness of this situation I was invariably told: 'Don't forget, he is an orphan.' To this day I am almost ashamed to admit that there were times when I felt that being an orphan was a wonderful kind of privilege.

Across the road from my grandparents' house lived the Lefkovits family. They were not only distant relatives, as were many of the Jewish families in Vary, they also had horses. Indeed their business was to breed and buy and sell horses. And such was the economy of that part of the world that the price of horses was never the same in Czechoslovakia as in Hungary. Thus it came about that one of my first practical skills was the somewhat unexpected ability to smuggle horses.

Hungary was no further than the far side of the Tisza river. At night, a group of horses would be led to the river bank. There, generous amounts of sacking were wrapped around their hooves, and even more generous bags of oats hung on their necks. Once every possible precaution was taken to make and keep the horses quiet, they were led on to a waiting raft. And trusting that those who were deputed to entertain or distract the armed border guards further along the river were doing just that, silently we floated to the other side of the river. As soon as we landed, the waiting Hungarians quickly took the still feeding horses and led them behind some tall bushes, paid one of the Lefkovits men and within minutes we were floating again, sitting on piles of empty sacks, back to Czechoslovakia.

There were other occasions when we crossed empty and returned with the horses to Vary, and while it may be true that all horses look the same in the dark, I sometimes have the feeling that some of the horses we bought in Hungary were none other than the very horses that were sold a few months earlier. Occasionally I heard people in Berehovo speak of the men of Vary as nothing but a bunch of horse thieves. Young as I was, I quickly rose to their defence. 'You simply do not understand,' I would say, 'there is a world of difference between a smuggler of horses and a thief, and my friends are no thieves.'

Many, many years later, my wife Jackie and I attended a unique gathering of Holocaust survivors in Israel. One of the evening functions took place in the huge indoor basketball stadium on the outskirts of Tel Aviv. It was a hot night and although we arrived early, I wanted to be near an open window, so we climbed up to the very last row of this arena which was eventually filled with eighteen thousand people. One of the last to arrive was a man who had 'American' written all over him, and the only seat he could find was the one right next to me. Soon we were in conversation, and by way of establishing his credentials, he gave me a business card which told me that his name was Robert Leroy, and that he was the president and founder of an organization called Witnesses to the Holocaust Inc., in Elgin, Illinois. I asked him if this was his full-time and salaried occupation, and by way of reply he gave me another card. It carried a picture of a horse and described Robert as a breeder of horses. He added, 'I bet you have never met a Jewish horse breeder before.' When I told him that he was quite wrong, and that I had actually grown up with, as it were, horse breeders in our backyard, and proceeded to tell him where and how it came about, it is not difficult to imagine my thrill when he told me: 'Well, before I was Robert Leroy, I was Otto Lefkovits, and I was probably the one who taught you all you know about smuggling horses.'

During most of my visits my two young uncles, Hershi and Icu, were generally at home. They were delightful, gentle and funny, but they often had to rest. I became conscious of the special looks that passed between my grandparents when one of them began to cough. From time to time I was allowed to spend an entire weekend in Vary and it was in the course of one of our Shabbat afternoon walks that I came to understand fully the nature of the shadow that I had sensed and felt hovering over the family for a long time.

My grandfather was a heavy pipe smoker. His assortment of pipes hanging below his full grey beard were almost part of his face. Not being able to smoke from sundown on Friday until at least three stars appeared on Saturday made him quite tense during Shabbat.

The Friday evening meals were always pleasant – a delicious meal accompanied with the best of his wines and interspersed with *zemirot*, an assortment of delightful melodies set to ancient religious poems, created a mellow and truly delightful mood. So much so that I cannot ever remember actually going to bed, only waking up in the morning, covered by an always crisp and ample feather-bed. Going to the synagogue service in the morning with the men was also a leisurely affair and I was always proud of the respect that was shown to my grandfather by all the other members of the community. But soon after the brief nap that he took after another Shabbat meal, my grandfather's tension grew by the minute. His addiction to tobacco was only exceeded by the strictness of his Shabbat observance, and it was mainly to ease the tension that we would go for a walk in the village or, to be more accurate, we used to race around the village.

It was on one of these walks, with my grandfather clutching one of my hands and Icu holding the other, that I became aware of an unnatural sweat on his face, and even the palm of my uncle's hand, who was still only in his twenties. Soon we had to stop because Icu had another violent fit of coughing. I was shocked and fearfully anxious at the sight of the blood that quickly filled his large white handkerchief. Slowly we returned home. Once Icu was in bed, my grandfather took me outside and sat with me on a bench and, as calmly and quietly as he could, explained to me the nature of tuberculosis. 'It is the curse of our family,' he said. Both of the younger sons were infected with it, as Patyu's mother had been as well. For the first time I saw him cry.

When they were well enough and sufficiently strong, both Icu and Hershi worked with my father, mostly supervising the cutting of timber in the more distant forests where the fresh air was thought to be good for their condition, or sometimes working in the office of the sawmill in Berehovo.

Icu was the first to die, though he was the youngest. When it happened, Hershi, who was in a phase of remission, was working on a project near Jasina* at the far end of Carpathia. It was decided that on no account was Hershi to be told of the death of his brother. The risk of an emotional upset that could bring about another tragedy was just too great. When the seven days of mourning and sitting *shiva* in Vary came to an end, my father set out to visit his younger brother. I was allowed to go along, but I had to promise to be normal and cheerful and, if it became necessary, even to lie about Icu.

My father had greater problems. To disguise the fact that he was in mourning, on the way to the station we stopped at the barber's to have over a week's growth of beard cut with clippers, rather than be shaved and in that way violate the prohibition against shaving for the first thirty days. It was not his usual clean-shaven look, but close enough not to arouse any awkward questions, and although it was a warm day, before the train reached Jasina, he put a pullover over his waistcoat which featured the large traditional cut on a mourner's garment that followed the burial.

On the way up to the site in the forest, we even rehearsed in the horse-drawn carriage the topics and the kind of news

* Kőrösmező in Hungarian.

that we would tell him. In the event our visit went off better than we had expected. Hershi himself did not ask any difficult questions, and nor did he think that there was anything the matter with our appearance. He looked well enough and he was quite cheerful. We even managed to look quite pleased when he took out his violin and played some of my favourite tunes after lunch, although I knew that the playing and even the hearing of music in that period of mourning was against tradition. To make sure that he did not return home until at least the thirty days of intense mourning were over my father invented a series of urgent tasks for Hershi that would keep him safely in the mountains and so postpone a little longer his inevitable and intense pain.

I was not there when Hershi came back to Vary, but before long his tuberculosis, coupled with a dreadful injury that he suffered in connection with Hungary's occupation of Carpathia, led to his death when he was just thirty years old.

Hershi's great love was music, and it was always thought that he had the making of a great violinist. He had a very fine instrument, said to be a Stradivarius. Certainly many people came to see it, and if Hershi was satisfied with their musicianship, he was quite willing and pleased to let them play a few notes on it. His own teachers were part of the small Gypsy colony who, like the Jews, were an integral part of the population of Vary. But unlike the Jews, they lived in a camp, as they still do, at the edge of the village.

At that time I knew very little about their origins or occupations. The popular image was that of an easygoing group of men and women who were not quite to be trusted. My own impressions were entirely different. Perhaps this was because it was Hershi, with whom they had a deep and affectionate relationship, who introduced me to the Gypsy camp. They were certainly cheerful. They were also warm and friendly, always tempting me to eat dishes which they knew I had to refuse. 'A little bacon would do you good. It will make you

tall and strong.' But since none of them was particularly tall,
I was not very impressed by this argument.

There was something little short of magical about those
evenings I spent in their company. Sooner or later there was
music making. They understood instinctively Hershi's great
passion and need. Two or three of the men would join him
with their violins and sometimes they would be accompanied
by a cimbalom as well. Mostly they just improvised, weaving
melodies and harmonies, giving the most popular and com-
monplace songs a freshness and an excitement that touched
me to the core of my being. Quite late one evening, after such
an impromptu concert, we were sitting around a warming
campfire, by the edge of the Tisza. The moon was full and
the sky filled with stars reflected in the gently flowing river.
One of the older men kept looking up at the moon, and after
a while leaned over to me and said, 'Listen hard, and you will
hear King David himself play the violin on the moon.'

Even after the distance of some fifty years, I can still see
and feel that scene; the stillness, the warmth, the large yellow
patch on the river and I am quite sure that on that night I did
hear King David play his violin on the moon.

Hershi's decline could not be controlled. He spent more
and more time in bed, and because it was winter, I had to
wait until someone could drive me to Vary so that I could
visit him. When his end came, my parents were in Budapest
and I was at home with my brother and a maid. A telephone
call came from Vary, where there was only one line at the
post office. It was from my Uncle Lajos. He told me the names
of some drugs and injections that Hershi required urgently
and he added, 'You had better tell your father that our brother
does not have much time left.'

Despite the heavy snow and icy roads, I quickly cycled into
the town centre and got the medication from the pharmacist
who knew all about Hershi and his illness. I gave the package
to one of the taxi drivers waiting outside the Royal Hotel and

asked him to deliver it to Vary as quickly as possible. I assured the driver that my father would pay him in a few days' time.

I was not quite sure how to make a long-distance telephone call. Our phone had to be cranked, and when the operator finally answered, the number had to be given to her and the connection was made from Central. I did know that to call Budapest I needed the help of the *interurbán* operator. My good fortune: the operator turned out to be a very sympathetic woman. At once she understood my anxiety and my dilemma. She found the number of the hotel where my parents were staying, but when the call reached the hotel my parents were out and it was the operator who left an urgent message for them to call me back at home.

About an hour later, my father returned the call. By that time I had rehearsed a little speech. Its solemnity and formality have remained in my memory to this day. 'I deeply regret to inform that your dear brother, Hershi, is very severely ill. I am also instructed to advise you that you should make your way to Vary at the greatest possible speed.' My father assured me that he would do just that and hung up. To this day, I remain touched by the *interurbán* telephonist who called me a few minutes later. 'I was listening to you,' she said, 'and you handled a very difficult job well.'

Very late that night my father arrived home in a Budapest taxi. As my mother was still out shopping, he had left her a note asking her to pack their luggage and take the train home. He then took the very first taxi and probably gave the driver the biggest fare of his career. The only stop they made was to buy a blanket for a bit of extra warmth in the back of the cab.

Naturally I was still wide awake when he arrived. After paying the driver and getting the maid to give him a meal, my father got on to a local taxi man, and by the time he had washed and changed clothes another car had arrived.

Sensitive to my distress, he let me accompany him to Vary. Thus I was present at Hershi's end. The two of us joined my grandparents in his room, lit only with a small oil lamp. His pale face was framed by large white pillows. Suddenly he coughed and thick blood was splattered all over the pillow. Then he was still and I knew that he was dead. For what seemed a long time, every one of us wept. I can still hear my grandmother Hani sobbing, 'Dear God, another of my children!'

This was the second tragedy that I had witnessed at my grandparents' home. The first one, which was, in a curious way, connected with it, occurred more than a year earlier, in October 1938. The betrayal and dismemberment of Czechoslovakia in Munich* was already a *fait accompli* and 10 November was the date set for Carpathia to be handed over to the Hungarians.§

In an attempt to soften up the population who were about to be 'liberated', a terrorist organization was formed. Presumably because they were the lowest of the low, they were called the *Rongyos Gárda*, or Ragged Brigade. On that night, their target was Vary. So easy to reach from just across the Tisza river. No doubt they had information about the village and its social structure. The Magyar majority of the village would have seen to it. Their target was the Gryn household.

When Hershi heard some commotion coming from the cowshed, he went out to investigate and as soon as he reached the doorway, one of the terrorists spotted him and buried his sharp axe just below his shoulder-blade. Hershi was left there unconscious, and it was only when my grandfather made his way to the cowshed soon after dawn for the morning's milking that he was greeted by the terrifying spectre.

---

* Munich Conference, 29–30 September 1938.

§ The Vienna Arbitration on 2 November 1938 agreed to Hungary's annexation of the area known as 'Felvidék', comprising part of Slovakia and part of Sub-Carpathian Ruthenia, including Berehovo. Hungary took possession of the rest of Sub-Carpathian Ruthenia – a briefly autonomous region known as Carpatho-Ukraine – on 15 March 1939.

His son was half-dead and, with a senseless brutality that still defies reason and understanding, all the cows and a couple of calves pointlessly slaughtered. They were slashed open from head to tail. It must have been a friend of the family who telephoned us in Berehovo still before breakfast. My father was still wearing his *tefillin* and was in the middle of his morning prayers.

Within an hour we were in Vary. By this time the stench of dead cows filled the air. Even worse was the sight of Hershi, who was by this time lying face down on his bed, breathing, but not yet able to speak, and being tended by the local doctor who kept muttering 'Murderers, murderers, all of them.'

Many years later, at an exhibition of Francis Bacon's paintings, I not only recognized the shape and the texture of those blood-covered carcasses, but somehow even their smell reached me across the decades and I had to leave the gallery for fear of vomiting all over again.

By this time many friends were on hand, members of the Lefkovits, Kosher and Deutsch families. A group of men were digging deep trenches near the river bank, wordlessly pulling the carcasses towards them and the women comforting my inconsolable grandmother.

Perhaps it was the memory of this scene that, a few weeks later, made me probably the only person who was crying when the population of Berehovo lined the frosty road that led into our town from the Hungarian border, to greet the arrival of our new masters.

Today there are no Jews left in Vary at all, and long ago the synagogue became a warehouse. Nor is there anything left of my family's property. Patyu and his young and very pregnant wife, Joli, had returned to Vary after the war and were living in the house. A sudden and violent flood, on the eve of New Year 1949, washed absolutely everything into the Borzsa river. They stood on the bridge a few steps away, watching, with just one blanket left between them.

The fields were even bigger than I had remembered. There is
still a Gypsy camp on the outskirts of the village. The houses
have a more permanent look about them, certainly newer and
bigger, and also equipped with electricity. The Gypsy Judge*
was welcoming, and delighted to arrange for a bonfire and a
dance, but the music was provided by an electric guitar.

The Jewish cemetery had been neglected. Many stones were
missing. I was shocked to discover that some of them had
been used for pavements and that a nearby farmer used some
other stones for the extension of his cowshed. Perhaps it
was a vestige of sensitivity that made him face the Hebrew
inscriptions inward. But Esther's tombstone beckoned like a
light and we were touched to find that there were some fresh
flowers on it. The only emotional breakdown we experienced
came to us in that cemetery. Naomi was first to break down
near that grave; soon Rachelle and I joined her. For a long
time we held each other and cried.

* The head of the Gypsy, or Romany community.

8

ARRIVAL OF THE
HUNGARIANS

I remember that November day in 1938 when Berehovo's life, as I knew and loved it, came to an end. Indeed, I remember it as if it happened yesterday. Early in the morning, the sight of the Czechoslovakian flag, which was taken down in a very muted ceremony in the centre of the Big Market, put me into a very depressed mood. That flag was the only thing I could draw properly. The flagpole itself was surrounded by a small group of soldiers and their officers, who looked every bit as dispirited as I felt. Slowly they marched to waiting lorries around the corner, climbed into them and on to a few motor-cycles, which had sidecars as well, and drove off in the direction of Mukačevo without any fanfare.

By this time my teacher Mr Václav was gone. But before he left, he had come to our home to say goodbye and the farewell present he gave me was a biography of Masaryk. There was then about an hour's strange quiet in Berehovo. In company with a couple of friends we cycled around the town, aimlessly. By then Gabi had his own small bicycle and he tagged along.

Practically all the shops had signs in two languages and I began to notice that their owners, perched on ladders, were busy printing over the Czech words. Some were inside the shop windows themselves, busy removing tags that had Kčs* prices on them.

* Abbreviated from *Koruna československých*, Czechoslovak crowns.

By chance as we passed the courthouse, the biggest and architecturally the most distinguished building in town, an enormous Hungarian flag was being rolled down from its top windows, reaching almost to the pavement. They must have been busy preparing it for days. Like lemmings, suddenly from every direction, men, women and children came pouring into the streets, dressed in their finest clothes and many wearing traditional Hungarian folk costumes with ribbons flying from head-dresses and jaunty hats. They were heading up Main Street and Bocskay Street towards the railway line. Some carried flags with St Stephen's crowns embroidered or painted on them. Many boys were wearing Levente caps modelled on Hungarian military headgear, even some Jewish kids. But only Christian youths were ostentatiously showing white socks, which had become the peculiar symbols of Nyilas,* or fascist sympathizers.

The parallel poles of the rail crossing, now in their upright position and already covered in flags, and the large 'Welcome to the Liberating Heroes!' poster marked the head of the reception line.

On one side of the road there was a platform for the dignitaries. My friends and I parked our bicycles in a nearby yard and found a place directly across the platform. By now, the crowds were enormous. Pretty well everyone must have been there. As eleven o'clock approached, the announced time for the formal entry of the Hungarians, you could feel the excitement in the air. A small local marching band had taken their place next to the platform and intermittently played patriotic melodies, repeating the 'Rakóczy March' over and over. In between the brass band's numbers, a small Gypsy ensemble entertained with Hungarian folk songs, which the crowd was only too happy to sing.

Among the officials and community leaders jammed on the

* The Arrow Cross Party.

platform and trying to look both important and nonchalant, I noticed with some astonishment our rabbi, Solomon Hirsch, wearing his First World War uniform, freshly cleaned and bedecked with medals he had earned as a chaplain in the Austro-Hungarian army. Since no one ever threw anything away in Berehovo, that should not have surprised me, but I doubt that he had expected to wear it again. In my eyes, he looked and felt completely out of place.

Not much less astonishing was the presence of Uncle Deszö in a group of other men, standing below the platform. They too were wearing officers' uniforms, veterans of that war. My uncle was a lieutenant, and like Rabbi Hirsch, richly decorated with medals.

It was a cold, misty day. At eleven o'clock on the dot the sound of more distant bands began to be heard, and soon we could see on the grey horizon the leader of that stately parade, which had come to 'liberate' us. He was a high-ranking officer, riding on a beautiful stallion, wearing a steel helmet and with one hand holding his unsheathed sword against his shoulder. When he reached the platform, he stopped. Behind him, the military band also stopped playing. One of the men who stood on the edge of the platform said some emotional words of welcome. Bouquets of flowers were thrown from the crowd. The General Brigadier replied quietly, with his sword sweeping in the direction of the town.

As he moved off, the shouts of the townspeople all but drowned out the sound of the bands. Behind them came columns of soldiers, some on horses, some on the backs of lorries. Then came a line of horse-drawn cannons, more soldiers with rifles slung across their backs, riding slowly on motorcycles equipped with sidecars. More horses were pulling large cooking vats on wheels and finally, hundreds of foot soldiers, with their officers riding alongside, waving at the tireless, yelling crowd.

To all intents and purposes this was a folk celebration. The kind I had never seen before. The only parades I had seen before were on May Day when I would bedeck my bicycle with elastic red paper and join the marching workers carrying banners. They too shouted slogans and sang different but equally patriotic songs, but none of them came anywhere near this kind of popularity and excitement. With the experience in Vary only a few weeks earlier, and of what Hungarians were capable of doing still so painfully vivid in my memory, as far as I could see I was the only person in the vast crowd who was crying. Ever since my earliest childhood I had been given to premonitions, but I could not even begin to guess how fearfully right this premonition would prove to be.

It was not long after the arrival of the Hungarians that all kind of changes could be seen. There were the obvious things. The shop signs became exclusively Hungarian and the prices were now in pengő.* There were hordes of new officials who came, believing that there would be very rich pickings in this newly conquered part of their country. As far as the majority of the population were concerned – not speaking so much now about the Jewish community – for them this really was a kind of liberation in terms of language, culture, and also the sense that they would now have the opportunity to run the town along lines that were more congenial to them.

Since the majority of Jews in Berehovo were also Hungarian speaking, they believed at this early stage that their situation would not change radically. We knew that in Hungary proper there had already been years of so-called 'Jewish Laws' at work. Of course they were really anti-Jewish laws and very much modelled on the Nuremberg Laws, already operational in Germany since 1933. There were some Hungarian 'Jew Laws' which had started as early as the 1920s. They limited the number of Jews in higher education, in some of the learned professions, and ownership of certain kinds of land. But if the

* Hungarian currency from 1926–1945.

Jewish community of Hungary had come to tolerate them and somehow work out a *modus vivendi*, it was widely believed in Berehovo that in time, so would we, because it was not very long before some of these 'Jew Laws' also became operational in Carpathia.

The first of these laws, which had a sudden and most unwelcome impact on the Jewish community, concerned licences for business and workshops. The Hungarian word *ipar* was on everyone's lips. It became necessary to go to the town hall, wait for hours and sometimes days before one could see the right official, bring every conceivable proof that would establish the applicant's right to the premises and that he was able to do the work for which those premises were to be licensed. This applied in all cases, from the large brick factories to the smallest shoe repair shops. It also became very clear that those Jews who had non-Jewish partners, or who were prepared to take in non-Jewish partners, had the licence granted to them a great deal quicker than those who were working on their own or who had only Jewish employees. There was also a great deal of talk about bribes and that the new set of officials expected generous financial considerations in order to sign and stamp the necessary piece of paper that would allow you to function in your work.

My father had a partner in the share of the sawmill that formed part of his business. His name was Emil Szusz, and by this time they had worked together for a number of years. Emil and his wife had no children, and some members of his family had emigrated to Canada some years earlier. While their application was going through the lengthy process, Emil must have discerned the writing on the wall, and virtually overnight he left Berehovo with his wife to begin a new life in Canada. I do not know if he took any capital with him, or whether he and my father made any agreements or arrangements about the transfer of some of their funds. I do remember receiving one or two letters some months later, but from that time until the present I have not heard about what became of Emil Szusz.

A Hungarian book-keeper who had been employed by my father for several years was asked to accept a nominal partnership in the business. He readily agreed and within days, the *ipar* was granted. As far as the development of timber, its preparation in the sawmill and marketing was concerned, business continued more or less as before.

Business licences were not the only vital documents required. It became much more urgent and important for everyday living to have a nationality. It had to be Hungarian, and in order to obtain it, proof had to be brought to another set of even more greedy officials that the applicant's family had lived in Greater Hungary ever since 1850. For the majority of the Jewish community this was virtually an impossible task. Many had arrived after that date, others came from small villages where record keeping was not of a particularly high standard. It was something of a concession on the part of the authorities when they permitted the use of internal Jewish communal records to be brought for this purpose. This proved to be of some advantage because virtually every community kept a *pinkas kehillot*,* and as far as the Jewish community was concerned, everything possible was done to help with these applications.

Állampolgársági was another word which suddenly became familiar to everyone. It meant the citizenship document which had to be produced, whether it was for registering home or field or vineyard. It was necessary when a child was about to be enrolled in school or to register any kind of vehicle, and of course an absolute prerequisite for anyone who wished to apply for a passport or travel document.

We were lucky enough, and my father obviously generous enough to obtain both the official citizenship document for the family, as well as a set of passports for every member.

---

* Written record of the community's births and deaths.

Soon there was a joke making the rounds in Berehovo. On the crosses and crucifixes outside the churches of the town as well as on the small roadside shrines, the four letters 'INRI', namely, *Iesus Nazarenus Rex Iudaeorum*, was given a new and bittersweet twist. It was said that those four initials really stood for *Indulok Nazaretba Rendezni Irataimat* which means 'I am leaving for Nazareth to arrange my papers.' The situation was sufficiently ominous that most heads of Jewish families made a point of checking that one way or another they were inscribed in the *pinkas kehillot*. The officials in charge of the Jewish community readily cooperated, but in the event, this could not help everyone.

The biggest change in my life clearly had to do with education and schooling. All the primary schools had now become formally Hungarian, and while in my own school modern Hebrew continued to be taught, the teachers responsible for non-Jewish subjects had to be recruited from among the newly arrived 'liberators' from Hungary, who saw their role more as colonizers than educators. The teacher assigned to my class was a short fat woman who lost whatever friendship or loyalty I might have developed for her within hours of setting foot in our class. She told us that Hebrew was a useless, dead language and that the sooner we became patriotic Hungarians and 'not waste time with your funny old-fashioned customs', the better it would be for us.

There were no more opportunities to read or speak Czech, and while I kept all my books and periodically rearranged them on my shelves, they were gradually being moved higher and higher and being read less and less. We had to learn the poetry of Petőfi, learn the geography of the Hungarian Puszta – a part of central Hungary that was as barren as it was boring – and learn every possible detail of the life of the great Hungarian leader of the day, Admiral Horthy. His naval rank in a completely landlocked country was just one more unexplained mystery to me.

By this time I greatly enjoyed the company of a very bright group of friends. My own cousin, another Hershu – the son of my uncle Marci – was intense and intelligent. He and I spent a few hours together every week studying and testing each other on that week's Torah portion. I spent time with Teller Öcsi, who was my age but much bigger, and therefore an increasingly important ally in the street fights that became a fairly regular occurrence when Christian boys turned on us. This friendship also enabled me to visit his father's large carpentry workshop and there was particular pleasure in watching some of my father's timber turned into exquisite furniture by Öcsi's dad. I was very fond of Czuker Yossi.* His big sisters were among the most beautiful girls in Berehovo and his home was very near my *cheder* which made frequent poppings-in congenial.

Berner Laci was another close friend. We were distantly related. He was very good looking; always beautifully dressed and because his father owned one of the town's night clubs I considered him the very epitome of sophistication. Although I was not allowed to enter the night club when it was open for business, I visited it as often as I could, got to like the stale smell of alcohol which never seemed to leave that basement, and when only Laci and I were around I got great satisfaction from trying to play the drums.

My closest friend was Dénes, good-natured, funny, intelligent and probably much better read than I was. We never tired of each other's company. When he visited my house it was only natural that when it was time for him to go home, I would walk with him as far as his own front door, but our conversation was usually so engrossing that he would then walk me back to mine. This we did perhaps half a dozen times until finally and almost in desperation, we would agree to

* In the original text Hugo made sporadic use of the Hungarian convention which places family names first. His inconsistency has been preserved.

part when we reached the cinema and then everyone would go back to his home on his own.

In the summer we would go as a group to the Strand, a clearing on the banks of the Verke river on the outskirts of Berehovo, which was equipped with sand, deck-chairs, and even a few beach huts, and where the river was sufficiently deep that we could actually swim. By this time too we had all become painfully aware of the fact that the lives of our families had become immensely complicated. We often spoke about the anxieties of our parents. Our fathers had to work harder than ever, our mothers had to mend and repair clothing instead of buying new things, but the thing that we found most painful were the humiliations that began to creep into our lives. *Zsidó* or 'Jew' was becoming an unpleasant word. Most hurtful was the adjective 'smelly' which was often shouted at us even when we passed the houses of neighbours, who only a short time ago had seemed quite friendly.

More and more non-Jews, and particularly young boys and girls, began to wear the insignia of the Nyilas party, and it was becoming clearer to us by the day that the kind of Jew-hatred that erupted in Germany on Kristallnacht in November 1938* was gaining supporters and sympathizers in Berehovo itself.

It was not that unusual to see swastikas and the crossed arrows of the Nyilas party appear as graffiti in different parts of the town, but they were soon whitewashed or erased, and by a kind of unspoken, but common consent, not much was made of this. As I did not have any Christian friends to discuss these matters with, my friends and I could only speak about how we thought they might be feeling. We were anything but happy about the conclusions we reached.

On our last visit to Berehovo there were only two of my school friends among the thirty-five Jewish families who

---

* 'Night of broken glass'; 9–10 November 1938.

comprise now the entire Jewish population of the town.*
Gyuszi, who still lived a few doors from our own house, was
already retired from his work as the manager of the exchange
shop where people brought their unwanted goods. He had
always done the best that he could to get them decent prices
and therefore he was a well-liked character in the town. A
disease of his back had made him progressively smaller giving
him the appearance of a hunchback; he had been much taller
when we were children. Since his mother, who had also
survived, died about three years ago, he had been living
entirely on his own and I believe that I was the first person
who was actually invited and permitted to enter his home. It
was spick and span, indeed sterile, and he was proudest of
his greatly worn copy of Will Herberg's book on Western
philosophy, which he kept in a brown wrap and carefully
hidden in one of the cupboards. He confided in me that wild
horses could not drag him into the synagogue, for although
he was conscious every minute of his life of his Jewishness,
he believed that God had let him down very severely. It was
very sad for Naomi, Rachelle and me to see him at lunchtime
on Shabbat sitting lonely and isolated in a restaurant, so
broken in body and seemingly oblivious to the world around
him.

Teller Öcsi was my other school friend who was still in
Berehovo. He was still powerful and still busy in his father's
carpentry business, with a couple of marriages behind him
and children scattered in Hungary and Carpathia. He was
now the *rosh kahal*, the head of the small Jewish community,
an office neither of us would ever have expected him to
fill. He did not make much of his difficulties during the
intervening years. It is a measure of his indomitable spirit
and sense of humour that he told us of the postcards he had

---

* According to a national census in 1989, there were 140 Jews still in
Berehovo. Since then, many have emigrated to Hungary or Israel.

to send from time to time to relatives that he had 'enjoyed a cup of tea at the Donat Hotel', since all the recipients of these cards knew that Berehovo's once most modern hotel had become the headquarters of the KGB. The tea that was being served there was beyond any kind of sweetening. He did not know how much longer he would remain in the town, but assured me that as long as he was there, he would see to it that there remained a vestige of Jewish communal and religious life.*

Berner Laci also survived, as did his mother and sister, and soon after the war they made their way to the United States. Sadly he suffered a severe mental breakdown when he was still in his early twenties and for many years he was institutionalized. My last visit to him took place in the intensive care unit of a Los Angeles hospital where he was in a coma for several weeks following a massive heart attack. His doctor assured us that he was brain dead and I had relatively little hesitation in supporting the decision that the life support machinery should be switched off.

For many years I had believed that Yossi Czuker had perished in the *Shoah*. I last saw him on one of the death marches in the spring of 1945. It is difficult to describe that night of Chanukah in 1988, which celebrates the miracle of the spirit, when Yossi – now known as Jan – a very successful businessman and most generous philanthropist in Los Angeles, visited our home in London, together with his wife, Suzi. In virtually every sense it was like finding a long-lost brother.

By the time I finished the first four years of elementary school, in the early summer of 1940, much of Europe was already at war. The able-bodied young men of the town had all been drafted into military service – the Christian population into the Hungarian army proper, and the Jews into forced labour battalions. For the first time I was directly

* Öcsi Teller died in 1998.

affected in a personal way and I had to do a great deal of rapid growing up in the course of that summer.

The *gimnázium** in Berehovo followed the anti-Semitic rules of the Hungarian regime. It had a very strict quota system, called *Numerus Clausus*,§ which limited the number of Jewish pupils in the school to three per cent. The annual intake of the school was a hundred new students every year and in earlier years it was not at all uncommon for seventy to eighty of them to come from the Jewish community. Now no more than three could be admitted to this more rigorous and academic education. All others had to make do with the *polgári*¶ school where tuition was completed by the age of fifteen or sixteen, and none of the boys or girls who attended it could aspire to higher education. Matriculation, which was a prerequisite for entering any kind of university, was only available to those who completed, at age eighteen, the *gimnázium*.

There was no question in my mind, nor in the mind of the family, that I was *gimnázium* material and I was therefore duly enrolled to take the entrance examination. My friend Dénes and I took our places in the large school hall, filled to overflowing on that May morning, and spent two or three tense hours writing compositions, solving arithmetical problems and answering questions concerned with Hungarian history and literature. A few days later I was invited for a personal interview. The teacher conducting the interview was tall and skinny, he wore thick glasses and repeated every question two or three times. Throughout the interview, he never called me by my name, but only 'Jew boy'. He also

* Secondary school.

§ The *Numerus Clausus* law, limiting the number of Jews in the free professions, was introduced in Hungary on 3 May 1939.

¶ Higher elementary school, where students received four years of technical training.

asked me many unpleasant questions about my family, which I answered as clearly and with as much dignity as I could muster, but I was fighting tears much of the time. When he asked me what I wanted to do when I grew up, and I answered that I thought of a career as a research chemist, or possibly in forestry, he told me: 'Does a Jew child like you really expect to gain admittance to a university?'

He ended the session by telling me that if I came by the school in three days' time, I would see the names of all those who were successful posted on a notice-board outside the school gate. I slept very little and ate even less in the course of the next three days. The atmosphere of the interview hung over me like a thick heavy cloud. Dénes too was moody and in between our outbursts of anger and frustration, there were long periods of silence. My parents said very little, and Gabi did the best that he could to assure me that, in his opinion, I was bound to be successful.

On the Friday morning, Gabi and I bicycled to the *gimnázium*, but he managed to get there a few seconds ahead of me and with his small hand covered the small column which was headed 'Jewish Students'. He had a big smile on his face. Yes, my name was one of the three, and so was Dénes's. By lunchtime I was in floods of tears. I had proved that I was clever enough or perhaps just persuasive enough to get a place, but the prospect of a career as a token Jew in a school that was blatantly antisemitic and where I knew I was not wanted filled me with dread.

My father usually spent Friday afternoons doing his paper-work in his study at home, but that day we spent hours walking up and down our long garden, discussing advantages and disadvantages, pluses and minuses, my prospects and my fears, and a little of his ambitions for me as well. I was conscious of my mother watching us, with some anxiety, from the veranda window, and by the time we had to bathe and get ready for Shabbat, we had a perfect understanding.

While I was still relaxing in a hot tub, he was busy on the telephone talking to friends and acquaintances, making a list of schools which might serve as alternatives to the *gimnázium* in Berehovo.

Still before Shabbat, he managed to contact the directors of the Jewish *gimnázium* in Mukačevo and in Užhorod. They could both accommodate me as a fee-paying student, but neither school had boarding facilities. Commuting daily by bus to Mukačevo was considered, but dismissed on the grounds that in the winter it was sometimes impossible to get through. We also considered the possibility of my boarding with one of my father's two sisters living in Užhorod, but they both had young children and relatively small homes, and I was very glad when we gave up on that.

But the Jewish *gimnázium* in Debrecen, which was in Hungary proper and only three or four hours away by train, had boarding facilities and its director, Dr Vag, assured my father that he would be able to find a place for me in the school. The last call was to Dr Kardos who owned the *internát*, the boarding school attached to the *gimnázium*, and when my father did not demur at the fee required, I was offered a place on the spot. A different but much more welcome excitement filled me by the time Shabbat came into Berehovo that day.

The formal letter of acceptance arrived a few days later, together with a long list of requirements, about clothing and footwear, bedclothes, towels and toiletries. There were regulations about visits and holidays. Even about pocket money. More than anything else, there was the promise of a warm welcome.

That summer was filled with preparation. My mother engaged a seamstress to work at our house, sewing machine and all, measuring me for shirts and even underwear. Everything was monogrammed, including the socks. My father's cousin, Hershi, one of the best tailors in Berehovo, required my presence for trying out new suits and my great-uncle

József made a plaster cast of my feet to get some new shoes and boots perfectly right. Never before was I the centre of so much attention, nor so elegant. Under the apricot tree behind our kitchen, I read chunks of *Tom Brown's Schooldays* in Hungarian to a patiently listening Gabi, by way of emotional preparation for my life ahead and for the separation that would be the most difficult part of it.

The war was going on. Newspapers reported the march of the German armies across Europe with pride and enthusiasm. Our main source of information was the radio, especially the news from the BBC in London. The four muted drumbeats which preceded them stopped all activity and conversation. It was hard to reconcile the images of air raids and devastation with the relative tranquillity in Berehovo.

But we had already seen a little of the effects of war. In late autumn of 1939, Polish refugees had streamed through the town. Most of them were non-Jews. For several weeks the hotels, and even some public places, were temporarily converted into dormitories and they were all filled to capacity. I was particularly intrigued by their elongated bicycle seats and made no secret of my wish to own one myself. It was well known that these refugees had very little money, and the local population was not averse to picking up some bargains. Once, when my mother filled a basket with cooked meat, cakes and fruit, and asked me to take it to the feeding centre that was set up in the synagogue courtyard, she added: 'And don't you dare come home with a new bicycle seat!' Gradually the Poles left and we heard no more of them, nor was anything said about the Jews in Poland.

There were other refugees in Berehovo as well. A part of Carpathia, the area north-east of us, remained an independent region,* but the regime was avowedly fascist and violent. Those Jewish families that could, fled to the greater security

* Carpatho-Ukraine; see footnote on page 74.

of those towns and villages that had already been incorporated into Hungary.

A few doors from our home we rented a house for our relatives, the Grosz family, who had arrived from Sevluš and we became very close. Their oldest son, Micky, had gone to Palestine many years earlier. Two more sons, Ernő and Imi, would soon do likewise. The journey was dramatic to say the least. Their group which included another cousin, Ajzi Goldstein, hired a boat that would take them to sea via the Danube. It was in the winter, and while passing through Hungary, the river froze. For weeks they were stranded on board. When they reached Haifa, they were interned by the British as enemy aliens.* Eventually they were freed and joined the Czech army with understandable dedication. The youngest Grosz boy, Gyuri, became a very good friend. His accounts of atrocities he had seen made me realize that even the Ruthenians had become infected by the antisemitism that was sweeping across Europe. When all of Carpathia had become part of Hungary, they returned to their home in Sevluš, but at least once a year we visited them, mostly at my insistent urging.

An older sister, Manci, got married while they were our neighbours. The ceremony was held in our garden. Gyuri, Gabi and I made the *chuppah*, the marriage canopy, out of my father's *tallit* and four carefully cleaned fence poles, and we were publicly thanked by Nándor Polák, Manci's bridegroom. Tragically neither Manci nor Gyuri survived the Shoah, but another sister, Gizi, did. By chance, I was present again when she married her widowed brother-in-law, Nándor, in Prague.

---

* To illustrate the anti-Zionist sentiment prevalent among rabbinic authorities in Carpathia, Hugo often cited how Ernő's father was a *dayan* – a judge – in the Beth Din, and when Ernő sent his father a postcard to say that they had arrived relatively safely in Palestine, his father was fired because his son had become such an out-and-out Zionist.

Early in September 1940 my trousseau was ready. Before leaving for Debrecen, I visited Silce and Vary to say farewell to my grandparents. I was given both gifts of money and advice and felt very grown up making those trips on my own. I also went to say farewell to Rabbi Hirsch, who gave me only advice and was glad that I would have a decent Jewish education in my new school.

He also gave me the name of a friend of his with whom he had studied at his *yeshiva*, and as it turned out that friend was to give me extra tuition in Talmud all the time I was in Debrecen. My mother also prepared a list of all our relatives in Berehovo, and it took me two full days of cycling, cake-eating and hand-kissing before every name was crossed off on it. The night before leaving, Gabi and I talked most of the night. Because his birthday was in November, we realized that it would be at least four years before he could join me at boarding school. We agreed that unless my experience was really unpleasant we would both insist that he followed in my footsteps. Then, for at least four more years, we would be together again.

The last thing I saw of Berehovo early next morning was Gabi, waving his wet handkerchief and running alongside the moving train. My mother also cried as she saw us off. The last promise that I had to make was that I would write at least one letter a week. But since I had already spent time away from home when I was still younger – on an experimental stay with a famous doctor relative in Vienna – she assured me that I would not be homesick. Unlike me, she chose to forget that the experiment had been a short-lived failure.

My father and I were experienced fellow travellers, and as he had a first-class rail pass, we were comfortable and I slept most of the way. A taxi took us to the *internát*. After we were shown around and I was given one of four beds in the dormitory reserved for new boys, my father and I embraced intensely, but without tears, and I was on my own.

The actual school was a spacious and purpose-built structure. It was very well equipped with classrooms, laboratories, a fine gym and a newly opened art studio. The Kardos *internát* was a brisk ten-minute walk from the school. It too was purpose-built. I believe it was the property of the Jewish community and leased to Dr Kardos. The day-to-day running was the responsibility of Dr Laci Gonda and his wife Kati. He was tall and attractive, invariably kind and amusing. He also had a fine voice and when he discovered that I was familiar with the liturgy of the daily and Sabbath services, he quickly taught me the popular local melodies and enrolled me as one of his assistants in conducting the services for which he was also responsible. Kati was more strict. Her hair was closely cropped, and she was calm and efficient. Whenever she was not busy running the school and supervising homework, she was busy reading the Tauchnitz editions of English classics.

Dr Kardos was a little more distant, but greatly respected for his fairness. His academic field was Hungarian and world literature. He was fully qualified for university teaching, but because of the 'Jew Laws' which had already been in operation in Hungary for several years, he could only get work in Jewish schools. Most of the other teachers were in a similar position, and even at that age I understood and appreciated the remarkably high level of instruction.

We all had to study the classics, including Latin and Greek. Dr Sós made sure that to this day I can recite reams of Ovid and Catullus. Hebrew, classical and modern, was also part of the curriculum. Dr Rosenfeld was particularly proud of our singing, unaware that what motivated our lusty rendering of every Zionist song known to man was our desire to drown out his own off-key leadership. Our art teacher, Mr Ádler, was himself a well-known painter, but even the extra lessons for which my parents gladly paid, could not get me up to a decent standard. That our son, David, is a fine artist is living proof that some apples manage to grow at great distances from the tree.

The gym teacher was Károly Kárpáti. He was the Hungarian wrestling champion in the 1932 and 1936 Olympics. As a Jew he could no longer compete in national events. He often told us how lucky he was to get such a decent job and how sorry he felt for so many other fine Jewish athletes who had to make do with any menial work that they could get. In formal classes he taught us to climb poles and ropes, to vault over French horses and throw the medicine ball. But he also took us in groups after school hours to train us for self-defence and street fighting. This was certainly no academic exercise. Debrecen was a Lutheran town, with its own university and Lutheran *gimnázium*. Our school's only concession to uniform was a dark blue Levente-style cap, with a distinctive metal badge that had *Debreceni Zsidó Gimnázium* enamelled on it.

It was not difficult to recognize us as Jews on the streets and walking was fraught with danger. Often we, as smaller boys, were attacked by much bigger and much larger crowds of Christian boys. The Kárpáti lessons enabled us to give as hard as we got, and to take with as much fortitude as we could muster. I know that our headmaster made formal complaints to his Lutheran colleague, but without much success. Although I once spent a great deal of pocket money to buy a switch-blade and honed it to perfection, I did not have the nerve – or whatever it takes – to use it.

In my second year in Debrecen a formal and official humiliation was introduced. All secondary schoolboys had to do some sort of military training: learning to march, becoming familiar with rifles and bayonets as well as military history. But this national programme did not apply to the Jewish schools. Instead, we had to go every Wednesday afternoon to the local gasworks. We were accompanied by some of our teachers, and once we got there a Hungarian sergeant took charge. Our drill was to march with shovels and spades which the school had to purchase for every one of us. Instead of saluting we had to practise removing our caps in unison. When the instructor was satisfied that we knew how to hold our tools in every conceivable style and position, we were put to practical work. Week after week, rain or shine or snow, we marched in formation from the school, across the city, to the gasworks. On the way, we were jeered at by the Lutheran boys who also had training sessions on Wednesdays, marching in the opposite direction, with swords and rifles and sometimes with bands. We became sure that this was no coincidence when our sergeant made us wait at a road junction for a long time in the cold drizzle, and only shouted 'Forward march!' when he saw the Christian columns approaching. When we reached our destination, we were put to the most pointless task imaginable. Those who had spades had to dig holes and ditches, and when they were perfectly round or oblong or square, they had to be filled in again. Those with shovels had to move mounds of coke and cinders from one spot to another and then return them to their original place.

I felt very sorry for those boys who were in the last year of school because after matriculation they would be drafted into labour battalions, then taken to the Russian front to support the fighting units and endure unspeakable suffering. I knew this to be the case because on holidays in Berehovo I would meet older cousins and neighbours who were on leave from their battalions. I saw their frostbite, heard how they were being used as human mine-sweepers and understood why they and their families were obsessed with food packages.

Yet life in Debrecen was enjoyable. I had no trouble with schoolwork and in the *internát* there was a friendly and supportive atmosphere. It took me a while to get used to drinking water instead of the wine which was always part of our meals at home. I was also the object of an undeserved slander. It was a rule that everything on your plate had to be finished. I had indicated that I did not like the skin of boiled poultry and as a rule I was served portions that had no skin. But one Friday night, the main course was goose, and the huge wing I was given was almost all thick skin. The vegetable that evening was puréed spinach, which I liked and ate without problem. Stealthily, I removed the goose skin, wrapped it in a napkin, and put the whole package in my pocket. I did not count on Kati Gonda's hawk eyes. No sooner had we finished grace after the meal when Aunt Kati – as we called her – made me get up, empty the offending pocket and announce that this was the first time that the school had had a spinach evader.* It was a reputation that stuck to me for years. In her termly letter to my family, she had also repeated this story. Everyone but me thought it was very funny.

Yet Kati and I not only had a firm friendship, I also became her unpaid and unofficial assistant, as I was her husband's. Rationing of many foodstuffs had become a way of life and the bureaucracy that came with it was complicated and very time consuming. Though I was still very much a junior boy, it was my responsibility to take the lists of almost a hundred people to the various offices scattered throughout the city, answer questions posed to me by forbidding officials, explain changes and special needs, and make certain that I returned with the right coupons and vouchers for sugar, butter, meat and even clothing. Usually this was done in the afternoons when the other boys were doing their supervised homework, but I was more proud than resentful of the fact that I had to do mine, often all alone, in the large dining-room after supper.

I had three passions in Debrecen. The easiest to satisfy was my liking for pickled peppers stuffed with sauerkraut. A stationery shop near the school always kept a small barrel of them. The two dark, sad-looking sisters who owned the shop,

---

* We have to assume that Aunt Kati did not check the contents of the napkin.

not only let me pick the ones I liked, but also let me charge it to my account. Kati was the banker for pocket money and the weekly amounts I drew out invariably covered the cost of five pickles.

I also needed money for the theatre, which was an even greater passion. Debrecen had its own repertory company, and its elegant theatre featured touring companies as well. I loved everything about the theatre, beginning with any clever bits of scenery, all the way to the leading ladies. In Berehovo, from the age of about seven, I never missed one performance of the Yiddish troupes that visited from time to time, nor any of the amateur productions put on by the Jewish dramatic society. The problem in Debrecen was that I was not allowed to go to public places without permission and, probably because of the antisemitism throughout the city, such permission was not given if you wanted to go alone. More difficult was the fact that the only possible time for me to attend the theatre was Saturday afternoon matinée, for which permission was out of the question. For one thing, it implied the violation of the Shabbat injunction about spending money. My solution was simple, even if it was risky and costly. During the week I would buy two tickets for one of the very small boxes on the highest tier. After lunch, I would join one of the groups of boys going for the traditional Shabbat walk, leave them as soon as I could, and run as fast as possible to the theatre. There I would make my way to the box and, lest I be recognized by some of the teachers of our school who might also be Sabbath-breaking theatre lovers, I sat on the floor of my box until the lights were lowered and the curtains went up.

Lehár operettas were a staple diet, and so was a succession of vaguely French farces. From time to time they presented slushy dramas, written and played almost to a formula. About the Hungarian officer wounded and on leave, assuring his fiancée of undying love that was second only to the love of his country. When the acting was good, even I cried as the hero, restored and elegant again, bravely left for the front. But most of the time I was conscious of the labour battalions' stories and what real Hungarian officers could do and I was almost ashamed for being there. But not ashamed enough to stop going. Remarkably, my escapes into this fantasy land were never discovered and the few friends in my dormitory who knew about them never betrayed my secret.

My third passion, which remained totally unrequited, was for a girl who was known to all of us as Tehénke, or 'Little Cow'. She was a local girl, beautiful and bright, a student at the Jewish secondary school for girls. Everyone knew that she was my girlfriend, and through the network of school rumours, I understood that the feeling was reciprocated and mutual.

When we did go on Shabbat afternoon walks, usually to the Great Forest on the edge of Debrecen, we would always trail Tehénke's group. There were looks and smiles, but such was custom and the power of inhibition that I never actually spoke to her. I have always regretted this failure of opportunity and nerve. Sadly, I can no longer remember her real name, nor can I recall the names of most of my fellow students, even those with whom I shared a room for more than three years.

The official and more or less regular 'entertainment' offered to all of us in the Kardos boarding school was the Sunday morning outing to one of the city's cinemas. It was a special showing of the feature film of the week. Many of the films were American, British and French, with Hungarian subtitles. *The Wizard of Oz* must have been the first colour film I saw, and Judy Garland became an instant favourite. For a time I tried to walk and sound just like Mickey Rooney. I even asked the hairdresser who came to clip us once a month at the boarding school, to give me a haircut 'just like Andy Hardy's'. I cried over Jean Gabin's torment in the trenches of the First World War and developed a lasting crush both for Karády

Katalin, a sultry Hungarian actress, and for Greta Garbo. During school holidays my brother and I invented all sorts of scenarios in our summer kitchen which we turned into a fantasy film studio. They all had to include the familiar 'Ninotchka, I looove you!' line that was spoken to Garbo.

During one of the holidays, my father took me along for a short business trip to Budapest. My favourite treat on that particular trip included a visit to the sophisticated department store – the *Párizsi Divat Ház*, or Parisian Fashion House – where I was rewarded with a pair of Zeiss binoculars for a reasonably good school report. The other was dinner in a restaurant famous for its fisherman's soup. As we had long ago established that this delicacy was free of any forbidden shellfish, I had almost no religious qualms about enjoying its spicy, paprika-rich flavour. The one reservation had to do with the cutlery and plates which had obviously been used for out and out non-kosher or *traif* dishes – but this was Budapest after all . . .

To my embarrassed surprise and delight, not only was Miss Karády in the bar at the entrance of this elegant restaurant and on her own, but she and my father obviously knew each other. Indeed they were on Géza-and-Katalin terms – and, yes, she was happy to join our table for dinner.

My father was a handsome man. He had thick, wavy hair with just the right amount of silver on the side and piercing blue eyes. He was always immaculately dressed and his generous tipping made us always welcome in hotels and restaurants. It also guaranteed attentive service. Katalin, of course, was well known and before long I was conscious of the fact that virtually all eyes in that restaurant had focused on our table. It was a memorable evening for me – meeting a flesh and blood film star – though I was so impressed with the occasion that I could barely utter a word of intelligent conversation.

It goes without saying that my father rose to new heights

in my estimation. On the way back to our hotel, I was even more fascinated to learn that he knew many other well-known Czech and Hungarian actors and actresses, but they were almost never the subject of conversation at home. I would have loved to have boasted about this encounter when the holiday was over and I was back in Debrecen, but showing off went against the grain in our school, and if this was not showing off, what was?

It was during one of the Sunday cinema outings early in my second year at Debrecen that I experienced another powerful intimation that, while so much of our life was normal, there were ominous and dreadful events brewing in our immediate world.

A few months before, on 26 June 1941, Hungary had formally entered the war against the Soviet Union. Within days there was a decision to expel from Carpathia all those Jews who could not offer clear proof of Hungarian citizenship. They were to be passed on to the German authorities in Eastern Galicia. Between 14 July and 12 August, more than 10,000 men, women and children were rounded up, including many families in Berehovo. Some had arrived in our town only a short time ago as refugees from Poland, and stayed with relatives and friends, hoping to move on to Palestine. Some of those who were rounded up in what was now called 'razzia', were families who had lived in the community as long as I could remember.

We were on holiday in Siófok, a pretty resort town on the shores of Lake Balaton, and rapidly becoming a great favourite for the entire family. When we returned, neighbours told us about the deportations and that the people from our town had been taken to Kőrösmező,* not very far from Berehovo itself. Some thought that they might be allowed to settle there and perhaps return soon to collect the bulk of their belongings,

* Jasina.

which had to be left behind. There were those who felt that they would be moved still further, perhaps to Galicia and the Ukraine, as the Red Army was retreating.

Before the feature film came on, there was a newsreel. It showed the victorious Hungarian army moving east. Tanks and trucks loaded with soldiers alternated with horse-drawn field guns and smiling warriors waving at the camera. My eyes, however, were drawn not to the military scenes we were meant to applaud, but to the side of the muddy road with long lines of civilians. They were all carrying bundles and many of the men and women were holding their children's hands. Their slow movement and the weary, dejected look on their faces made a dreadful contrast with the cheerful marching music in the background and the grating voice of the commentator. These Jews, he explained in a rapid aside, would now have to put behind them their comfortable, parasitic lives and work hard to help achieve victory for the Axis forces.

Suddenly I recognized many of our neighbours. There was one family who sat near us in the synagogue, another who ran a small grocery – the only shop on our residential street – and still others who I must have greeted in the streets of Berehovo when I last came home for the school holidays. They were certainly not settling in Kőrösmező and it needed no special sensitivity to realize their desperate situation. That afternoon my compulsory weekly letter to my parents was filled with my account of the newsreel. I also wrote about my feelings of sadness and anger, that we must never trust the official explanations, and ended with my premonition of a great tragedy. My mother's reply, a few days later, tried to be reassuring. Many people in Berehovo had received postcards from those who were deported via the Red Cross and that they seemed to be well, she claimed.

Many years later, I was able to piece together the full horror of this episode. How SS Gruppenführer Franz Jaeckeln assured a meeting of his colleagues in Vinnitsa on 25 August that he personally would see to the killing of the Jewish arrivals from Carpathia by September. And how the massacre did, in fact, take place on 27 and 28 August 1941.

When I was working as an executive of the American Jewish Joint Distribution Committee in New York twenty years later, I found in its archives several letters from Paul T. Culbertson who was the Assistant Chief of the Division of European Affairs in the Department of State in Washington. Dated 25 July 1941, he urges the Joint Distribution Committee 'to intercede with all possible authorities, including Hungarian representatives in the United States' to enlist public opinion and to get relief to those Jews who were being deported to the 'newly acquired Hungarian military territory in Galicia'.

In another letter, dated 26 September 1941, Culbertson informs the AJJDC: 'According to a trustworthy Hungarian officer, at least 2500 deportees plus 8000 Galician Jews have been massacred in the Kamenec-Podolsk [sic] region by German soldiery cooperating with Ukrainian bandits. The number killed is placed as high as 15,000 according to other reports. Fleeing people and praying Jews in synagogues were machine-gunned. Corpses are reported floating down the Dniester River, with little attempt made for retrieval for interment. August 27 and 28 last were declared mourning days among deportees.'

The JDC file contained no information about any possible measures that may have been taken between these two letters. But while researching for Chasing Shadows, Naomi found a copy of a newsreel in German archives which was the same one that I first saw in Debrecen. Watching those scenes again after so many years and recalling my mother's trusting letter served to remind me not only of the Kamenets-Podolsk tragedy, but also how naïve we were, and how unsuspecting we remained, for more than two years afterwards.

In Debrecen, school life became more and more demanding. Latin, mathematics and Hebrew literature were my favourites. Algebra seemed hard at first, and then suddenly it all made sense. In one term, I astonished my teacher, Dr Sebős, when, instead of turning in the homework for a particular lesson, I had gone ahead and solved all the mathematical problems listed in our textbook for the entire year.

Chaim Nachman Bialik's poem, 'In the City of Slaughter', describing a pogrom, haunted me for many months and my Hungarian translation of it earned the commendation of Dr Kardos himself. It was the only praise I got from him and I treasured it because he already had a reputation as a published author and translator of classics. For a time I was sure that I would be an author myself. I sketched out several possible plays but none got further than that. Drawing and painting continued to bring the lowest possible pass marks, despite Mr Adler's tutorials, but in a moment of inspiration I volunteered for fencing lessons, for which there was an extra fee, and my grades in physical education jumped from 'satisfactory' to 'good'.

Dr Sebős was also our form master during my last two years in Debrecen. Like so many of his colleagues, his earlier career as a university professor was cut short by the 'Jewish Laws'. He was a mathematician to his fingertips, and equally at home with philosophy and literature. While Dr Gonda was a kind of role model for appreciating music and laughter as well as the pleasure of prayer, Dr Sebős was the intellectual model. He was a short man with a rasping voice, and not easy to please.

The only weakness that he had and which was clear to us, was his fondness for touching the boys as he moved from bench to bench looking at the progress of his students' work. As we got nearer to the final examinations in June, boys who were slow or worried about their algebra or geometry were known to sit in their shirt-sleeves with two or three buttons undone, but this may have owed more to the malice of school-boys and their fantasy than to the supposed predilection of our teacher.

My reason for remembering him so much more vividly than most of my other teachers has to do with an encounter not in Debrecen, but at Siófok. As it turned out, it was our last holiday there, very soon after my Bar Mitzvah. I managed to persuade my father to buy me an expensive fishing rod, as I wanted to graduate from home-made sticks and string with bits of bread melting off the simplest of hooks in minutes, to something more professional. My new equipment had a reel, lead weights to keep double and triple hooks under the water, even a green net for the hoped-for catch. It then turned out that I had to have a fishing licence as well, which cost almost as much as the equipment, and that too was arranged. Finally, I was in heaven. Sitting day after day, on the sunny shores of Lake Balaton, with a tackle that was virtually professional dangling in the water, a book in my lap, and beside me a Thermos flask filled with a mixture of raspberry syrup and ice-cold water.

One morning I was both embarrassed and delighted to look up and find that Dr Sebős had quietly sat himself next to me. He, too, was on holiday in Siófok, and soon we were in the deepest conversation I ever had with any of my teachers: about the war, the inevitability of Hungary's defeat now that the Russians were at last moving west, and about what was happening to the Jews. Although no newspapers ever reported any of the atrocities, Dr Sebős was a regular listener to the BBC in London, and had all sorts of contacts with friends and former colleagues in Palestine and Switzerland. He spoke about his fears for the Jews who were trapped in those parts of Europe that were under German occupation – which was most of it. And about special Nazi units in Poland and the Ukraine whose particular job was to terrorize the Jews. When I said how lucky we were that, despite the official antisemitism of the country, we could still lead normal lives, he was silent for a time and then said something which I still recall as if spoken yesterday. 'I have this terrible feeling that, sooner or later, the fate which has overtaken our fellow Jews outside Hungary will catch up with us as well.' Despite the sunshine, suddenly I felt cold and afraid. Not only because of what he said, but because as he spoke tears were running down his cheeks. Dr Sebős crying was unthinkable.

It was, I know, a coincidence, but for me it was hauntingly symbolic that the one and only sizeable fish I ever caught happened while my teacher was still sitting next to me. Our conversation ended as the sight of this large, wet fish thrashing about my feet filled me with another and more immediate terror. Suddenly, all I wanted to do was to release it and have nothing to do with its death. Dr Sebős knew no more than me about fishing, but while he was holding the fish down I managed to release the vicious hook from its mouth, pricking my thumb in the process, and I was greatly relieved to see it swim away.

My career as a fisherman was over and so, I felt, was something of my childhood as well. I did not see Dr Sebős again on that holiday, although I looked for him all over the town, hoping to invite him to join us for a meal in our pension. He was my form master again when the next term started, but he never referred to our meeting in Siófok. I learned much later that before the end of that school year, which was the final one for the Debrecen Gimnázium, he had committed suicide.

One of the very few family photographs that survived the war is a picture of my brother and me, together with Neiman Boriska, taken at Lake Balaton that summer. Boriska was my father's beautiful young cousin and she was our guest on the holiday. She was a talented pianist, who introduced me to Liszt, Chopin, and most memorably to Beethoven's 'Moonlight Sonata'. By then she was engaged to Neufeld Lajcsi, my mother's first cousin. Conveniently the Neiman shoe store was right next door to the Neufeld textile shop in Berehovo, but at this time Lajcsi was serving in a forced-labour battalion in the east. He was taken prisoner by the Russians, and after a while joined the Czech Army in the Soviet Union. He survived the war, but Boriska did not.

The photograph is included in the film, *Chasing Shadows*. When the film was first shown at a film festival in Jerusalem, Boriska's closest girlfriend, Kain Erzsi, was in the audience and recognized Boriska in the photograph. In a letter to Naomi she reminisced both about her friend and the 'charming young boy who is now your father'. Those are her words, not mine!

9

BAR MITZVAH

The last time our family were together was on the occasion of my Bar Mitzvah. It was to take place on the Shabbat after my thirteenth birthday which, fortunately, coincided with the end of term in Debrecen. Arrangements were made many months earlier, not only with the Chazan and the other officials of the Great Synagogue, but also with Rabbi Hirsch, as my parents hoped that he could be present as well. Gonda Kati was also informed at my boarding school because extra lessons had to be organized and an eye kept on my preparation.

By then my relationship with Kati had become more of a working partnership than simply student and matron. As food rationing was becoming more and more severe, my contacts with officialdom and expertise at form-filling had greater usefulness than ever. I also knew the regulations and had discovered that leaving a few pengő on the official's desk as a present 'from our house master, who so appreciates your concern for our well-being' almost always resulted in a handful of extra coupons for sugar or butter. At first Kati was angry with me, but when I offered to take the money from my own 'bank' she relented. There were many mouths to feed and I had already experienced the fact that as soon as an unknown official saw *Debreceni Zsidó Gimnázium* on my school-cap's badge, they were not only insulting but found all sorts of ways to cut our legal entitlement. If anything, it was I who had to rearrange my busy afternoon schedules to fit in the Bar Mitzvah lessons.

There was no question that my Talmud teacher would not also be the Bar Mitzvah tutor. The extra lessons for which I had to visit his home ever since I first came to Debrecen were always enjoyable. My only objection was to the smell of cooking which never seemed to leave the book-lined room where we had our Talmud lessons. Though Mr Schwartz had *semicha* from one of the great *yeshivot* in Hungary and was therefore an ordained rabbi, he seemed entirely content with his career as a teacher. In the mornings he taught religion in the girls' school and his afternoons and evenings were busy with boys like me. My impression was that I was one of the few who went eagerly rather than to please the devoutness of parents.

The letter I brought to Mr Schwartz from my mother gave him the date of the Bar Mitzvah and the request that he not only prepare me to read the Torah portion and the prophetic Haftarah reading, but also that he should coach me for the speech I was to deliver on that occasion. During the next few sessions we went over the Torah reading, which concerned Miriam's affliction with leprosy in the Book of Numbers as a punishment for gossip. I did not think it very appropriate as my grandmother's Jewish name was also Miriam (though she was always called Mariska) but there was nothing I could do about it.

The Haftarah was from the prophet Zechariah, starting with the line 'Sing and rejoice, O daughter of Zion, for behold, I come and I will dwell in your midst, says the Lord.' And sing it I did – over and over – much to the annoyance of those boys who had to have their bath after me. For several months before the Bar Mitzvah it became my habit to sit in the tub and not even begin to soap myself until I had chanted it through, including the blessings before and after. To this day, I know it by heart and in the course of the years Zechariah's vision and conviction 'Not by might, nor by power, but by My spirit, says the Lord of hosts' has become very much part of my personal credo.

Mr Schwartz would also listen to me reciting the readings, but his main concern was the speech. One day he gave me four typewritten pages that he had composed patiently and with great erudition. It began with: 'My dear parents, grand-parents, family and friends . . .' followed by lengthy quotations from the Talmud in Hebrew and Hungarian, all on the theme of right speech and the rules of evidence in court cases. While I understood the connection with the Torah portion and Miriam's unhappy experience with careless and wounding speech, and was truly impressed by its elegance of argument and language, I also felt that it would be heavy going for most of my family. It was also not my style, nor did it have anything to do with my ideas or concerns. When I began to raise some polite objections, the look on my teacher's face ended all discussion.

To please him I learned the speech off by heart in a matter of a couple of weeks. Mr Schwartz not only rehearsed his text with me, but also where to pause and for how long, what gestures to use and how I was to kiss my mother's hand first as I concluded the speech.

At the same time I started to work on a speech that was to be my own. This time I had not only to sketch it out and begin – as I had done with my attempts at play-writing – I had to finish it as well. I took as my theme Psalm 114 – 'When Israel came out of Egypt, the House of Jacob from an alien people . . .' – partly because we had just been studying its Hebrew text in Mr Rosenfeld's grammar class and were made to sing it on several ceremonial occasions and partly because I believed that our situation was every bit as desperate as that of the Israelites in their time of discrimination and slavery. My hope was that just as God had redeemed those early Jews with His strong hand and outstretched arm, so God might rescue and redeem us as well. Instead of the Talmud, I quoted Bialik and a rabbinic legend about Nachshon ben Amminadab. Nachshon was a boy who stood with his people on the shores of the Red Sea. Behind them came the pursuing Egyptians, ahead of them the deep and dangerous waters. When Moses urged Israel to move forward, they were fearful and hesitated. But Nachshon jumped and it was only then that the waters parted. My speech ended with the thought that thanks to my parents' and grandparents' love and example I would gladly jump myself and so would my brother Gabi and, of course, I thanked everyone for their generous gifts and for honouring our home with their presence.

The reference to the 'gifts' was a pious and confident hope and on the whole I was pleased with my work. My manuscript was carefully hidden away among the pages of a volume of Latin poetry. In this way everyone would understand why my lips were moving as I bent over that book, even when I studied it after lights-out in the dormitory with the aid of a torch under the bedcover. I continued to practise that speech on the train back to Berehovo and by the time I arrived home I was able to assure my mother that I was completely prepared and that she had nothing to worry about.

A few days later the great event arrived. The Berehovo relatives opened their homes to members of the family arriving from other towns and villages. Our grandparents stayed in our house and there were also rooms booked both in the Royal and the Donat Hotels. Although I could not attend most of my own friends' Bar Mitzvah celebrations because I was away at school, they were generous in their support. At least two boys accompanied me to Uncle Hershi Gryn's tailor shop for a final fitting of my new suit, and later to collect it. My plea for long trousers when it was first ordered during the Passover holidays went unheeded. The tradition was no long trousers until matriculation at eighteen and the fact that there were even twelve-year-olds in Debrecen who wore them made no difference! Uncle József had made a pair of new shoes which fitted like a glove and to my delight my feet had become big enough to fit my father's large collection of shoes as well. There was a haircut on the Friday morning which was accompanied by a full shave. It may have been intended symbolically, but it was a joke since my cheeks were completely smooth.

Despite the presence of many guests, I had to be in bed early to be fresh in the morning. The anticipated excitement and Gabi's account of events in the family and the town guaranteed that I hardly slept at all.

In the synagogue all went well in the morning. The Chazan greeted me in person. Before the service started the Shamash* led me to the Rabbi's seat where he shook my hand with solemnity, wished me well and invited me to join his special *minyan* the next day when I would put on my *tefillin* for the first time as befits an adult member of the community.

When the Torah service started all the senior relatives had honours, some to open the ark, others to take out, carry and undress the scroll. My grandfather Jacob was called third to recite the blessings over the Torah, which was the most honoured position, and my father was last but one so that he could stand next to me when my turn finally arrived. The gentle red-bearded Shochet who usually chanted the Torah portions stood aside. I had gone to greet him after my haircut the day before at his place of work in the poultry abattoir and when I asked if he would allow me to chant my own brief portion he readily agreed. He waved aside my offer to recite it to him there and then. 'If you say you know it,' he said, 'then I am sure you know it! Just take your time and don't be nervous.'

I know I did well, both with the Torah portion and the Haftarah. Before the Torah scroll was taken away to be

* Synagogue caretaker.

dressed, my father recited the formula: 'Blessed be He who has now absolved me from responsibility for this one!' – though in Hebrew it is only three words. He said them loud enough for me to hear. While the Chazan recited the *mi sheberach* – invoking God's blessing in my name on all members of the family, each of whom he was able to name without any prompting from me or my father – I looked at the women's gallery high behind the reading desk. There I saw my mother leaning over the veiled balustrade, my grandmothers on either side of her, and as I waved with as much sophistication as I could muster in their direction she returned the greeting with a handkerchief which I knew would be tear-stained.

When I finally finished, there were shouts of '*Sh'koach!*' – 'Well done!' – and I returned to my place by way of the Rabbi's seat again, shaking his hand and the hands of a sizeable proportion of Berehovo's male population. When the service ended, there were more affectionate greetings from the descending women and at last we were on our way home.

As the guests arrived there was a brief *Kiddush*.* My suggestion was that Gabi recite the blessings over the wine and the two specially large, plaited loaves. Drinks of wine, brandy or slivovitz were served and soon all the adults were seated in a semicircle in the dining-room, with children filling every bit of floor space. My older cousins stood just inside an adjoining bedroom. Other than a few of my friends, all the guests were family. Soon there was an expectant silence that, in time-honoured fashion, had to be filled by my speech.

I stepped forward and spoke as eloquently and feelingly as only a middle-aged thirteen-year-old (who had picked up some of the most dramatic habits of a provincial theatre company) could speak. There were pauses and gestures – and a deep seriousness as well – and the words that I had written and

* Ceremony that sanctifies Shabbat and most Jewish festivals.

practised so painstakingly came tumbling out. There were
nods and smiles of encouragement from grandparents, aunts
and uncles, but gradually I became aware that my mother's
face was getting darker and darker. She was fidgeting with
her hands and, completely out of character, looking not at
me but through me. I knew I was doing something wrong but
for the life of me I could not imagine what it was. Mercifully
the speech was over. I had delivered my lines, remembered
all the quotations and had every reason to be sincere about
my thanks for the generous present.

There were shouts of '*Sh'koach!*' again and hugs and kisses
instead of handshakes. But as I bent over to kiss my mother's
hand, she hissed in my ear: 'That was *not* the speech we paid
for!' In a flash I understood it all and during the next few days
I was many times and powerfully reminded. Mr Schwartz had
not only sent a bill to my mother for the Bar Mitzvah tuition;
perhaps in justification for his fee he had enclosed a carbon
copy of the speech he had written as well. By that fatal Shabbat
my mother knew it as well as I did. My attempts to reason
and to explain that what I had said was the 'real me' made no
impression. When her own brothers and sisters complimented
her on her son's fine *drosha*,* she shrugged it off with: 'Don't
congratulate me – tell him! *He* did it!'

One of the more unusual Bar Mitzvah presents ever given
was the large bottle of cherry brandy which my aunt Violka
thrust into my hands as she arrived at our house. For reasons
that remain as mysterious as that present was, soon after
lunch my friends and I moved off to the far end of our garden.
There, in the space of about an hour, we drank every drop of
it. When Gabi found us and insisted that I return to the house
because everyone was waiting for me to cut the specially
ordered *dobostorta*,§ I had immense difficulty in walking and

---

* Talk on weekly Torah portion.
§ Hungarian 'box' cake, topped with a layer of caramelized toffee.

17. A street in Berehovo, 1938. [*Roman Vishniac*]

18. Pre-war view of Berehovo. The two market places were separated by a row of shops. Rozsoskert Street is behind the courthouse on the upper right-hand side.

19. Berehovo, 1989. Rozsoskert 72, the house where Hugo was born. [from *Chasing Shadows*]

20. The courthouse, 1940s. The biggest and architecturally the most distinguished building in Berehovo. [*Géza Ignáczy*]

21. Before 1944 the markets were busiest on Sundays, Mondays and Thursdays, but on Saturdays the area was deserted. [*Géza Ignáczy*]

22. Main Street, Berehovo. The Donat Hotel (the white building down the street) was once the most modern hotel in Berehovo. Later it became the headquarters of the KGB. The *mikveh* and the Great Synagogue were on the left and behind them the courtyard which was once the heart of the Jewish community. [*Géza Ignáczy*]

23. & 24. Shops on the market square. Neuman's, a textile shop, belonged to Hugo's uncle, Samuel. Right next to it was another uncle, Jószef Neufeld, who made shoes and boots that were guaranteed to last a lifetime. [*Géza Ignáczy*]

25. & 26. The Berners were also distant relatives. Berner Laci, whose father owned the nightclub where Hugo liked to practise on the drums, had a mental breakdown after the war and was institutionalized for many years. [*Géza Ignáczy*]

27. The Great Synagogue, or *Nagy Templom*, where Hugo celebrated his Bar Mitzvah in June 1943 and where his father kept his own seat.

28. Berehovo, 1989. Hugo with his schoolchum, Öcsi Teller, in Berehovo's one remaining synagogue. Öcsi was still working in his father's carpentry workshop and, to Hugo's great surprise, had become the head of Berehovo's tiny Jewish community. [*Naomi Gryn*]

29. Under Soviet rule the Great Synagogue was
encased in concrete and turned into a cultural centre.

31. On Friday nights the former
synagogue is now the scene of
Berehovo's weekly discotheque.
[from *Chasing Shadows*]

30. In front of the cultural centre
the Communists erected a
golden statue of Lenin.

32. Mukačevo, 1938. The second day at *cheder*
for the boy in the middle. [*Roman Vishniac*]

could barely hold the knife. For the second time in my life and hers, my mother saw me drunk.

I still do not know how the day ended or how my friends – who were in no better shape – got back to their homes. But word of this episode must have reached Rabbi Hirsch as well. Early on Sunday and again wearing my new suit I was in his home for the morning service. The *tefillin* I strapped on my arm and around my head, that had a wonderful smell of new leather, were my grandmother Mariska's present. Her late husband was my *kvater*, or Godfather, as well as my grand-father and that was the traditional gift. Rabbi Hirsch made a point of inspecting me and invited me to lead the first part of the service. But when the prayers concluded and all the men made their way to a long table in the back of the room for a glass of schnapps, Rabbi Hirsch quietly but knowingly whispered in my ear: 'It will be best if you only have a glass of soda water!'

It was many years later when I visited my mother in Karlovy Vary that we reminisced about the Bar Mitzvah. Like me, she recalled every detail about it. Perhaps because it was the last time that both of us had seen all our family. She even remembered the clothes and the jewellery her sisters and sisters-in-law had worn that day. Certainly every conver-sation and comment. 'Were you really mad at me?' I asked. 'Very!' she said. 'I had already written to Mr Schwartz a thank-you letter. I had told him how much we all enjoyed the beautiful words about honesty and truthfulness. I even enclosed an extra banknote by way of appreciation. And there you stood, making a liar out of me!'

10

ESCAPE PLANS

Before I returned to Debrecen for another school year in September 1943, we had one of the few secret and family-only conferences that I can recall.

As a rule our home was open. No doors were ever locked, other than the gate that led into the street and that only when we were away. Not even the bathroom had a lock or even a bolt. If visitors had to use it, a quiet word from one of our parents guaranteed privacy. It was understood that confidential conversations remained within the four walls of the house and I cannot remember a single occasion when Gabi or I had to be reprimanded for being in any way indiscreet. By this time radio sets belonging to Jews were confiscated and we were well aware of the danger in having a Telefunken radio hidden in our cellar. Indeed I could time almost to the second how to run the aerial wire from the set through a small window into the garden and so have the best possible reception for the daily BBC news bulletin. To this day whenever I enter Bush House in the Strand in London I can almost physically hear the muted drumbeats, '*da-da-da daah*', followed by 'This is London, London calling . . .' and then the news delivered in Hungarian. We knew that anything heard in this way was not to be discussed with anyone outside our trusted family circle.

Nor did we ever refer to the two metal boxes known as the 'if necessaries'. Each contained a bundle of Hungarian banknotes as well as American dollar bills. One was hidden above the wooden rafters in the summer kitchen and the other in a specially prepared hole under the floorboards of the house in our vineyard. My brother and I were shown the hiding places and the contents a year or so earlier, and once this was done we neither asked nor expected any questions about them.

But now, just a few weeks after my Bar Mitzvah, the four of us were finishing an early supper under the apricot tree, and in a voice that was instinctively lowered my father made a surprising announcement. With the help of business friends in Budapest and some costly introductions to various officials, on his next trip to the capital he expected to bring home a set of visas to Turkey. Gabi had already started lessons in Hungarian history and his text book had obviously given the Ottomans a bad press. 'Aren't they as cruel there as the fascist Nyilas here?' was his immediate response. With a superior knowledge that came from the Lexicon given to me as a Bar Mitzvah present – I was already addicted to it – which had an early entry on Kemal Atatürk, I was able to assure him that Turkey was both modern and much more liberal than Horthy's capricious regime. And, as an avid reader of the weekly Jewish newspaper, I could recall no accounts of anti-Semitism. 'But why go to Turkey?' was my question.

Our parents had obviously been discussing and planning for some time. The tide of the war had turned. It was only a matter of time before the Russians would push the front westward and Carpathia with its mountain passes was bound to be a battleground before too long. My mother – usually the optimist of the family – also felt that as food-rationing and other shortages would increase, the condition of Jews could only deteriorate. She also believed that the Jewish Agency for Palestine had an *aliyah** office in Istanbul. 'With a little luck we may not have to stay there very long and wouldn't it be

* 'Going up'; Hebrew term for immigration to Palestine and, after 1948, to Israel.

wonderful if we could get to Netanya?' she said. The inside of the door of our summer kitchen was plastered with fading postcards and photographs, sent by her cousins, the Grosz brothers from Sevlus, showing the beaches of Netanya and – to us – exotic orange groves.

That night I read the Lexicon entry on Turkey over and over again until I knew by heart the names of all its major cities, its products and the number of square kilometres it occupied on both sides of the Bosporus. Before going to bed I suggested that we get a Turkish-Hungarian dictionary as soon as possible, only to be told that under no circumstances were Gabi or I to so much as breathe the word 'Turkey' outside our home. In fact, there was virtually no mention of it inside the house either. Within a short time of this conversation I had to return to Debrecen for what turned out to be my last year in the school. When I next came home for Chanukah, my discreet question about Turkey was greeted with even more discreet silence and it was clear that the plan had been dropped.

In any case, my thoughts and energies were focused in a more direct and urgent direction. Just before leaving Debrecen, the Director of the *gimnázium*, Dr Vag, addressed the entire student body. He told us that unless the school could find a great deal of extra money it might have to close. Many families were unable to pay the set fees, costs had gone up dramatically and, he hinted, that all sorts of 'war taxes' had been levied on the school. He asked that we – the boys – do whatever we could to get donations from relatives and friends. Specially designed subscription forms were distributed and, moved by Dr Vag's heartfelt appeal, as well as my experience of the avarice of the city's officials, I took two of them.

As usual, all the family came to our home every night during the festival of Chanukah. The *menorah* candles were lit, my mother's potato *latkes** were served, the children

---

* Fried potato pancakes – later one of Hugo's own culinary specialities.

withdrew into a corner to play their *dreidel** games and soon
my aunts and uncles as well as my parents were busy playing
'Twenty-one', the one card game everyone was familiar with.
That year I made a little speech about the needs of the school
and to my delight it was agreed that who ever had any win-
nings, at least half of it would be given to the *gimnázium*. By
the eighth and last night of the festival my two sheets were
almost completely filled, most of them signed only with the
initials 'NN' which meant 'anonymous', but the amounts
were quite respectable. I also visited more distant relatives'
shops and work rooms and even non-relatives whom I judged
to be sympathetic and generous. I was very conscious of the
fact that my polite but persistent appeal for money caused no
surprise. By then Jewish institutions of every sort had such
acute shortages that collectors of support were a common-
place, daily experience.

By the time I returned to Debrecen in early January, an old
handbag my mother gave me for this enterprise was bulging
with banknotes and silver coins and I was touched and proud
to receive a handwritten note of thanks from Dr Vag himself.
He also informed me that my efforts had resulted in the largest
single amount of all the gifts the boys brought back. This did
not surprise me in the least because the night before my
return to the school my father looked at the two long lists,
quickly added up the figures and, with the last NN entry,
doubled the total.

About a year later, we were on the first of our forced marches
from Lieberose, a miserable and relatively small concentration camp near Cottbus in Upper Silesia, to the main camp
of Sachsenhausen on the far side of Berlin. It would be more
appropriate to call it a death march, because of almost three

* Four-sided top with a Hebrew letter on each side, used for gambling
during Chanukah.

thousand of us who left Lieberose no more than eight hundred reached our destination alive.* Snow and slush covered the roads. We moved in rows of five. At the side of every two rows there marched an SS guard with his rifle pointing at us. At dusk we stopped, made a left or a right turn, walked a few steps into a field lining the road and spent the night sitting or lying down there. At daybreak those who could get up moved up the road again, but only a few hundred yards. Some of the guards stayed behind and we shuddered at the sound of the rifle and pistol shots which executed those too ill or exhausted to continue to move.

Blankets were at a premium; inevitably they became wet and as the marching got under way they became heavy to carry. Ahead of our column was a much bigger group of American prisoners-of-war who also found their blankets a burden. By early afternoon my father insisted that we pick up one or two blankets and in that way have a measure of protection for the coming night.

The only traffic that passed us consisted of German troop carriers, usually in long convoys. When they approached, we had to move to the side of the road, get splashed and if the guards believed that high-ranking officers were passing us, shouts of '*Die mützen auf!*'§ went up and we had to remove

---

* In a statement Hugo made in German to *Heim des Landeskomitees für Deportiertenfürsorgs* (office of the regional committee for the care of the deported), in Budapest, on 4 July 1945: 'After we left the hospital was set on fire and the people in the hospital all died. With the remaining prisoners with whom we found ourselves in Lieberose, we formed a detail of 1400 men when we marched away from Lieberose. When we arrived in Sachsenhausen, only 900 remained of the 1400; the remainder had died on the journey.' His figure of 3000 is closer to the entire prison population of Lieberose at the time of their evacuation, including those who were massacred before they set off towards Berlin.

§ Fifty years must have erased many of the Fraülein's German lessons; this should be '*Die mützen ab!*', 'caps off!'.

our caps. One afternoon, on the third or fourth day of this bizarre and painful journey, a yellow truck passed us with the words 'Géza Gryn Timber Works' still painted on its side. The only thing that was different about the truck was the addition of a wood-burning stove behind the driver's cabin which now fuelled it. My father and I looked at each other and it was one of the few times when I saw him cry.

My memory went back to that warm August evening a year ago and the many might-have-beens. When the convoy was out of sight, I asked him the question that often crossed my mind: 'Why didn't we go to Turkey?' It was several minutes before he answered and I can still remember every word of it. 'I had everything arranged. Passports, visas, train tickets. We even had sleeping-car reservations for the two dates a week apart. Then I went to see my parents in Vary and the next day we visited your grandmother in Silce. It was to be a kind of farewell. But when we sat down at home and realized how much they depended on us – not just the old people, but our sisters and brothers and their families as well – we just could not go through with it. I am so sorry. But you understand, don't you?'

ding? Yet there was something sinister about the whole place. Now, I know, what is was; but at the time I only felt that something was not quite as it should have been.

The officer came round, and he stopped in front of me. I was just undoing my shoelaces, but my hands trembled.

"How old are you?" he asked me.

"Ni... ni... nineteen" I lied (but I was beginning to believe it myself.)

"Why are you here?" he inquired further.

"I... I was told by that 'Herr' that I should come in." came my reply.

"Your Block?"

"Block 7, in Camp 'D'." I answered.

"Put your clothes on and 'schies in Wind' ('buzz off')" he ordered.

He went off and I felt relieved. I dressed again, but slowly, because I was curious to see what would happen next. The children lined up in twos and the double-door was opened. A strong smell came out of the hall beyond it. It was a smell I never ~~felt~~ experienced before. Sweetish – yet not sweet. The hall was lit by electricity and ~~pipes to~~ beneath the ceiling ran the usual metal pipes, but from where I stood, I could not see much of the interior. (the floor, I noticed, was dry.)

The children went in and Karel waved to me as he entered. My dressing, however, was completed and the man who asked us in made signs at me, ~~if he and~~ at the front door. The meaning was obvious. As I passed him he said something like: "Are you lucky!"

As I opened the front-door, the double-door behind me was closed by the officer. Outside I took a deep breath. I was glad to be out again. It was inexplicable ~~inexplicable~~ – but I ~~felt~~ very relieved. It was curious, I thought, that no soap was given to the children; and only two people supervised their showers. When we showered, there was a whole army of bankers and other 'assistants' swarming around the place. Very curious!

Going back to the square I went the other way round. The

II

THE BRICK FACTORY

The next three chapters were written by my father when he was a 21-year-old student rabbi in Cincinnati. He was then very keen on thrillers, which perhaps shows in his prose style. It should also be remembered that English was still a relatively new language for him. After my father's death, I found the chapters buried in a drawer in his office at the West London Synagogue.

... the monotonous rattling of wheels fills my ears and my mind refuses to think. Save for an occasional groan from my companions, nothing disturbs this summer afternoon. All appears to stand still. Yet I know that our train is racing with time itself and its destiny is still a complete mystery to me and to all around me. But I do not grasp the meaning of it all. Everything is confused. Think!! I must think. So much has happened to me lately and all happened so quickly that there was no time left for meditating. Looking around now in this goods wagon, seventy-five faces are probably figuring the same thing as me. No, not quite seventy-five. There are about a dozen children as well, who cannot think. Not as I do, anyway. They notice that they are squashed, and the absence of air and food and water is perhaps more unbearable to them that it is to me. But on the whole this trip must be quite a novelty to them.

   'Mummy is watching over you . . .' comes a tired lullaby

from the corner farthest from me. Yes, mummy is still watching over you. How long will she be there, though? The baby must have similar thoughts to mine, for now it has started weeping. Like a sign for action, four or five other babies join in too. How can anything be so cruel as listening to babies cry? It sounds like an overture to a drama that is about to commence. God, how I wish it was the finale! It is certainly time this whole business was over. Much more I cannot endure. Escape . . . yes, that's what I'd like to do. Run away! Break down the carriage-walls and jump. My imagination is definitely jumpy today. We are crossing a river now. The bridge below echoes and re-echoes the sound of the train. I hate that sound. It infuriates me. I wish the bridge was undermined and blown up. Now.

Through a peeping hole, no bigger than the size of four slices of bread, I can see the river below and green bands on either side. There are some workmen walking along the line. The sun still radiates its heat, but for these workmen the day is probably over. Now they shall go home and eat and rest, and perhaps they will have a bath later. A bath. A steaming tub of water. I should gladly give five years of my life for such a bath now. The last one I had was exactly three months ago. It is not the dirt that really bothers me. The sensation of getting into the water and relaxing is what I really long for.

Now the train passes by an orchard. Look, ripe apricots all over the place, and some kiddies trying to climb a fence to get at them. One of them is going to make it. He is already halfway across, but what he can't see is that a man with a stick is coming down. I wish I were that boy who will now get a hiding for trying to pick some apricots. Or maybe the man knows him and he will get his fruit without punishment. Who knows? Wish I could have stayed there to watch. The longer I stay by this window, the more depressed I shall get. Or can I get any more depressed? I shall sit down. Sleep . . . yes, that would be nice, to sleep. For hours and days. Right now I have just enough room to stand, or sit with my legs between my brothers and Mummy and my back against Dad's chest. And the smell! Those babies have hardly had anything to eat. But they keep on being sick and mucky. Not that we are any better, but at least we go to the corner and pile everything in one heap.

Of the seventy-five, I know about thirty. No less than twenty-four are relatives of mine. Uncles, aunts, cousins, second cousins, neighbours, friends. People whom by no possible stretch of the imagination could I have pictured in a similar position. They look so ridiculous. Sitting on a filthy floor, some silently, others trying to make conversation, and quite a few weeping. Where they get all the moisture for tears I am unable to understand. They have had no water for twenty-four hours. About five people tried to talk about water, but they were all hushed down. In novels I used to read about men in the Foreign Legion who fainted when there was talk of water in the desert. Pretty soon I will choke, not faint.

Dad is amazingly calm. On the whole my family, with one exception, all take things pretty calmly. Or maybe they, too, are troubled. I guess we all are. Although by now none of us would really be surprised at anything. Three months* of jail can show one quite a lot. It can teach one how to dodge jailers' blows, how to push in or out of crowds, how to keep silent. After the first week, we gave up trying to make conversation and became accustomed to the daily routine.

If only I knew what was going to happen next! This terrible uncertainty is worse than anything imaginable. But then, so was everything before. We never knew what tomorrow would bring. We had constantly hoped for something better.

* Hugo and his family were forced into the ghetto in Berehovo on 20 April 1944. Their transport left six weeks later on 28 May and arrived in Auschwitz on 31 May, according to the statement he made to *Heim des Landeskomitees für Deportiertenfürsorgs* on 4 July 1945.

Unfulfilled hopes and wishes. One after another was shattered and a new one always took the place of the old. From high hopes we gradually sank to lower and smaller ones. Instead of peace, we would have gladly accepted personal freedom, and finally we have arrived to the stage when a slice of bread and a glass of water is the only thing we – or at any rate I – hope for.

Mummy's head is in front of me. Her new dress is still on her. It is the only one she has had for three months. By now it looks more like a charwoman's worst overall than one of Budapest's most elegant and expensive dressmakers' work of art and taste. On the whole Mummy has been wonderfully brave up to now. Sometimes I think all this confusion and hardship is but a matter of course to her. Never a word of grumbling from her. Had I not seen her crying sometimes, I would say she does not notice what is going on. Even when she cries she does it silently and unobtrusively, lest she should disturb anyone. If there was anything I could do to make things easier for her . . . As if there was anything or anyone who could.

Then there is Dad. Calm now, he looks thoughtful and only the beating of his heart assures me that he is still behind me. His thoughts must be thousands of miles away. Perhaps they are not in this world at all. I can never tell what Dad is thinking about. He never talks about his thoughts. In fact, lately he has hardly talked at all. His suffering must be very hard on him and humiliating. All he has worked for and achieved is now shattered and he is no more than a lonely straw on a huge wave of destruction. He could have avoided all our troubles quite easily. And if ever he does speak, he always tells us that it is all his fault, for not being more foresighted. It is quite useless to tell him differently. 'Had I not been so selfish . . .' Poor Dad. He selfish! Never have I heard him to refuse anything. To us maybe he did, sometimes. He had his own ideas about child-upbringing. But no beggar has ever been turned away empty-handed. All this sounds like a nineteenth century novel, but sometimes these things do happen in reality. Perhaps it is not very common nowadays to find someone unselfish, and even if we do come across one, we seldom appreciate it. Even less often do we stop to think about it. Oh, but what on earth am I talking about. Pretty soon I'll be giving myself a moral preaching.

Just relax, Hugo. How I should like to do that! Relax. Be full of emptiness. Care not one damn. So easy and simple to say it. Complications start when you try to not care. Somehow all the brain cells in my mind seem to have conspired against me.

I should like to recapture the old home atmosphere. If I could do that only for a minute, then this heavy strain might ease a bit. It is not so much the physical discomfort that troubles me – I am quite used to that. The mental strain is the unbearable one. My head feels like a barrel of gunpowder, quite conscious of its liability to explode. One little spark and it will go with a bang! If only this spark did not take so long to come. Come and have done with me. Fate certainly takes its time over these 'sparks'. Who knows when (or if at all) all this will come to an end. Will it be soon? Much longer it just cannot last. Until it comes I must try to escape from my own present thoughts. Any more brooding over myself will only make things worse. Like pouring petrol on to an already blazing fire.

Maybe if I let, or forced, my mind to take me back a few years, more pleasant memories would mingle with their present, and harsher, colleagues. Not that anything really pleasant did occur for the past three years. At the time, I suppose, they were not so bad. Compared with the present they certainly were 'good times'.

The whole world, or rather my whole world, began to go wrong when the war against the Soviet Union was declared.

Quite clearly, I remember we were going to visit my grandparents, or rather my grandmother, who lived in a small village
in the Carpathian mountains. A better and finer morning can
hardly be imagined. We started out fairly early. The sun was
bright, but not yet hot, the road quite deserted (it was a Sunday,
I think) and we were about halfway when Dad switched on
the radio and the news was just coming on. The exact words
fail my memory, but the announcer sounded quite agitated
(or did he?) when he announced that the 'Governments of
Germany, Italy and Hungary have declared war on the Soviet
Union, and joint forces have already gone into action, cap-
turing such-and-such places, with hardly any cost to "our"
people.'

By then we were speeding at about sixty [miles an hour]
and had Mummy not cautioned Dad we would surely have
had an accident. 'Six weeks' was Dad's forecast 'and that
swine (Hitler) will address a crowd of bloody Nazis from
Moscow's Red Square.'

Dad was never an optimist. Sometimes his forecasts did
not go far wrong either. My knowledge of international affairs
was quite negligible, but I did know that it took the Germans
a week or two to defeat any country. Only a few months
before that I had stood in the streets watching wounded Poles
staggering through our town and lots of women and children
came with them. For a loaf they would give a bicycle or even
a camera. They were telling us some pretty terrible stories,
about towns being levelled to the ground in a matter of hours,
and whole crowds of people being machine-gunned. It all
sounded quite fantastic to me.

In those days my idea of warfare was quite a naïve one. We
had a picture at home which showed a group of riders going
into action and a small boy with a drum. My ambition was
to be a similar drummer boy and I rather thought that waging
war was something worthwhile doing for the fun of it. Like the
Romans used to fight. The Romans were my ideals anyway. So

if fighting was all right with the Romans, it was all right with me, too. The Polish war did not sound quite as good, but I guessed the Germans were a pretty filthy lot, so one could not really expect them to be sporting in a war. Had it been the English, it would have been quite different, I thought. (I was a great Kipling fan at the time, and often played 'jungle hunting' riding my elephant, i.e. my older cousin.)

My mind certainly does wander. But to get back to Granny's: that Sunday was first of the 'strenuous days'. I could feel that there was something in the air. Everybody talked of war, bombing, airplanes. There was even talk of gas warfare. The general opinion was that Hungary (and we lived in Hungary at the time) would become an important base. Suddenly everyone sounded wise – or tried to, anyway – predicting the absolute defeat of Russia and Germany respectively. The lunch at Grandmother's was not a success. Early that afternoon we set out on our return journey to town, one week ahead of schedule. In town something like a panic was the first thing that struck me. The usual cinema crowd was about, and people were grouping in front of public notice-boards, on which the headline 'STATARIUM' ('martial law') was visible from our car.

'Well, that settles it,' commented Dad quite philosophically. 'Mobilization, listening to foreign radio stations forbidden, yes. "Peace in our Time" is not altogether impossible, but we shall be pretty aged by the time it comes. Should we still be alive to welcome it.' As I said, my father was not an optimist.

In a few days' time his predictions were realized word for word (except for the very last 'futurism' which is still pending).

The rest of that summer in 1941 was not at all pleasant. Neighbours and friends were called up, and it was not long before official notification started arriving. 'Your son (brother, husband) was killed (captured) on such and such a day, while serving his country. His memory will be treasured by the whole nation.' A fat lot of good that did.

My cousin, Imre, was called up as well.* He came home in uniform, his artistic long hair cropped short, and there was a definite air of depression about him. (In a surprisingly short time my ideas about war had changed completely.) I felt sorry for Imre. I felt I might never see him again, and at the station I kissed him in front of everyone. My family have never called me an affectionate child, and this sudden wave of affection took everyone aback. Three months later (during Christmas holidays) my aunt talked to me about that kiss. 'Hugo, you were the last one to kiss my darling.' Imre was killed in November, in active service 'somewhere in occupied territory'. My aunt was very fond of Imre. So was I.

Imre, you were the first one of the family to die. I shall never forget or forgive you for that!

Back at school the war played only a small part. Some of the professors were soldiers and we thought it was rather fun to see our geography master in a shabby uniform. He was stationed quite near to Debrecen (where I was at school) and whenever we saw him in the streets, we stood at attention and saluted the 'hero'. He was quite young, and our sudden manifestation of respect often embarrassed him. I do not think he was quite sure about the sincerity of our respect. I ask you to forgive me, Professor, we were making fun of you. The Professor was killed one year later 'while defending his country'.

Being slightly aware of hard times, that year I worked hard. My report was good. I thought Dad would be cheered up at least. When I got home and showed him the report, he patted me on the back: 'Hugo, I should like to be present at your graduation.' 'Why, Dad?' I asked, rather surprised. 'I should like to be alive in ten years' time.' He was very still as he

---

* Presumably Imre was drafted into the Hungarian labour battalions.

spoke, and, as if regretting what he had just said, quickly continued, 'Here, take this money and buy yourself a book. I never know what to get for you.'

I went to buy a book. It slips my memory what the book was about, but I remember quite distinctly thinking about what my father had said, and before going to bed I prayed that we might be together in ten years' time – alive. Praying was not a very frequent habit of mine, but the way Dad spoke that afternoon persisted in my mind and has stayed there ever since.

Dad seldom spoke to me about general topics. He was always reserved. Deep in thought, he would hang his umbrella on a coat-hanger and dump his coat in the umbrella stand. Not very tall, and getting broader with his years, he always looked very handsome. His wavy hair was quite thick and half-black, half-silver. He had grey temples at the comparatively early age of twenty-five. In the evenings he used to sit by the radio and duly listened to the Russian, English and German news bulletins. Before going to bed, he would remark: 'The only thing they all seem to agree on is that there is a war on. Funny thing about this war – neither side seems to suffer.'

To us, personally, nothing remarkable had happened. We went to Lake Balaton for the summer. News still reached us about the happenings in our town.

In the middle of July 1942, about two hundred families were notified to produce 'Citizenship Papers' by the end of the week. Those people were born and bred in Berehovo (the name of the town) and never before had they been asked for any documents. 'Citizenship Papers' indeed! Of course, not knowing what would happen if they did not produce the necessary documents, they tried hard to get some official certificates. It seemed all civil servants (Hungarian imports with the 'liberation' of 1938) had conspired against them and the only thing they managed to get was a scornful laugh, or in the more persistent cases, a kick in the backside. By the end of the week, they were pretty confused. One thing seemed certain to every one of Berehovo's twenty thousand citizens: that there was something up the Authorities' sleeves. Just what that was gave Berehovo its first but by no means last, shock. On Saturday morning a lorry stopped outside every one of the 'First Two Hundred' (as they were later named) homes, and each family, with twenty pounds of luggage, was huddled into the waiting lorries and, with a gendarme on each motor, they started out. They were given no time to say goodbye to anyone, and I am convinced that they had no idea what it was all about.

All this news had reached us whilst we were still on our holiday. In the hotels and restaurants German officers (convalescing and otherwise) became an alarmingly frequent sight. Not only did they completely ignore difference of age and sex, but on one occasion (I was present), they actually beat up an aged couple who occupied a table near the orchestra. When I saw this, I felt a queer sensation in my throat. Something was choking me, and I felt I would cry. I had known the couple quite well. I often got a paper for the old gentleman who lived in the same hotel as us. But to see him stagger out with a bleeding nose, humiliated and shocked, was too much. Not only for me, but for a good three-quarters of the diners and musicians. In absolute silence we got up and started for the exit, amid the drunken laughter of the Nazis. That was my first encounter with the *Herren Volk*, * as they really were.

Back in Berehovo, after our holidays, I found some of my friends were included in the 'First Two Hundred'. News had filtered through from time to time and this we learnt: that straight from their homes they were transported to the Ukrainian border and deposited there. They were allowed to

---

* So-called Master People.

go off, on their own this time, and wander amid ruined villages. Most of them died of starvation and later of cold. My elders talked about a lot of sadism and sheer brutality, but it did not convey much to me.

Through a newsreel, however, I did learn quite a lot. They showed a lot of ragged people trying to fight their way to a water cart. The commentator announced them as 'victims of Soviet aggression who now find themselves homeless and without a single hope for the future'. Not only I, but most people in the cinema recognized in the crowd ex-citizens of Berehovo. They looked like anything but human beings. Unkempt hair, torn shirts, sunken heads and eyes staring mutely. It was a horrible spectacle. 'Victims of Soviet aggression indeed!' was the general comment. On the following night, and on many more, the picture kept haunting me. I could see myself in that crowd, fighting for a drop of water, and when I did get some it was generally knocked out of my hands.

The following term at school I was very quiet. My schoolmates began to make fun of me, and some of the more patriotic ones tried to beat me up one night. It was on my way back to the college from an afternoon walk that about five or six boys rushed out from a dark alley and quite literally dragged me back with them. About three boys came from my class and the rest were all older, though from the same *gimnázium*.

'You filthy foreigner,'* said one, 'you will be sorry that you have ever attacked Hungary.' They searched my pockets and one of them examined my new Montblanc fountain pen.

'I think we shall ransack the enemy,' he said and duly pocketed my pen. I tried to protest and broke down completely. I just could not help crying, and although I did not actually cry for help (it was a very dubious street anyway) they must have become frightened. So after each one kicked me wherever they could reach, I was left alone. When I got back to

* Perhaps because Hugo was from Carpathia.

the college, I was still sobbing and my general appearance was pretty ruffled. The headmaster asked me to go with him to his study, where, after a little persuasion, I told him my story.

Dr Kordo* (the headmaster) was a great friend of mine. I suppose in a way I hero worshipped him, but he was really a very good man. When he heard my story he patted me on the back and I remember his words still.

'Hugo, you will find little justice in this world, and you must learn to be tolerant. It is much more important that you should learn this than anything else. Latin and mathematics may help you with your career, but you will achieve very little if you are not tolerant. When some great injustice is done to you, you must tell yourself that they don't really know what they are doing. When you are a grown-up man you can do your share to prevent injustice. Meanwhile, you must be very brave.' Dr Kordo probably did not know himself just how much tolerance I was going to need.

Next day I was asked to identify my attackers. I picked out five, and needless to say they denied it flatly. They said they had sat at the pictures all evening. However, Dr Kordo searched them and my fountain pen was found on one of the boys. It was returned to me, and later I heard that the boys were all caned. Somehow it gave me no satisfaction at all. I do not suppose it was so much the physical pain that left its mark on me, but the shock of suffering for no more than being a foreigner (and automatically an enemy to be distrusted). I avoided those boys for the rest of the term, but I did have various threats conveyed to me through some of the others.

It was during the Easter holidays that the war – or perhaps not so much the war as the Nazi ideology – touched us directly. 'Touch' is a moderate word, 'stab' would be more direct.

On my way home, at Királyháza, a number of wagons were

---

* Known as Dr Kardos in Chapter 8.

attached to our train and a horde of German soldiers got into our carriage. I gave up my seat and went out on to the platform.* It was raining and cold, but by then I had an unconscious fear of anything military, especially if they were Germans. Just before the train got into Berehovo, I went back to get my luggage and I noticed that the Germans were getting ready to alight as well. Cautiously I pulled down my suitcase and started for the door again.

'Hey, you,' shouted one. 'You going to Berehovo as well? Say, have you got a sister?' By then they all laughed and I felt I was blushing wildly. 'No, I have no sister,' I stammered in German and raced out.

Mummy was at the station to meet me. 'Look, Mummy' – I pointed at wagons marked 'DR' – 'a surprise for Berehovo.'

I believe Mummy must have felt very much like myself. Agitated, and certainly not too hopeful as to our future prospects. 'Come Hugo, they are probably only in transit.' Mummy, unlike Dad, was an optimist. 'We have a small party waiting for you at home. We will celebrate your homecoming.' How was poor Mummy to know that it would be the last time we celebrated!

At home, my brothers§ started jumping at me, and searched my bag for presents. There were some neighbourhood children present as well. Soon I was telling them of my trip and the things I did at school. We were quite gay and as I liked to talk of my school experiences, I for one, was enjoying myself.

We were interrupted by Dad's arrival. I jumped up and rushed to embrace him. He did not look a bit like himself. Nervously, he just patted me on the back and, almost rudely, asked my guests to go home. Dad never could manage to be

* The wooden porch at the end of the train carriage.

§ In fact, Gabi's twin brother, Kálmán, had died in infancy (see Chapter 3), but in this account, Hugo – for reasons known only to himself – chose to resurrect his long-dead brother.

completely rude. It was very unusual for Dad to take such action. There was no doubt about something being wrong. All of a sudden, I was convinced it had something to do with the Germans.

I was right. They had come to Berehovo for good. Two local schools had been given notice to quit and make room for them. Save for a few Nyilas (the Hungarian Nazi movement), the whole town was agitated. The ordinary man-in-the-street had no illusions about Nazi befriending methods.

Stories, if not quite through official channels, had been leaking through. They were the kind of stories – very well known to wartime residents in Europe – that had no origina- tors. No one could tell where exactly he had heard these stories, but he was convinced that these were not just unfounded rumours. An occasional slip in the more liberal papers only strengthened the belief that after a Nazi set his foot in a place, even grass refused to grow. Thus we knew of the brutal treatment of Poles, Russians (there was no secrecy about that), Frenchmen, Czechs and, of course, Jews.

Dad had a friend in Dachau, and on one occasion we had a letter in which he told us that he was 'being interned, but had received the most considerate treatment. A small food parcel, however, would be most welcome.' That was the last we heard of him, but not quite the last we heard of Dachau and Theresienstadt. I realize that I was a child, as I still am, but I cannot help thinking that we had been living in a fool's paradise ever since 1939.

Dad must have known that we could not possibly survive the war without being directly involved. Why then didn't he try to seek refuge in Britain or the US? Financially, he could have afforded it. But he would not leave my grandparents. I could understand that I, a child, should love my parents, but it puzzled me to see Dad being so fond of my grandparents. Somehow I could never imagine Dad being attached to anyone really. The very picture of independence. Of course he loved

us, but we were his children. Yet it never occurred to me that
he must have had the same feelings towards his own parents.
However, he never manifested his feelings verbally. When it
came to action though, he was quite ready to sacrifice anything for the sake of his parents. Up till now this did not
make any sense at all, but I think I know now how he must feel,
because as I watch my parents now, hungry and humiliated, I
know I would do anything to help them. It is not even entirely
unselfish that I should feel that way because in them I always
did, and still do, see my own self.

Oh, how I should like to do something very brave to get
me out of here! Futile thinking.

> Futile, futile, all is futile!
> This fearful present;
> And unpromising future.
> From such weary thoughts
> In past shadows I seek refuge.

Back to Berehovo, then! Back to the first night of the German
occupation. A highly strained atmosphere and on top of it –
rain. Rain pouring from every corner of the sky. As if Nature
was lamenting with us.

'. . . Heaven and I wept together!'

Only the Heavens knew just what that night was going to
bring. At about nine o'clock, just as we were trying to listen
to a foreign station, someone rang at the gate. Never before
did I realize that the shrill sound of an electric bell could be
so full of warning. Suspense followed the ring. The set was
switched off immediately and after the bell rang a second time,
Dad went out to see what was up. Next minute Mr Rosner came
in. We sighed with relief to see that it was only a friend, but Mr
Rosner was hardly relieved. In fact, he was hardly himself. A
middle-aged man, an exemplary family man with six children,
is rather an unusual sight when he is seen weeping.

He was sent by the Elders of Town on a special mission. His wife and children, together with some sixty more women, children and very popular men had been taken to the Nazi headquarters (established six hours previously). They were held as hostages, and the fee for their release was one million pengő (pre-1946 Hungarian currency). There was a time limit as well. The hostages – so the Nazi message warned – would be executed at 6.15 a.m. should the million pengő not be delivered by 6.00 a.m.

One million pengő! People with a thousand pengő were among the rich. But in Berehovo the majority of people were not rich.

It was Mr Rosner's mission (being a relative of hostages) to act as a collector. He appealed to my father as I have seen no other man plead for anything. Dad was not one to despise the value of money (in that respect I am very unlike him), but he realized the danger that would befall not only the sixty-odd hostages, but the entire population, should the money not be paid. He gave 10,000 pengő cash, and another 10,000 worth of jewellery. This one contribution was the largest Mr Rosner had collected up till then, and he took his leave amid tears of gratitude.

The rest of the night was panicky and filled with the strange atmosphere of the unknown. We did not go to bed at all, in spite of Dad's pleading. At midnight, the collection was not more than 200,000 (Dad went to the Town Hall every thirty minutes). Another six hours to go and 800,000 were still to be obtained. I could not imagine how so much money could ever be obtained. I never asked for a lot of money, probably because I never needed it, but if I was given ten pengő by some big-hearted uncle, I generally gave half of it to my brothers, not knowing what to do with it.

Now they had to get a million. A big chest was used for storing the jewellery, which consisted largely of rings, earrings and necklaces, with an occasional brooch or gold watch. I saw it at 2.00 a.m. and it was a pitiful collection. Every piece in the chest must have had a little or big story of its own. I tried to picture their owners when they first received them. Most of them were presents, I thought. How overjoyed those people (especially the women) must have been. Probably they got them for some memorable occasion, like an anniversary, or engagement, or even wedding. And now they had to part with it for good. There must have been tears in every house that night.

At about 4.00 a.m. there was still half a million to be collected, and the collectors (whose numbers had by then increased about five times) were running about wildly and panic-stricken. They went into every house and they refused to leave without some contribution. From time to time a German officer appeared, smiling and offering cigarettes to those looking least worried and inquiring occasionally about the situation.

'It will be very sad to see seventy-five funerals tomorrow. No?' He said this smiling and, adjusting his monocle, he took up a handful of jewellery and slowly let it drop back, one by one, while the people, filled with terror, stood silently. The officer was eventually asked if they would accept bankbooks, as there was not enough cash in the town. He said they would accept bankbooks, but only for half their value. 'We Germans are not such bad businessmen, eh? We make good bargains. No?'

There was a renewed wave of collection. People were strained and they would have given anything for the night to be over. Bankbooks, savings of a lifetime, were taken out from beneath stacks of shirts or linen, and shaking hands offered them to the collector, whose voice by then was a hoarse whisper. I had a bank account as well. Dad opened it for me when I started going to school at the age of six. It was to finance my university studies.

'You will not want that any more, Hugo,' said Dad, and I

noticed his hands were trembling as he reached for the books in his drawer. There was a gun in his drawer, too. I noticed him clutching it for a moment, but when he saw us standing around, he pushed the thing into the back of the drawer, and without further talk he handed the books over. The total value of the three books was 90,000 pengő.

At 5.30 a.m. the collection was over. On the horizon the first signs of a new day were beginning to take a visible shape. Another day was coming and what it would bring was another of Fate's secrets.

I stood by the window gazing at the horizon and watched the sun rise. It is a very solemn process to watch. At first the sky turns orange and it looks reluctant to part with the earth, but the sun gradually has its own way and sharp rays begin to break through. One by one they appear, like heralds riding in front of a sovereign's procession. Then the top of the sun appears, emerging from its night's rest in the earth. It is not strong enough yet, so one can still gaze at it. It is a very majestic picture. To see it come out completely like a red-hot sphere and watch passing clouds adopt its colour, only to get rid of it when they are a safe distance from it. The sun, however, is in no hurry. Slowly its glow becomes more powerful and our mortal eyes have to turn away from it. The sun will not let itself be mocked by mortals!

It was six o'clock when I had to turn away from the sun. Dad came in again. He had helped carry the chest over to the Nazis. They had released the hostages, but did not comment on anything. The hostages were tired and hungry. Some of the men had turned grey overnight, and two women fainted when they were released.

There was a momentary sigh of relief all over the town. There were no rich people left. But at least there were living people left. A morning service was held in every church and synagogue. The danger was now over, and God had to be thanked for giving enough courage.

As I said, the danger of the moment seemed to be passed. We knew, however, that the financial ransack would not satisfy the Nazi thirst for blood. The following days passed very slowly. The population (except for the Nazi colony) was not allowed to be on the streets after 9.00 p.m. All radio sets had to be taken to the Town Hall and the keeping of a set was punishable by death. The slightest blackout offence was also rewarded by shooting. Letters were censored and all travel stopped.

For myself, I was scared. I dared not go out at all. Once I attempted to visit my aunt, but I was about halfway when I saw German soldiers raiding houses, dragging out men and young women and lining them up in the High Street. They were only a working-party whose duty was to clear up the Nazi headquarters and soldiers' quarters. Afraid that I might be taken in as well, I turned around and started racing back home. That was my only attempt to break the blockade and I admitted failure by not attempting it again.

My school report was forwarded from Debrecen. It was a very good one and the headmaster enclosed a note of sympathy and offered to keep me a place at the school should I wish to return at any time. Poor Dr Kordo! As if he did not know that I could not return. My good report from school, however, left me quite unimpressed. Day after day I just sat in our garden, and I don't even know what I did. Thinking was no good. There was nothing to think about. War had come to us and it intended to stay.

Then we heard rumours that all 'suspicious' citizens would be deported, as Berehovo was declared to be in the War Zone, where 'enemy aggression was imminent'. Of course we would be 'suspicious' Dad decided, and the thought of deportation gave me a very queer sensation. Best way to describe it would be by saying that there was a constant pressure on my chest and every time someone shouted or the front doorbell rang, this pressure increased tenfold, and I could not even breathe properly. I was not the only one. The whole family, and the whole street were in constant fear.

We heard tales of heroic resistance in other parts of the Ukraine and in all other occupied countries, and my mind was thrilled with it. A year or two ago, it had been my greatest joy to listen to someone who came from the Underground, or had met someone from the Underground, but now all those heroes seemed like fictitious characters. How could anybody *think* of resistance? Now, I see that it was the thinking of a cowardly child, but I am a coward. If I were anything else, I would not be in this wagon.

Anyway, three weeks passed since that unforgettable Friday night and rumours of deportation became more than rumours. There were notices on every street corner saying that 'householders and their families must keep indoors all day now (shopping time 10.00 – 11.00 a.m.) and await a "commission" which would call on every home'.

Why these 'commissions' would call was not explained, but there was no need. We were certain that it meant eviction. The question was which homes would be visited?

We did not have to wait long for an answer. They called on us just forty-eight hours after the notices were put up. During those forty-eight hours, I prayed and even wrote a pledge. It ran something like this: 'I, Hugo G, solemnly promise to offer myself in the services of God, should my entire family in five years' time meet together.' I named all my close relatives name by name, and I hid the slip of paper under a very big log in our backyard. I had made my bargain with God, and it was up to Him now to see the deal through.* It was a very childish

---

* While Hugo was doing this, Bella was also doing some hiding. She brought together her Sabbath candlesticks, Géza's *kiddush* cup, their *chanukiah* and Hugo's school report, wrapped them into a waterproof piece of material and hid them in a hole in their garden. 'When I came back my things were gone, but my mother's treasures survived and they are still in our home and used Sabbath after Sabbath and year after year. And I also sometimes think: how strange, that one way or another I did try to make

thing to do, as I now realize, only six weeks later. I was never very religious, and I certainly tried to look even less so when I was with my friends, but within myself I always respected God, and when in trouble I did not hesitate to ask Him for help, which I expected unconditionally. (The fact that I never received any help is an entirely different thing.) But it was too late to do anything now. The 'commission' called on us on 21 April at 9.30 a.m. It consisted of two rough-looking policemen, one German SS man and two civilians who spoke the language of the *Herrenrasse*.*

Their first request was that we should give up all our 'jewellery, firearms, cameras, field-glasses, microscopes, foreign currency and local currency over 100 pengő'. They took Mummy's earrings and some other bits of jewellery, including two of my own silver cups which I had won at school (one for swimming and one for being in the winning football team). I noticed that Dad did not give up his gun. When I heard that all cameras were to be given up as well, I stole into my own room and taking my Leica camera, I stealthily made my way to the bathroom, placed it inside the oven, and covered it with ashes. Back in the sitting room I noticed Dad making signs towards me. I went quite close to him and he pointed at his back pocket. It took me a second to get it, but when I did I reached in and pulled out a bundle of banknotes. I slid it under my pullover and tried to make my way out to the yard.

'Hey, you,' said the SS man, 'where do you think you are off to?' I stopped and must have looked a shocking sight. I know I was trembling and I tried to answer, but only a hoarse whisper managed to find its way out.

---

much of my life something of a life of service to God's cause and the cause of my people and how I wish that God would also have kept my bargain with Him' [from the film, *Chasing Shadows*].

* Master Race.

I muttered something about going to the '*Abort*' (lavatory). The Nazi must have been used to frightened boys like me, and let me pass. Once outside, I hid the money under the tree trunk where I had put my note of pledge as well.

Meanwhile the 'commission' started going round the house, taking down pictures and rolling up carpets. Suddenly one of the men looked at his watch and, in a matter-of-fact tone, told us that we had exactly fifteen minutes in which to pack as we were going to be 'evacuated'. Each one of us was allowed to take 25 kilos (about 50 lbs) of belongings. Vaguely, I remember Mummy gave me three shirts to put on and two pairs of socks, plus a few pullovers. When I was ready in my overcoat with a bundle of food on my shoulders, I must have weighed double my own weight. I certainly looked double. Nothing, however, seemed to surprise our 'commission'. I presume they were used to such sudden gains of weight.

At the end of the fifteen minutes we were told to line up outside the house and wait for a lorry that would pick us up.

Things have happened so fast that, until we stood outside, we did not realize that we had been thrown out of our own home with practically nothing. I do not quite know whether I took a proper farewell of the house or not, but I do know that I was crying when the lorry arrived. There we stood on the pavement, humiliated in every respect. None of us spoke. There was nothing we could say. We were all thinking the same, but our thoughts were so gloomy that we dared not speak them.

The arrival of the lorry was both painful and relieving. The strain was too great on us. Whatever was to happen would be a change, and we all needed that change – very badly. I helped load our packs on to the lorry and climbed on top myself. It was then, for the first time, that I felt there was no point in my living any longer. All that was dear to me was going to be left behind.

Our street was a long one and as the road was not too good

it took the vehicle about five minutes to get out of it, and so I had five minutes in which to bid farewell to our home, garden, street, neighbours and friends. The latter stood by their windows, some crying, others waving after us. They must have had fears themselves and I felt sorry for them, because they still had 'evacuation' coming to them, whereas we were already on our way.

The lorry, meanwhile, passed by the football ground and the school. As an ardent footballer and a not too reluctant schoolboy, I was sorry to leave both places. It was then that I began thinking about my brothers. Younger than myself, they could not have been aware of the danger that surrounded us. In fact, it must have been rather fun for them to live in constant excitement, so far from the everyday quiet routine that was part of our home. I was particularly embarrassed (anyway I blushed) when Gabby* (my youngest brother) asked one of the soldiers – the Hungarian one – to show him his rifle. Strangely enough, the soldier obliged and for a few minutes they were busy examining the secrets of a rifle. It was rather ironical, I thought, that the soldier, just before robbing us – or, at any rate assisting in the process of robbing us – should behave like a friend, and I am sure Gabby was convinced of the man's friendly intentions. What Gabby did not see was the other Hungarian soldier pushing Dad with his rifle-butt.

Looking at my brothers now, I feel very sorry for them. Gabby is still fair (we are all dark and he is expected to follow suit). He is a skinny little boy, but always full of beans. My forehead is full of scratches, his 'homework' on me. Although he is my brother, he is very unlike me. First of all he is a good musician. He surprised the whole family on one occasion when he sat down to the piano and started playing Schubert, without one mistake. Apparently Boris, my cousin, taught

* Usually spelt 'Gabi' or 'Gaby'.

him behind our backs. He was given piano lessons afterwards
and it was not long before he appeared at charity concerts.
He is, in fact, our Child Prodigy No. 1. Clem,* his twin, is
darker and more like me. His instrument is the violin and he
is quite good at it, too. Here, I think I should mention that I
have tried my hand at the cello, but I am no good. The three
of us, Gabby, Clem and myself, in spite of our occasional
disagreements, are very fond of each other. In our better
moments we have decided to settle down together when we
are grown-ups, and I was unanimously elected as the eventual
leader, which flattered me more than I ought to say. But right
now they look dirty and hungry, not at all resembling those
two clean and mischievous children who were known in
Berehovo as 'the twins'.

To get back to the lorry (my mind is certainly jumping to
and fro), we noticed it did not take us out of town, but turned
on to a lane which led to the local sawmills (the owners of
which included Dad), and the brick factory. The lorry drove
into the brick factory, which was surrounded by barbed wire
and Hungarian soldiers patrolled all around. There were a few
people already in the place. They lived in what used to be the
stables. We got off the lorry and went to see the officer in
charge of the factory. He greeted us quite politely and told
Dad that he expected us, and in fact thought that Dad could
give a hand with the administration of the place as ten thousand people were expected.

'Ten thousand?' ejaculated Dad, quite taken aback. 'Do you
mean that half of Berehovo will be evicted?' Dad asked. 'Oh,
probably more than half,' he answered us with a beautiful
smile, 'but we only have room for ten thousand. We shall
convert the drying huts,' he went on, 'and although there are
no walls around them, I think there are enough bricks lying
about to put up some loose walls. You won't need them for

* Hugo's wishful reincarnation of Gabi's real-life twin, Kálmán

long – I mean,' he added hastily, 'as a temporary arrangement it will be good enough. You' – he turned to Dad – 'you shall have a room for yourself and your family. You can get plenty of straw. I am sure you will be comfortable. Well, I must go now to meet a transport.' With that, we were dismissed.

Our room was quite bearable. We had just put down our luggage when we heard wailing from outside. Dad and I rushed out to see what was up and a more pathetic view I have never seen before. About twenty horse-drawn carts came driving up. On them sat old people and children, each holding on to a little bundle and beneath them some bedding, grey from the journey on the dusty roads. The younger and the middle-aged walked beside the carts and on either side of them walked armed guards with their guns resting on their arms, level with the stomachs of the people they escorted. The wailing we heard came from the women who must have felt that they were in grave danger. I imagine they had been crying ever since they left their village which was six miles outside Berehovo (that I learned later). Dad was crying. It is a painful thing to watch a grown man weep. His whole body shook and he laid his arm on my shoulders. I felt they were trembling. Next thing I noticed was that I was weeping too. Silently my tears began to roll down and I felt the salty moisture on my lips. Silently we turned back, but we did not go back to our room. Instead, we took a walk round the lake which was situated just behind our room.

It was late in the afternoon when we returned to find our room tidied up and Mummy preparing some food on a smoking stove. The room was bare, or rather its walls were bare, and in one corner Mummy had made a bed of straw, covered with blankets. There was a table in the room, too, but it had only three legs and was propped up by bricks. Some old chairs were arranged around it and our luggage was neatly deposited in the corner opposite our 'bed'. The stove stood in the corner opposite the door, so that every time the door opened a fresh

wave of smoke filled the room. There was only one window
and one of the glass panels was missing. A newspaper was
placed there to prevent draught.

We ate in silence and went to bed early. I hardly slept a
wink and judging from the general moving about, neither did
Dad or Mummy. Gabby and Clem were, however, sound
asleep. Even if I had tried to go to sleep, I could not have done
so because of the crying of babies who were not used to
sleeping in sheds without walls.

Morning found me tired, but glad to be able to get up and
around. I decided to make a tour of the place and so passed
the morning. There were two rows of sheds on either side of
the road that led up to the building which housed us. Only
one shed was occupied and the occupants were busy putting
up a wall and hanging curtains or sheets to make their own
cubicles. The occupants of the cowshed were already 'old
timers' and they had a hand in the kitchen which was converted from a dressing room for the workers. It was not compulsory to eat from the communal kitchen, but once
provisions were gone, we would be obliged to get our soup
and bread from there. At the end of the road stood the gate.
It consisted of a long pole with weights attached to its thick
end to balance it. When a vehicle came in, the pole was lifted
and then it dropped by itself on a Y-shaped piece of metal,
hammered firmly into the ground. Outside stood a uniformed
gendarme with a bunch of feathers in his topper. He was
armed with a gun and a rubber truncheon. Inside the gate
stood a young boy (about eighteen) – one of the 'inmates' –
whose job was to lean on to the end of the pole in order to lift
the thing. When I came near the gate the boy made signs at me
to go away, but no sooner had I started to retreat when the
gendarme called me up to the gate. Not too happily I advanced,
and when I got as far as the pole he snatched my ear and began
to twist it – hard. I yelled and he twisted it harder.

'That'll teach you, swine of a child, to put your nose into

things that don't concern you,' he blared at me. I could see his red, coarse face. He had a big hanging moustache and a filthy ear. When he let go of my ear, I turned around and ran away as fast as my feet would carry me. On my way, I could hear him laugh and felt I could kill him.

Next I went behind one of the sheds. About ten yards from the sheds ran, parallel, the railway line. But there was a barbed wire fence between the line and the sheds. A bit further up some people were digging a hole. I went up to them and asked what it was going to be.

'A latrine. And you can give a hand,' said one of the men. But as they did not pay any more attention to me, I decided to walk off. My next destination was behind the opposite row of sheds. There were a number of piles of bricks and another lake, bigger than the one behind our room. In this lake, some of the older inmates of the camp were having a swim and for a moment the scene reminded me of a summer outing to a pleasure beach. But the illusion was soon dispelled by the shrill sound of the factory sirens.

Having got over my shock (that it was not an air-raid siren) I rushed back to our room, but on my way I met Dad and Mummy going towards the 'Plaza' (as we called the square in the centre of the camp). There were about a thousand people already standing there and I thought for such a large crowd they were remarkably silent. It took me another few seconds to notice a high-ranking German officer who was standing on the steps leading to the 'surgery'. Apparently he was waiting for everyone to assemble and about five minutes after our arrival he began his speech. You could hardly call it a speech, but it went something like this: 'You probably know that you are here because of your unreliability. You are not prisoners, but you are under martial law and that means that you must not be outside your rooms after ten. Also you must not leave the factory grounds – at any time. If, however, you make such a futile attempt, you will be fired at. And your guards are all very good shots indeed. Your Commander will be Captain Nagy of the Hungarian Army, and you shall also have a leader from amongst yourselves who will communicate with Captain Nagy, should any problems arise. He will be appointed by me. I do not know how long you will stay here, so there is no point in asking such stupid questions. And,' he added, 'even if I did know it [the answer], I would not tell you. You can dismiss now and go back to your jobs.' Thus the speech came to an end.

It was also time for lunch and I was rather hungry. During the meal we heard some more lorries and carts drive up, but the novelty of it had worn off, and I continued to eat. We had brought provisions with us, but we knew that we could not make it last for ever. So our portions were considerably reduced. According to Mummy we had enough calories and vitamins, but I felt hungry just the same. Still, I did not say anything about it, nor about my earlier encounter with the gendarme, but went out to play.

There were some boys of my age in the camp and I decided to make friends with them. I was surprised to find one of my schoolmates carrying a bucket of water to one of the sheds. He, too, looked surprised to see me in the camp and right away I offered to give him a hand with the bucket. He came from a nearby farm. His father was a 'gentleman farmer', but he was called up as early as 1939, and became a prisoner of war soon after the outbreak of war with Russia. The boy's name was Paul. Paul Gross to be exact, but in Debrecen we called him 'Tata', largely, I think, because of his enormous hands and feet. He was a dark boy with very thick lips and he supplied us at night with sexy stories. He was a very good mathematician and his aim was to become a textile engineer, as his uncle had a weaving mill somewhere in the USA. He was an only child and had been taken with his mother first to the nearest village and from there to our camp. His mother was a small, fragile woman, also dark, but otherwise not at all like Paul. She had a very high-pitched voice and I did not take to her very strongly. She greeted me warmly, and hoped that Paul and I would be good friends. Her next question was whether we had any cooking facilities and I told her of our stove.

'Your father always was a lucky man,' she said. 'I hope your mother will let me use it. Would you like to ask her for me, Hugo?' I said I would and then she asked me if I thought that Paul could have supper with us as she had not yet unpacked her food. As it was only about three in the afternoon, I was rather surprised at her request, but I said I would ask my mother, knowing that she would not refuse. Before she could ask any further questions, I proposed that Paul and I should go for a swim, to which she graciously agreed, after warning us not to go in the deep end.

Later on, I did ask Mummy if Paul could have dinner with us, and she agreed wholeheartedly, but quite frankly I did not like Paul's mother. I had an idea that she was trying to 'plant [palm] him off'. Still it was good to have an old friend around.

During the next few days the population of the camp grew to its maximum capacity and yet, day after day, loads of people – old and young – kept coming in. There was no longer room in the 'barracks' (as the wall-less barns were called) and a number of young people decided to put up tents of a kind and even the actual drying chambers, which had no windows at all, were occupied. The number of self-supporting families had gradually decreased and queues outside the kitchen became very long indeed.

It was decided that a communal stove be established, and with the aid of some of the money the 'committee' was able to collect, food was bought from outside. The authorities must have been aware of the shortages, because they allowed us to buy the stuff and on many occasions they even encouraged it. I have an idea that they were responsible that we should not starve, and it must have come as a godsend that we (meaning all the inmates) were willing to put up the money and thus they could save the official allowance.

These shortages, however, did not affect us (meaning my family) because some of our friends outside managed to send in some food every day.

About ten days after our arrival at the factory, I felt quite at home. I became friendly with some of the gendarmes and there was one who was – I used to claim – not at all a gendarme. He was – again I quote – 'an ordinary human being'. Quite rare in the Nazi-Hungarian Gendarme Force. Anyway, this man talked to me a lot and when we discovered that we both knew Debrecen, he proceeded to tell me a number of dirty jokes in connection with the Big Forest, on the outskirts of Debrecen. One day I asked him if it would be possible for me to go out for a few hours, as I 'had some business to settle' in the town. At first he flatly refused, but when I offered to give him one hundred pengő (I still marvel at my courage for being able to offer a bribe), he agreed, but said: 'We must be very clever about it.'

The plan was that I would go out while he was on duty on Thursday evening and come back when he was next on duty – Saturday noon.

Amidst my family's best wishes I set out on my expedition. The object of it was to recover the bundle of notes I had hidden during the search in our home and take it back with me, as we had discovered that money had not lost its power, even in the factory. The gendarme shook hands with me and told me that when I came back, I should not walk up the road, but come behind the bushes and whistle three times. If he returned the signal I should proceed, but if he whistled twice only, then I should just wait. If, however, he whistled four times, then I had better scram and not come back until Monday evening.

The road leading out of the factory was quite familiar to

me and in spite of the darkness I managed to find my way quite easily. As much as it was possible, I tried to evade the main streets, and about an hour later, I was standing outside our house. It was a very queer feeling – I had to break into my own home. I did not remember until it was too late that the front gate had a seal stamped on it. I realized this only after the gate was open and the seal broken.

Although the gate was locked with a key, it was child's play to open it. One only had to lift it and then push it sideways. The hinges were loose enough to let the gate slide back a bit and the feat was achieved. On my way to our house, I did not see any sign of life in the streets, and as I went up the drive to the log (under which lay the money), the pebbles under my shoes made such noise that I should have accredited them more to a cannon.

To confess, I was scared to death. My hands must have trembled as I reached under the log, and it was with great relief that I groped a soft bundle which, in the moonlight, revealed itself to be 'it'. Hastily I made my way back through the front gate, closed it carefully, and started walking up the road – whistling.

Ever since I could first whistle, I have used this knowledge as a sort of weapon if I had to go anywhere in the dark. For, I argued, if anyone wanted to attack or rob, he would not choose somebody brave and not scared. And the most obvious manifestation of calmness I could think of was to whistle some dirty song. I had great faith in this since no one has ever attacked or robbed me at night – thanks to my whistling. It was now past midnight and gradually I became hungry and tired. I decided to spend the next day in our vineyard. There was a small house in the yard where we used to spend week-ends in the summer. It would be locked, but one of the windows was quite easy to open. Anyway, even if I had to break in, who cared? But before I started making my way towards the hills, I remembered the absence of food. It was too early in the season to hope for fresh fruit, and if we did have some stuff left in the house, it was sure to be rotten by then. Just as I was trying to find some solution to my food problem, I was struck by a bright idea.

It was customary in our district to employ 'hill guards' around the year. They were armed and their job was to keep the uninvited off the premises. There were generally five or six on duty at any time and they had a small food store in their guardroom. Of course they would not welcome me, but I hoped that an opportune moment might arrive when the hut would be empty. The rest seemed quite easy.

It must have been about one o'clock in the morning when the hut appeared within my range of vision. The night was one of those deceitful ones. One moment the moon illuminated all, next there was not a speck visible. Carefully, I approached the hut. There was not a sound in the night. The ground was soft and I got to the window without making a sound. Inside there was a paraffin lamp, turned low. The room was empty and there was bread on the table. These two factors were more than sufficient to induce me to enter.

The door made a terrifying noise. For some minutes I stood without making a move, but a reassuring quietness ruled in the hills. Then I tiptoed to the table and helped myself to a loaf and some raw bacon.* Having wrapped the food into a newspaper, I made my way to our own vineyard. Exhausted and hungry, I got there, and to my surprise the lock on the door was broken. Inside I found a candle and some matches and soon I got down to my meal. While I ate I noticed that a lot of light furniture, as well as some pictures and summer clothes, were missing. Being too tired to care, anyway, I lay down on the sofa and soon I was asleep.

Next morning – or rather noon – I got up, washed, and ate again. Then I went for a walk. Some of the trees were already

---

* Hugo expresses no remorse for eating the non-kosher meat.

blossoming and large crowds of blackbirds swarmed all over the sky. For hours I walked, aimlessly, trying to think, but only succeeding in asking myself questions. Of one thing I was certain. If all the men in the world had taken that same walk, there would never be any wars. Unfortunately, however, most men are too busy for such things as walks – hence the wars. It was all very illogical, but then I suppose logic is not always the decisive factor.

With sunset, I returned to the bungalow, finished the loaf and slept again. In the morning I started walking back to town. It was risky to show myself in daylight, but few people knew me and I had to take a chance. Walking down the hills I stopped frequently to look back and I had a funny feeling that I might never see those hills again. Perhaps my feelings were wrong, perhaps they were right. Who knows?

The town was not as busy as usual on Saturdays. Nazi soldiers parading along the High Street were the only things that moved. I suppose the absence of half the population accounted for that. Occasionally trucks loaded with furniture and household goods passed me. They were speeding towards the Mother Country: Hungary. On one lorry I thought I recognized our dining-room furniture. But I did not really care.

The chimneys of the brick factory were already within sight and I got off the road and walked behind a row of hedges. A few yards in front of the gates, I stopped and whistled. The copper on guard whistled back. Cautiously I peered out and ran across the road. I fell and cut my knee on a stone. I have cut my knee plenty of times before, but there was never any blood. This time it had to bleed. The gendarme came out, helped me up and practically carried me back. The shock of falling lasted for some minutes and I could not utter a word. I think I was under the impression that I had been shot, but the gendarme's swearing soon brought me back to consciousness.

Dad was glad to get the money. I suspect he was running short. I noticed a lot of young men were walking around with rubber truncheons and armbands with the letters 'CP' (Camp Police). The camp commander must have been a good psychologist, for all the recruits were of a tough sort and it seemed they were fond of using their truncheons as well. Especially on elderly people. What their exact duties were I never knew, but certainly they were the main chaos-creators. If the queue outside the kitchen was in a single line, they wanted a double one, and vice versa. I suppose they got a kick out of it. And so, for that matter, did the people in the queue. Literally.

Things were now going from bad to worse. Food was short and discipline very strict. On the Saturday following my return to camp, a group of SS soldiers came to the commanding officer's dinner party and afterwards, in a drunk state, went into the barracks and started kicking people. It seems they also raped several young girls and one man stabbed a soldier when he molested his wife. He was beaten up badly and had to be taken to hospital.

During the day rumours were spreading about everything from armistice to transports. One contradicted the other and groups of men were hotly debating throughout the camp. One Sunday morning, we woke up to find a long train of empty cattle wagons shipped on to the camp siding. During that Sunday the atmosphere was very strained. Were those wagons for us? Or was it a mistake?

But on Monday the mystery was solved. The wagons were meant for us, after all. Barracks 1 to 4 were to get ready. They could take as much as they could carry. Chaos turned into real panic. Where were they going? No one knew. They were to embark at noon on Tuesday, and at about 10.00 a.m. the commanding officer addressed those who were leaving, but of course everyone was present to hear his speech. He was very brief: 'You are going to Kecskemét where a large and comfortable camp is waiting for you. You will work on the land. Behave yourselves and you'll soon be back. Have a good trip.'

The embarkation began. There were a lot of feather-hatted

gendarmes swarming around the place. Kicking and swearing, they searched everyone and all valuables were pooled in a barrel. 'You'll get them back when you get to Kecskemét,' they said. Kecskemét, by the way, is somewhere in Hungary and famous for its apricots and brandy.

Relatives of the departing asked for a place to be kept near them, and waved handkerchiefs as the gendarmes ordered everyone, except those who were to travel, back into their barracks. I did not go back to our room. I was too curious to see what was going to happen. Soon I did. They had to form groups of seventy-five in front of each wagon. The doors were slid open and in they went. That is, the first forty. The rest squeezed in, and there were a few left over who were still to be added to the already crammed wagons. How they were going to lie down, I did not understand. But soon I could hear babies cry and general calamity. The doors were shut and a lock put on each one. Soon, faces appeared at the small square windows which had barbed wire on top of the iron bars.

A large engine puffed up the line and the gendarmes got into their first-class carriage behind the engine. Their carriage was marked MAV (the initials of the Hungarian railways) but the wagons had DR (German Railways) on them. The whistle went and a flag was waved. The engine started. Slowly at first, then gaining speed, in a few seconds it had taken the train out of sight. The first transport had left.

Rumour-spreaders now had a chance to display their ingenuity. According to one school of thought the train was blown up. This version was not acceptable, for knowing the Nazis as we did, they would not sacrifice railings and wagons unnecessarily. Others thought that the train was captured by Russians, although I could never understand how they could have come down from Stalingrad to Lower Ukraine in one day. Dad thought that the transport would have arrived safely to wherever they had gone – but he was certain it was not Kecskemét. He had travelled extensively all over Hungary and according to him Kecskemét did not need another two people, never mind ten thousand. Dad's sayings always go for me! He had never let me down – yet. If he said that a certain variety of cheese was good, I knew I would like it. That must have been due to some form of inheritance. As far as I understand my looks are not from him, but no matter what anyone says my taste in all things comes straight from Dad. He dislikes heavily made-up women, and I would not let any cousin of mine kiss me with lipstick on, etc.

The following Sunday night, a fresh train of wagons was shunted into the camp. Again, they were marked DR, and on Monday morning I went up to them. They smelled of strong disinfectant, but otherwise they looked quite clean. I climbed into a wagon at the rear and there was light enough for me to see carvings and pencil-marks on the walls. One pencil-mark read: 'Three days without water: God Almighty help!' Another went: 'If you read this, remember: do anything but do not get into this wagon.'

Needless to say these remarks shocked me. It sounded too much like fiction, but much stranger things were happening than anything in fiction. I made a note of the inscriptions and got out of the wagon again. On the side of it I noticed a small bit of paper. It was German and it was nailed to the wagon. On it I read: 'Auschwitz, Cracow, Prešov, Kassa, Csap'. I tore down the sheet and ran with it to Daddy. He was just in the middle of some discussion with my Uncle William.* Generally, I apologize when I burst in like that, but I was much too excited to do anything of the sort. I told them how I found the note on one of the wagons and showed them my copy of the carvings and pencil-marks. I must confess their reactions surprised me. They were not one bit excited. On the contrary, they just went on talking. The subject of their discussion was Bert who was our chauffeur. I pretended to

* Hugo's uncle Viktor Gelbman whose Czech name was Wilhelm.

look for something and so managed to overhear snatches of their conversation. It seemed Daddy was being cautious and he did not think five thousand would be enough. Uncle William on the other hand did not think that there was any danger at all, as long as 'he' was on our side. Two and two began to take the shape of four. If I had been excited before, by now I felt like jumping up and down just to quieten myself down. Dad and Uncle William were planning a getaway and escape!

Soon after lunch, Dad asked us not to tell a soul about anything we might see or hear in the near future. Solemnly we promised. He told us that we may be leaving camp pretty soon, and he looked at Mummy half-smiling, half-asking. Mummy just sat still and suddenly got up and went to a corner. I think she cried. Daddy wanted to go after her, but as he half-rose, he changed his mind and sat down again. He said something like: 'I wish you wouldn't, Bella. We've had this all out before!' I felt an urge to change the subject. I showed Dad the slip from the wagon again and asked for geographical information. He studied it for a few seconds, then he called to Mummy again: 'Here is proof!' Mummy came over and together we more or less deciphered it.

'Csap,' Dad went on, 'is an important junction in Carpathian Russia, from there Kassa is but a few miles. That's on the Slovakian border. Next you see Cracow. Well you know where that is. In Poland, of course. But the last stop is Auschwitz. I don't quite know where that may be. Sounds German all right, but why on earth would we have to go through Poland?' Dad looked very puzzled and after a few more minutes of meditation, he went for a walk. Soon I followed suit, and in the camp I noted a lot of consternation coming from Barracks 5 to 10. It was their turn next. Women were washing; men ran about with rucksacks and string, making parcels to suit all. Small ones for children, gradually increasing, until the grown-ups had parcels about as large as themselves. Of course, half of it would be thrown out before they embarked, and they knew it too; but funnily enough they all thought that they *might* get through with all their stuff.

They did not. Just as I had thought. After the train left on Tuesday, there were all sorts of clothing, kitchen utensils, brushes and even foodstuffs lying around the line. We were ordered to pick them up and pool them in the empty barracks. Hardly two thousand people remained now in the camp. The majority of those remaining consisted of the sick, doctors, the kitchen staff and a few of the camp 'elders', as well as the families who lived in 'private' rooms, such as ourselves. There were no more rumours. Everyone knew that in a matter of a few days we would have to leave too.

On Thursday morning, Uncle William came rushing in to us. 'Doctor and Mrs Vasas have committed suicide and they took the children with them,' he announced. I knew the oldest girl quite well. In fact, we had a chat only two days before this tragedy. She wanted to become a journalist, and now she was dead! She did not want to die. Of that, I am certain. Dr Vasas was quite a well-known man, and if he thought life was not worth living there must be something in it.

By Friday morning, six more couples had committed suicide. Five of the men were doctors and the sixth, the headmaster of the local grammar school. Dad said that the Commander was absolutely furious. His first reaction was: 'How dare they do it in my camp!' But of course, he could not get even with the deceased, so he ordered all knives to be given up. It was a ridiculous order, because there were so many knives lying about the barracks, now emptied of people, that we couldn't possibly collect them all within a week. But an order was an order and all day I was collecting knives. While turning out some kitchen utensils in Barrack 8, I found a book of verse which looked very familiar. Opening the cover I read: 'To Paul on your 13th. Hugo'. So he had carried my present with him. I was very moved. Though we were good friends, after a brief flare of friendship, we were not together much. With a little jealousy,

I had noticed him hanging around one of the prettiest girls in camp. Really, I did not blame him, but sometimes he would pass me without a word, and that hurt. Most probably, he had some reason for it, but I cannot think what it was. Anyway I took the book back with me and read it for a long time. There were bits of Goethe and Schiller as well as Petőfi and Ady. It was a sort of international anthology. All verses in their original. I remember particularly well a bit from Matthew Arnold:

'. . . Whether it will heave us up to land
Or roll us back to the sea, back to the deep waves of death,
We know not: and no search will make us know
Only the event will teach us in its hour . . .'

I learnt this bit off by heart. The 'it' was the 'huge wave of fate' and we were all 'poised on top of it'. Then I wondered what had become of Paul and of the eight thousand others. And what would become of us? I was full of forebodings.

Inside, Dad had another conference with Uncle William. By the look of them and the sudden silence which followed my entrance, I knew they were then discussing 'the escape' (as I called it).

'We can talk in front of him,' said Mummy. 'He is no longer a baby.' This remark will always make me feel very grateful to Mummy. She had told everyone frankly that I was 'no longer a baby'. And the conference went on. Dad even looked at me at times, and I felt he wanted me to approve, so I nodded. The plan was that Bert would bring along the lorry, and after sunset we would load our stuff on it and leave. Apparently the gendarme could be bribed and even the commanding officer was willing to 'listen to reason'. Uncle William was, of course, all for it. Aunt Rose and their two daughters, Isabelle and Eva* were not afraid. Neither was Mummy. My younger

---

* These two cousins also survived the *Shoah*. Itsa (Isabelle) now lives in Prague and her sister, Eva, lives in Los Angeles.

brothers did not have a vote, but Dad was not so keen. The front, he said, was far off, and he could not see how or where we could hide for such a long time. Uncle William suggested that we drive into Hungary – to Budapest if possible, with the rest of the convoys that packed all roads. We could always get some fake documents and the rest would be easy. Both Dad and Uncle William had property in Budapest and they could easily sell it. Dad even owned a block of flats, so there should be no difficulties at all. It was agreed that they would send a message to Bert to 'stand by' and to get as much petrol as possible.

On the following day – Saturday – Dad went to see the CO, but I never found out exactly what happened. The guard was quite willing to let us pass on Sunday night, and that same gendarme took a note to Bert, telling him to come fetch us at 7.30 p.m. on Sunday, bringing as much food with him as he could. The rest of Saturday and Sunday passed without any unusual incidents. I even went swimming on Sunday morning. I was wondering, as I lay in the sun, when I would get another chance to swim. Perhaps in Budapest, I thought, on St Margaret's Island, or in the Gellert Bath, where they had artificial waves every quarter of an hour.

My appetite at lunch was quite enormous, but as the afternoon advanced, I began feeling more and more nervous. And there was that queer merry-go-round feeling in the pit of my stomach. By 7 p.m. I was excited. Mummy refused all my offers of packing, saying that I was too worked up to be able to do anything. 'I wish we'd never told you anything about the plans,' she concluded.

Mummy was right. I should have been more controlled. Of course I knew I was not a baby, nor even a small child any longer, and I was beginning to realize that I had other responsibilities as well. Such as, for instance, looking after Gabby and Clem, or at any rate trying to keep them out of the way, and even quieten them if necessary. I made a resolution to become a real help and that I would do all I could to earn a good opinion from my mother.

By 7.30 p.m. I was standing at the gate, waiting to catch a glimpse of the lorry. The majority of people were already in bed, or at any rate in the barracks, and only a few young couples could be seen walking arm in arm, talking quietly and probably wondering what tomorrow would bring. A few minutes after the appointed time the lorry did become visible. It was not yet dark and the headlamps were not on. But it was already dusk and it was curious to watch the lorry grow bigger and bigger, as if it would emerge from the brim of the reddish horizon. It left a trail of dust behind it and I remember thinking what a waste that was, because in a few minutes it would be beaten up again – the dust, I mean. The gendarme opened the gate and as soon as the lorry entered camp, I jumped on the running board and gave him directions.

Mummy and Aunt Rose (they are sisters) had all our luggage ready and, with the aid of Bert, we had it loaded in a few seconds.

The incident which followed the loading is difficult to describe. I know my brothers were already sitting on top of a pile of clothing and both my cousins were ready, too. Bert was helping Aunty Rose get on the lorry, when Dad, followed by Uncle William, came running back to us.

'Quick, unload everything and get inside!' he ordered. 'There is no time to talk now, but for heaven's sake, be quick. Bert, you take the lorry a few yards further on, and remain sitting in it. If anyone asks you what you are doing here, tell them you were sent to collect some bricks for the "Town Defence". I'll tell you what to do later.' By the end of this speech, the luggage had been taken down and carried inside. Bert drove the lorry a bit further and inside we sat in the dark. Uncle William was telling us of the sudden happenings.

It seemed that three young men, one of whom was Dudy Klein, whom I knew quite well, had escaped on the previous night, and were caught at Csap by some SS men. One of the three jumped the train as they were being brought back to Berehovo and was shot at from the moving train. But the other two had been taken to the SS Town Commander, who had them flogged and interrogated. The commander himself brought them back to camp, and an extra fifty men came with him to guard the camp overnight. There was going to be a search as well, though neither Dad nor Uncle William knew what they were looking for. There was some rumour about partisan activities in a nearby forest, but whether that was true or not we knew not. Anyway, Uncle William thought that the Nazis were afraid of a raid which might be directed at the camp in order to free some of us.

Talking there in the dark, that horrible feeling of forthcoming disaster overtook me again and I shook like jelly. I did not say a word to anyone, due, I think, to my inability to speak. I was frightened in the worst sense of the word, and would have given five years of my life for some light. But they did not want any light lest the searching parties should come in. Exactly what happened afterwards I do not know for I fell asleep sobbing.

Monday morning arrived unceremoniously, and it was about seven o'clock when I awoke. I was not surprised to find myself undressed and in 'bed' because at home I regularly fell asleep fully clothed and always woke in bed. One thing struck me as obvious as soon as I opened my eyes. We were still in 'camp', so the escape plan had not worked. My brothers were still asleep and since we shared the same mattress I had to be careful getting up. Mummy was trying to get a fire going in the stove and it did not take me long to notice Dad's absence. I remember even the slightest details of that day – you see it was only yesterday.

Once the fire got going, Mummy made some coffee and asked me to dig out some cups. Our luggage was not yet opened. Dad came in soon afterwards. He looked very tired and unshaven. The crease in his trousers was missing and if anyone who knew him before had seen him then, I am certain they would not have recognized him at all. In a weary tone he informed us: 'We leave today!'

So that was that. No one said anything for a long time. We just sat there in silence. Gabby and Clem, who were awake by now, sat up on the mattress and joined our silence. They heard Dad say that we were leaving, and under other circumstances they would have jumped about at the prospect of a journey, but this time they must have felt that there was more to it than just travel.

As our bags were ready, we still had a few hours on our hands, so I went for a stroll. Though it only happened yesterday – just over twenty-four hours ago – it seems like months. It was not as if I had enjoyed that walk particularly, but at least I had plenty of air and room. First I went to the lake. It was deserted. Broken-down stoves, together with some handmade ones, decorated the bank nearest the barracks, together with some old pans and broken bottles, rags and even furniture. Some of the fireplaces were still smoking, probably they had cooked breakfast on them. What I felt exactly, I do not really know. But I felt lost and I will never forget the sight of those demolished and still-smoking fires. Perhaps my fate, too, will be similar to those fires. By now they are extinguished. And how long will I last?

As I stood on the lakeside, a young couple came down and went straight behind some bushes. They were only a few yards off, but because of the thick growth of the bushes, they could not see me. They must have been unaware of my presence, for they did not restrain their voices at all.

'Darling, this is my only chance,' he said, 'and I am not going to let it fly away. I feel sure they'll have me, and I wish you would come too.' There was a short silence, and faintly she said: 'I cannot come, Joseph. Mummy will need me.' Again they did not speak, but I think they kissed. 'Joseph,' she started after a while, 'you promise you'll come back here when it's all over.' Joseph promised and I felt comforted to know that there were at least two people who took their return for granted.

There was not much point in my staying there. They were probably making love, and as quietly as I could, I returned to the barracks. There were not many people left, but they were all over the place. Everyone was busy carrying something. The train was to leave at 2.00 p.m. sharp, and it was midday, or very near, and everyone was saying: 'Good God, I haven't even started packing!' Which, of course, was a lie, because they had been packing ever since the last transport had left.

Back in our room we sat down to lunch. We had some tinned soup, beef and peas, and some apple tarts. As the meal progressed I became more and more excited. During soup, I was quite calm, but when the beef and peas arrived I started thinking about this being our 'last supper' and by the time the tart was laid in front of me, my inside was feeling like a sea heaving with waves, especially in my tummy. Every time I am worked up it upsets my tummy most. It goes round and round, and just when I am on the verge of being sick it travels into some other part of my body. As a rule, my hands start shaking and I stammer wildly. When we reached the end of lunch I was shaking like jelly and I stammered.

However, there was no time to be lost, and soon I found a rucksack fastened to my back with a very heavy suitcase in my hand. Gabby and Clem had a bag each, and Dad had two suitcases on top of his large rucksack. Mummy carried some blankets and coats, and when I suggested that there would not be enough room for all this luggage in the wagon, I was hushed down.

The train was its usual size, but we had hoped that since there were fewer of us than previously, we would have more room. We had to form groups of forty-five in front of each wagon and the search began. It was very hot and we had a lot of clothes on. In less than five minutes I began sweating and needless to say, I was not the only one. The gendarmes had every bag opened and every pocket searched. Good shirts and shoes were thrown out and they did not have to explain why.

When they came to my belongings, I was again at the stammering stage and, without a sound, but with shaking hands, I opened the bag. My hands must have made him suspicious, for he spent twice as much time as with the others (or was that just my imagination?), but my bags were reduced to half their weight. He took especially long to examine the book of verse I had with me. He must have thought it was something precious, for he slit the cover open with his bayonet. But having satisfied himself that it was only a book, he threw it out with the rest. I was attached to the book but made no effort to reclaim it. Some people did go out of line and pick up some of their stuff, but I felt paralysed.

A young lieutenant was walking up and down in front of us. There was something unusual about him, but it took me several 'rounds' to notice that his pistol was hanging on a leather strap, instead of in its usual place in a case. Two wagons further on, I noticed a small man making his way towards a heap of linen behind them. His wife watched him with a small baby in her arms. He reached the heap and pulled out some white sheets, which I suppose were napkins, when a piercing scream went up, followed by a shot. I was looking at the man all this time, who dropped the napkins, raised his arms to his chest and fell to the ground. A small stream of blood was quite visible from where I stood, but my attention was drawn to the figure of a fainting woman: the same one who had been holding the baby and who must have screamed when she saw the officer aim. The woman was laid down by some of her friends, and in a few minutes a gendarme appeared with a bucket of water. Without much ado, he poured it over her. At this moment the baby started crying. It was not the usual sort of cry, but something quite horrible. My whole body was shaking. I have seen plenty of shooting in films, but it looked quite different in reality. The man who was shot must have died, though I could not see him since he was surrounded by gendarmes, who covered him with some white sheets and took him away.

The officer, however, did not seem to take much interest in these goings on. He murmured something like 'This will teach you discipline, you hounds' as he passed our group and very soon after we had to start our embarkation. Forty-five was not a bad number [for a wagon], really. There was a barrel of water in the wagon, and next to it a wooden box with a bucket in it which was to serve as the lavatory, and ten loaves of bread as well as some marmalade. We were the first to get in, and secured a corner. Most of the people in the wagon were friends of ours and we were confident that we would come to no clashes, though nobody entertained illusions about any pleasantness.

When everybody was inside, gendarmes came round and shut the doors. As it was still early afternoon, the light coming through the windows was quite sufficient, and soon everybody was preparing to settle down.

There was some whistling, and judging from the violent bumps we received, an engine was attached to our train. This engine was to take us all away, and who knows if we would ever return. Yet it did not move me too much. I stood up by the window as we started moving. The breeze coming in through the window was quite pleasant, after all that standing in the heat.

We were on our way. First the engine took us into the station, and there we were to receive a shock: the doors were opened again and thirty more people virtually thrust in. It seems they were under special guard in one of the schools (three hundred of them) and they were to join us wherever we were going. They did not complain about any discomfort, which was getting to be quite an acute problem, and as they sat down in the middle of the wagon, I noticed they looked strangely empty. As if no power in the world could move them or put some vitality into their veins. Dad knew one of them. He was a teacher and was known to harbour communist ideals. In fact, he used to make speeches on the first of May.

As the train started moving again, he told Dad that they had been treated like animals. Fifty of them had shared one classroom and food given to them only once a day. 'The food,' he added, 'consisted of one slice of bread and half a litre of pea soup, with a couple of kicks in your backside by some friendly gendarme.' They did not know why they had been picked out, but some asserted that they had been kept as hostages and should there have been any disorder in the camp they – in the school – would have had to pay with their lives.

Remarks such as 'It would have been a good thing if they did revolt' and 'Who asked them to spare us?' followed, but our attention was soon arrested by the speed of the train. I have been in fast trains before but never one as fast as this. We were heading towards Csap and, according to Daddy, the time taken should have been an hour, but we were there in less than thirty minutes.

The train did not stop, only slowed down a bit; we saw that the station had undergone an air-raid and most of the buildings were damaged. A number of burnt-out carriages and engines provided further evidence.

We were heading for Kassa, or Košice, and it was still daylight when we stopped in a sideline. In a matter of seconds, gendarmes were standing on either side of the train with their guns levelled horizontally. We heard the door in the next carriage opening and everyone was getting 'screwed up'. There were some shouts and even screams coming from our neighbours. Needless to say, the nervous tension did not decline in the least. About a quarter of an hour later, our door was pushed back and a party of two officers and two privates entered. One officer and a private wore German uniforms, the other two, Hungarian. The Hungarian officer addressed us: 'You are now on the border. We came to give some good advice. You will be treated well, but only if you give no trouble to these gentlemen' – here he pointed at the Germans – 'otherwise you will have a most tiresome trip.' He stopped and looked at us very significantly. 'The other reason we came,' he went on, 'is to request that you give up all your valuables, such as jewellery and foreign currency – dollars, pounds and even roubles – because you will have no use for any of those things. We will tell you how much the lot is worth and when you reach your destination you will be paid in local money. Now start giving it up.'

Of course we had already given up our valuables at least three times, but there was always some more they could extract. The ones who came from the 'school' did not have anything at all, but most of us did have some small things. Dad, for instance, gave up his fountain pen (and thus saved some dollars) and Mummy, a golden brooch.

At sunset we pulled out again, and soon we were tearing along the rails, as if we were hurrying to an appointment, but had found that our watches were slow.

After dark, I prepared myself for a rest. I tried to sit, but inevitably someone sat on my legs. I tried to lie down, but the thick dust from the floorboards nearly choked me, and besides, the clattering of the wheels on the rails was just about driving me out of my mind. In storybooks, I used to read how the villains tortured their captives by pouring drops of water monotonously on their victims' heads. Now I saw for myself what monotony really could do.

Finally, from sheer exhaustion, I did manage to fall asleep, in spite of the clattering and in spite of the babies yelling.

It was still dark when I suddenly awoke. The train was standing still and there was something, or someone, very heavy lying on my chest. I managed to stand up and, waking two or three people, established myself by the window. Out-

33. Carpathia was annexed by Hungary in November 1938. After Hungary entered the war in 1941 Jewish men between the ages of eighteen and thirty were drafted into forced labour battalions and moved with the Hungarian army.

34. A pre-war photo of the brick factory, where in April 1944 the Jews of Berehovo and all its surrounding villages were rounded up. They were told that they would be sent 'east' to be resettled and given 'agricultural work'. Hugo and his family were on the last transport to leave for Auschwitz. [*Géza Ignáczy*]

35. Berehovo, 1989. Hugo and Agnes Whyte with Éva Petricka (centre), a manager of the brick factory. Éva recalled how, when she was seventeen, she watched the Jews of Berehovo being brought into the ghetto. [*Naomi Gryn*]

36. From the *Auschwitz Album*, a collection of photographs taken in the summer of 1944 by SS photographers working in the Identification Department at Auschwitz. They document the arrival and selection of Carpathian Jews, including the transport that brought Hugo and his family to the death camp.

37. Those fit for work were sent to the right, the rest were sent to the gas chambers.

38. Hugo thought he recognized this man as his *cheder* teacher, Mr Jakubovics.

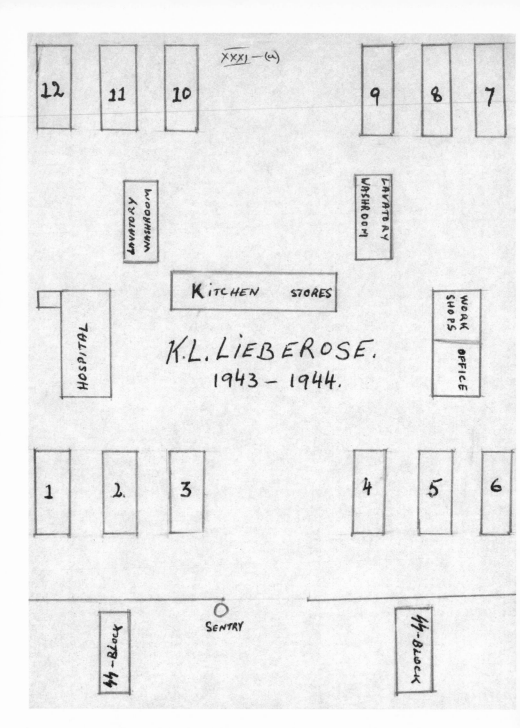

39. A map of Lieberose drawn by Hugo in 1951. His group was housed in Block 4. Six new barracks were added at a later date.

40. Lieberose railway station. Hugo arrived here in June 1944.
The camp was inside the nearby forest.

41. The Bauhof was an area near the railway where building materials were received and stored. Hugo was assigned to the Bauhof Arbeits-Kommando.

42. Prisoners from Lieberose building a power supply to Ullersdorf, a resort town in the forest intended for Nazi officers and their families, but which was never completed.

Taken by an SS officer in the summer of 1944, these photographs, originally in colour, were later used as evidence against Lieberose's camp leader, Wilhelm Kersten. He was sentenced to seven months in prison. Only two other SS officers from Lieberose were ever prosecuted.

KL.:

Häftlings-Personal-Karte

Häftl.-Nr.: 134278 U-Jude

Fam.-Name: G r ü n
Vorname: Hugo
Geb. am: 25.6.28 in: Beregszasz
Stand: ld. Kinder:
Wohnort: Beregszasz
Strasse: Rozsoskertstr.72
Religion: m.s. Staatsang.: Ungarn
Wohnort d. Angehörigen: Vater
Geza, KLM

Eingewiesen am: 30.5.44 Au, 5.6.44 Sa
durch:
in KL.: Mauth 26.2.45
Grund: Ung.Jude
Vorstrafen:

Überstellt

am: _____ an KL.
am: _____ an KL.
am: _____ an KL.
am: _____ an KL.
am: _____ an KL.
am: _____ an KL.

Entlassung:
am: _____ durch KL.:
mit Verfügung v.: _____

Strafen im Lager:

| Grund: | Art: | Bemerkung: |

Personen-Beschreibung:
Grösse: _____ cm
Gestalt:
Gesicht:
Augen:
Nase:
Mund:
Ohren:
Zähne:
Haare:
Sprache:
Bes. Kennzeichen:
Charakt.-Eigenschaften:
Sicherheit b. Einsatz:
Körperliche Verfassung:

KL.6 = 44 500.000

KL.:

Häftlings-Personal-Karte

Häftl.-Nr.: 134277 Ung.Jude

Fam.-Name: G r ü n
Vorname: Geza
Geb. am: 9.12.00 in: Vari
Stand: Vh Kinder: 2
Wohnort: Beregszasz
Strasse: Rozsoskertstr.72
Religion: mos. Staatsang.: Ungarn
Wohnort d. Angehörigen: Ehefrau
Ella geb.Neufeld,
KL Au

Eingewiesen am: 3015.44 Au,6.7.44 Sa
durch:
in KL.: Mauth 26.2.45
Grund: Ung.Jude
Vorstrafen:

Überstellt

am: _____ an KL.
am: _____ an KL.
am: _____ an KL.
am: _____ an KL.
am: _____ an KL.
am: _____ an KL.

Entlassung:
am: _____ durch KL.:
mit Verfügung v.: _____

Strafen im Lager:

| Grund: | Art: | Bemerkung: |

Personen-Beschreibung:
Grösse: _____ cm
Gestalt:
Gesicht:
Augen:
Nase:
Mund:
Ohren:
Zähne:
Haare:
Sprache:
Bes. Kennzeichen:
Charakt.-Eigenschaften:
Sicherheit b. Einsatz:
Körperliche Verfassung:

KL.6 = 44 500.000

43. & 44. Hugo and Géza's prison record cards from Mauthausen, now kept at Yad Vashem. While none of the given dates are reliable, the effort of the Nazis to maintain such precise records – even in the last weeks of the war – is remarkable.

45. Hugo with Bella shortly before he left for Britain in February 1946.

46. Bella rebuilt her life in Czechoslovakia and remarried. She died in 1964 and is buried in the Jewish cemetery in Karlovy Vary. Hugo always kept this photograph of her above his desk.

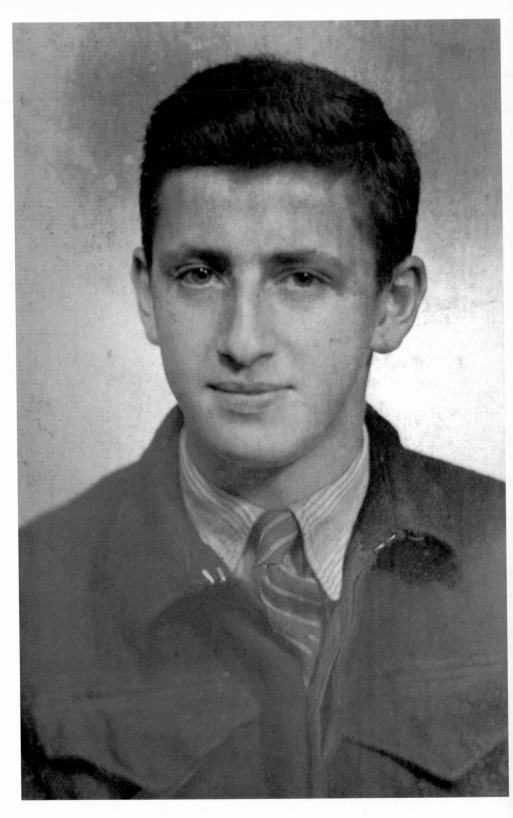

47. 'The sad truth is that tyranny and race hatred did not end when the Second World War ended, but the vision for peace did not die.'

side it was beginning to dawn and by that very slight light, I could just about see some vast fields in front of me. There was no sign of life anywhere. It was cold, dim and unfriendly. For at least another hour the train stood quite still and inside the wagon, only occasional yells disturbed the quietness. The engine let off excess steam from time to time, and the sound of this always brought me back to my senses, for standing by the window, I had to keep myself from collapsing.

The horizon was quite orange coloured by the time we moved off. Again, we travelled very fast. We were in Slovakia and very near the Tatra mountains. We passed a town called Prešov, or Eperjes, where we were supposed to have some relatives. There were not many people at the station and we could not see any of our relatives. I do not really know why we were looking for them. It was much too early – and they had no idea that we were passing – yet somehow we had hoped that they *might* be at the station. Quite illogical, but there it was.

During the rest of the morning we travelled across Slovakia, past the Tatra mountains. In the clear sunshine the hills looked majestic and strangely indifferent. What did those hills care about us? They had stood there for thousands of years, and seen generation after generation suffer and die, yet they had never moved. They saw us passing and the rocks did not tumble down on the line. They let us pass. Cruel things those mountains!

By noon, inside the wagon it was unbearably hot and the bucket in the box stunk to high heaven. There was plenty of food (hardly anyone ate), but the water barrel was nearly exhausted, and the little water that was still left in it was warm and full of dirt. Everyone was sweating and the odour of perspiring bodies, mingled with the other thing, was more than anyone was accustomed to.

The mountains were left behind and gradually the whole scenery changed. Meadows with cows grazing contrasted sharply with the high mountains. On the plain, I had the feeling that the picture confronting me was a very humble one and suggested peace. The names of the stations were spelled in a different way and German soldiers were more frequent. We were in Poland!

I sat down. There was not room for everyone, so we had to sit between each others' legs. Gabby in front of me and Dad behind. We were not talking. The train raced with time itself and I was beginning to go mad. The heat, the thirst, the dirt – everything seemed to conspire against me.

The time is now five-thirty. I must have slept for a while, but I am very thirsty. It is at this point that I started going back in my memory. Frankly, I do not feel any the better for it. I had hoped that it would help. It was a vain hope!

Since I started remembering things, we have covered a long distance. We are just nearing a big town. The place looks bombed out. The station has a lot of sidings and most wagons bear the 'DR' mark on them. When we get near the passengers' entrance I shall be able to see the name of this town. It reads: C ACOW. Obviously the R is missing and we are in Cracow, Poland. The route is – so far – in agreement with the note I pulled off the wagon in Berehovo – Csap, Kassa, Prešov, Cracow. According to the note, the next stop should be 'Auschwitz'. What on earth can this place, Auschwitz, be?

When we moved out of Cracow, I fell asleep murmuring 'Auschwitz, Auschwitz . . .'

12

AUSCHWITZ-BIRKENAU

At this point I shall change my narrative and revert to the past tense, for my account of the happenings is past – though it shall go on living in my mind for as long as I live.

The following account is true, almost word for word. Perhaps I am partial and prejudiced in (though unfortunately not ignorant of) the matter and therefore little exaggerations ought to be excused; but this is a personal account. As we all know, personal accounts always vary from the historian's, but the historian is not always on the spot . . .

When I woke up after we left Cracow, the train was standing still. It was dark, and from where I lay I could see two stars through the window. It was cold and very still. My parents and fellow-passengers were either asleep or just lying quietly, but there was not a sound from anywhere. Not even the babies pursued their heartbreaking weeping. I would have liked to get up and stand by the window, but there were people lying and sitting everywhere. There was not enough room to drop a pin, never mind a foot.

Suddenly the peace was broken. An engine gave a howling blast. It was not a whistle, but a very deep echoing sound which vibrated for minutes afterwards in my ears and, it seemed, throughout my being. I mention this blast because ever since that night, trains make me nauseous. These blasts were repeated at regular intervals. I counted up to five hundred, then followed the blast. Another five hundred, another blast ... and so it went on. Whether it was done intentionally or not, I shall never know; but after an hour of blasts I was just right for a strait-jacket. Strangely enough, not many people in the wagon were awake. Dad, however, gave a little shudder every time it sounded, though he made no comment.

The incessant blasts, however, gradually woke everyone up. The time was 4.30 a.m. I supposed that the engine had started its serenading at about 3 a.m. It was still dark, but I summoned enough courage to go to the window. 'Excuse me, but I have got a headache. I would like some fresh air,' I muttered as I stepped on various bodies, but eventually I got to the window.

In the dark I could just distinguish the outlines of a large town, or whatever it was. One thing was certain. It was very large. 'There are some factories here,' I whispered to a man lying by my feet. In three different directions I could see three tall trapeze-shaped* chimneys reaching into the air. They were smoking, but now and again large slashes of red flames shot out, illuminating the horizon. Besides these 'factories' there was no sign of life.

Gradually it became lighter and I could now clearly observe where we stood. The 'town' consisted of large, green barracks. There was a lot of fencing everywhere and the whole camp (for it could not have been a town) formed an unmistakable geometrical pattern. An inner and an outer square of tall 'nests' added curiosity to the picture. They were made of wood and stood on telegraph poles. The nest was large enough to accommodate two or three people. There was one fairly near our train and from the embankment (though slightly at a lower level), I could observe two figures swinging their arms round to their backs. An exercise, I supposed, which would keep them warm. Another curious feature about the nest

---

* Hugo must have meant 'trapezium-shaped'.

was a sort of pipe sticking out from each side. On closer observation, these pipes revealed themselves to be parts of machine guns. A discovery which alarmed me greatly, and secretly I prayed that we might soon move on. My prayer was of no avail. At 5.30 sharp, the camp suddenly became animated. People poured out of the barracks, rushed to another one, then returned. Some food was given to them from steaming barrels, and they lined up. There was some marching and soon after a group of them started busying themselves alongside our train. They looked very curious. They wore a pair of white- and blue-striped pyjamas and a similar coloured cap. They were pulling carts left and right, and although I could not see very far sideways, I was under the impression that there was a cart in front of each wagon.

Inside, everybody was greatly excited. There was not much doubt left about our destination. Bags were tied up, babies given the last drop of milk or whatever they were being given, men straightened their ties and, with their elbows, brushed their hats. Mummy supervised the family and my kid brothers were very reluctant to obey. The excitement increased further when the door was slid back and someone shouted: '*Macht euch fertig!*' ('Get yourselves ready.')

Then everything began to happen at once.

For as long as I live I will never be able to forget the scene that followed. Suddenly those near the door started jumping out, and the men in striped suits took away the luggage. We were going ourselves and I was reluctant to part with my rucksack. The man who took it away from me said something in Polish. I replied in German that I did not understand.

'You are nineteen and you are a mechanic or something like it! Don't forget, *nineteen!*' As he said this to me, he kept looking sideways lest anyone should see him. I told Dad about it. 'Well, perhaps you ought to say nineteen,' he commented.

Meanwhile we had to get into two straight lines. One for

women and one for men. As our wagon was near the rear, there was a very long line in front of us, and although this line moved fairly fast we had some time to talk.

'I am afraid they may separate us,' said Dad, and he went on, 'but try to contact us. Hugo will stay with me if he says he's nineteen, and if they believe him. You take care of the children and use the money if you can.' That was, of course, addressed to Mummy.

We were very near the gates, so quickly I went across to Mummy and kissed her, and kissed my brothers as well. It was instinctive. I felt I had to kiss. Goodness knew when we were going to see each other again!

Mummy was crying and that is how we left her. At the gates stood several SS officers. There were two on our side and two on the women's side. In front of me went an elderly man. 'How old are you?' they asked him. 'Fifty-six next week,' he replied. 'You go with the old ones, you'll like it!' said one of the officers. The old man went to the left.

It was my turn next and my heart was in my throat one minute, and in my toes the next. '*Wie alt bist du?*' ('How old are you?') asked one of the officers. He had a monocle over his left eye. 'I . . . I am nineteen,' I stammered. 'Have you an occupation?' asked the other one, and he felt my arm. '*Tischler und Zimmermann*,' ('carpenter and joiner') I lied, and I felt very hot.

'All right, you will go to work.'

'*Danke schoen!*' I muttered, and went right.

The interview could not have taken longer than a minute, or even thirty seconds, but it seemed like hours. As soon as I was 'passed', I looked back and saw Mummy running after Gabby and Clem. They were going to the left. The officer, however, ran after her and made her go to the right. I saw my brothers wave and Gabby started crying. I was too far to hear what was being said, but suddenly I felt Dad's arm on my shoulders.

'Come, son, we are on our own now!' he half-whispered, and he was at least as near to crying as I was myself.

We were walking along a sort of corridor with barbed wire on either side. Between the barbed wires ran lines of ordinary wire, and every pole to which they were fixed had a row of china knobs on it. 'We shall be surrounded by electricity,' remarked a gentleman behind us. 'Well, we won't want to escape, will we?' rejoined another. There was some laughter at this, but I could not see the joke anywhere.

The ground on which we walked was absolutely covered with bills, torn envelopes and innumerable contraceptives.* 'Our money is worthless, we'll have no correspondence, and women will be separated from us,' said the gentleman behind us. He was probably right, I thought. The walk took us a long time and there was ample opportunity to watch the goings-on.

Sounds of an orchestra reached us. They were playing the 'Rakóczy March', but we could not see where the players were. We passed a camp, which in spite of our bad humours, tickled us no end. A line of women stood and watched us. Some had white wedding gowns on, others wore anything from long multi-coloured evening dresses to two-piece bathing costumes – anything, except normal frocks. Another peculiarity was their baldness. Each one of them was bald. There is nothing as pathetic as a woman with no hair. I suppose we should not have laughed at that, but their costumes really were funny.

'I suppose,' said a man in front of us, 'they need a lunatic

---

* In an account of his arrival at Auschwitz written in the 1970s Hugo described how: '. . . the path itself was of hardbeaten earth and strewn with condoms and *tefillin* sets. The long black straps of leather and the opaque bits of rubber looked like obscene snakes and worms. They were totally meaningless and frightening at the same time. I compounded the irrationality of it all by taking out my own set of *tefillin*, kissed them with a recently acquired instinct and threw them to the ground with the others.' At Auschwitz hope in the future died alongside any hope in prayer.

asylum in a place as large as this.' Yes, we all thought that this was a local madhouse. But not for long.

'Uncle George, Uncle George!' shouted one of the women behind the wire. 'Rosie, Rose. What on earth are you doing in an asylum?' the man in front of us shouted back. 'This is no asylum, we are last week's transport from Berehovo,' came Rosie's reply. All the mocking and pitying was abruptly cut. It took us a few minutes to realize that within a short time we would all look like the inmates of an asylum.

The passage between the electric fences was long and exhausting, both physically and mentally, but eventually we reached a large building, in front of which we had to form columns of five.

The building, although very large, was quite flat. A number of people in striped trousers and without shirts were painting the roof with a steaming black concoction, the smell of which, mingled with a strong smell of chlorine, made our waiting even more unbearable. A number of people still had their watches by which we could tell that we had waited for two hours – standing. The heat brought out everyone's worst temper. People otherwise quite amiable, began to get irritated by the slightest thing you said or did to them. I took off my jacket and a pullover, but I still had on plenty of shirts and vests to make me perspire. And did I!

Everybody was guessing as to the purpose of the building and opinion was divided. Some said it was an office where they would issue us with local currency, ration cards, etc. Others, however, believed that it was merely a place of disinfection. The latter seemed most probable because of the smell of chlorine.

In the middle of this argument, two very short young men came out of the building. They wore the local uniform of white and blue stripes, but they had creases in their trousers and caps of similar material. The caps were flat and bulged in the front. Altogether they looked smart and efficient. They said something to a man at the front of the column and he, in turn, told us to stand to attention and then we were ordered to march inside. Once inside, we found ourselves in a very large hall with hangers all around the walls.

'Undress!' was the next order. So it was the disinfecting theory. Strangely enough there was no smell of chlorine inside. 'You can take your shoes and belts or braces with you, but nothing else!' said one of the short men in very broken German.

I was glad to take off my shirts, but I did not obey their orders exactly. Before we left, Dad had given me a beautiful penknife, with two blades, a corkscrew and a tin opener, with which I did not want to part. So I wrapped it in my belt, as well as a picture of the family, which I put inside my shoe. Then we proceeded into the next hall where a number of people stood waiting to cut off our hair. They used machines of various sorts, all of which seemed to pull like anything. Occasionally the barbers – obviously not qualified ones – dipped their instruments into a dish of liquid, and when they applied it to us again it stung. Our heads, armpits, and all other hairy parts were shaven – though for me it applied only to my head, not having hair anywhere else. The barbers spoke Polish and they were very rough. All the time they were questioning us if we had any *papierosy*, which I was told meant cigarettes.

From the barbers', we were ushered into another hall, and as we passed through the doorway a small bit of brown soap was handed to us. The hall had cement flooring and it was wet. A few inches below the ceiling ran a number of pipes with holes in them. We waited in there until everyone was inside, then one of the small men turned on a tap.

Within a few seconds everyone was soaking wet, and speaking for myself, it was the first thing I had really enjoyed. A hot shower! I washed myself and then Dad's back, and Dad in turn rubbed my back. This went on for a few minutes until suddenly the water stopped, but before we had time to say 'Oh, dear!' a fresh shower of ice-cold water came pouring down. That was hell! It lasted for another few minutes, but eventually stopped. The doors were opened into yet another hall, and as we passed through the doorway a man ran his spongy gloves all over our heads and other places where hair generally grows. The solution which he applied from the bucket by his side, was a murderous one. For at least two minutes I could not get my breath back. My head, stomach and armpits felt as if they were aflame, and judging from the sighs around me, so did the others'.

We had to walk around the room and *en route* we had to pick up our clothing. I was handed a pair of black pants, an outsized pink shirt, a complete suit (which could house three more like myself) and a cap. I made several vain attempts to change my outfit, but without any success. Dad had similar luck, with the exception that he got the biggest shirt I have ever seen. A Mr Mousekopf was less lucky.* He was a very fat man, ginger, with a very rough voice. Swearing was a second language to him, and during showers he was the only one singing. The lyrics were not the original ones, neither were they suitable for reproduction. Mr Mousekopf received a pair of trousers, too big for me, but much too small for him. The sight of him wrestling with his trousers cheered up everyone. Eventually he hit on a good idea. He split the trousers in the back and with the aid of some string it managed to stay put.

We all looked absurd and pathetic. Grown-up men looking like clowns at a fancy-dress ball.

Once more we stood outside in the sunshine, forming columns of five. As we were adjusting ourselves to our new appearances, a strange-looking group arrested our attention.

* According to Patyu, 'Mr Mousekopf' was in fact Sándor Donáth who survived the *Shoah* and later went to live in Israel.

They had on evening dresses and they were bald. We knew already that they were women, but these women seemed to be shouting at us!

'Dad!', 'Brother!', 'Joseph!', 'Henry!' and lots of other names were yelled at us. There was no doubt about the identity of the women: they were from our Berehovo transport, and Mummy was among them.

'Can you see her?' asked Dad. I knew whom he meant and I looked everywhere. A number of faces looked very similar. There was Judy, a little girl I was very keen on in the camp. She looked miserable. Her beautiful black hair had been cut off and she looked frail and, I suppose, ashamed. Other faces – all familiar, but hardly recognizable – turned towards us and they, too, were probably looking for someone dear to them in our midst.

Suddenly I recognized Mummy. She was waving at us and Dad must have recognized her at the same moment as I did. He clutched me on the wrist and kept a strong grip on it until we were ordered to move. Mummy had a pink dress on, and even without hair, I thought she looked the nicest of them all. She did not seem agitated and she waved quite resignedly. The distance between us was too great to be able to converse, and I do not suppose she heard Dad's 'Take care of yourself!'.

About noon we were marched off, and so were the women. We were depressed, yet glad to be away from the scene of our humiliation. The Nazi officers seemed to enjoy the perform-ance immensely, and their laughter only added bitterness to our already overflowing cup of misery.

Passing through a camp which had a big C on the gates, we noticed that the inhabitants were all Gypsies. They looked quite well nourished and first thing I noticed about the camp was the number of children playing in the dirt.

Others seemed to notice this, too. 'If they have their families with them, perhaps we shall be reunited as well,' said Dad. His optimistic remark surprised me because, frankly, I did not believe in any such reunion. In fact, I was afraid that I might be separated from Dad and told him so. We agreed, however, that I would give my age as nineteen and he would give his as thirty-five. We also decided that we would be 'cousins' if anyone asked.

After the Gypsy camp, we entered another one with D on the gates and one column stopped in front of a barracks which bore the number 7. The front doors were open and we could see long rows of three-storeyed beds on either side with a long stone bench running in the middle.

A fairly young man came out to meet us. He had an armband 'Blockälteste 7'* on his jacket. He wore civilian clothes, but a number in white cloth was sewn on to the front of his jacket, with the same number on his left trouser leg. He spoke German, but with a foreign accent. Later, we learned that he was a Pole.

In a short address, he informed us that for the time being we would be housed in Block 7, and that he was very particular about cleanliness. 'If you behave yourselves, I shall behave myself too. I am a fair man and I can help you a lot, having been an inmate of this camp for the past three years. Now, if you have any gold, watches or other valuables, give them to me, for if I find any, there will be plenty of trouble. You will not be happy with trouble around!' he concluded, smiling all the time.

It seemed he had two assistants and the three of them proceeded to line us up 'in proper order', as they called it. Five in each line. There were about seven hundred of us and by the time we 'learned' how to line up, dismiss, and line up again, we were thoroughly exhausted and very hungry. At about five in the afternoon, the two assistants and the Block-älteste went off with a large carrier and returned after fifteen minutes with bread and a small barrel. They went inside and

* Block elder; the prisoner in charge of a block.

for another half-hour we just hung around, sitting in the hot sand, or else walking to the lavatory and back.

There were about twenty barracks in the camp and only half were occupied. The inmates all looked very much like ourselves. None of them had been there longer than a fortnight. Some came from Holland; others from France, Poland, Slovakia and of course the Ukraine. The goings-on of the camp were as much of a mystery to them as they were to us. Dad made inquiries about the two previous transports from Berehovo, but no one could give us any information.

We were in the middle of a conversation with a few Frenchmen when *'Brotholen!'* ('bread-fetching') rang through the camp. The French, without any further ado, began rushing towards their barracks, and by the time we got to ours, there was a queue of seven hundred in front of us. The process, however, was not very long and in about half an hour's time it was our turn. We each received a small piece of bread with a spoonful of jam on top of it.

'You get soup tomorrow, but today no more left at the kitchen. This bread lasts for twenty-four hours,' rolled off one of the assistants. Being much too hungry, I ate up my whole ration and hoped for the best as far as tomorrow was concerned. I noticed Dad only consumed half of his and put the rest in his shirt (we had no pockets).

Again we were lined up and marched to the washing block, which consisted of two very long pipes with holes in them. I washed and drank some water from my palms, but the thing I remember most was the amount of pushing-around I had to suffer. Outside the washing block we were lined up again and marched back to Block 7. This time we went straight inside.

'You will share four to a bed. You should be quite comfortable. At night you are not allowed to go outside, unless you want to be shot at. There are some dishes at the back of the barracks which you can use as lavatories, but heaven help you if you use the floor or the bed. Goodnight! And no talk till six in the morning!' Here the Blockälteste gave us a significant look, and retired. The assistants took over and ushered us into bed. Ours was on the second storey and although there were four of us it was quite roomy. The beds were quite large and there was a 'mattress' filled with wood-pulp on each one and two blankets. Mr Mousekopf, a Mr Komp, Dad and myself were to share a bed. It was quite comfortable except for the constant shower of wood-pulp from the bed above us. Soon, from sheer exhaustion, I fell asleep.

When I woke, it was already dark, and there was a lot of talking outside. Something was up, and in a few minutes we were to find out what it was for ourselves. Another transport had arrived and they were to share Block 7 with us.

Shouts of 'Quiet!' and 'Order!' reached us from outside and then, suddenly, hell was let loose. Masses and masses of people streamed in, and in the dark they tried to find room. About six of them tried to invade our bed, but after four had squeezed in, Mr Mousekopf threw the next out. 'Jolly good thing you are with us,' remarked Mr Komp, obviously referring to Mr Mousekopf's size.

The newcomers spoke a Yiddish-German. They had come from the Ghetto of Lodz and the very first thing they asked us was if we had any bread. They were quite obviously old-timers, and after they told us that no place could be worse than Lodz, they went off to sleep.

We had to lie on our sides and there was not enough room to turn around. This time it took much longer to fall asleep, and although it was very quiet, the stillness had a very fright-ening quality. The smell of chlorine haunted us everywhere. It did not come from any particular place, it was just in the air. People we questioned about the smell either just shrugged their shoulders in an I-don't-know-and-couldn't-care-less manner, or else they looked very serious and would only say: 'Oh, there are all sorts of rumours!'

Next morning I was wakened by a series of very loud yells. *'Aufstehen! Raus! Raus!'* ('Get up! Out! Out!') In spite of being much more tired than the night before, I got up and together with Dad we got into a line in front of the beds. The Blockälteste came to inspect, but he looked much too sleepy to take any real notice. He pointed at several beds, and ordered the people who slept in them to remake them. After his inspection, to the washing block!

It was in the washing block that I obtained a proper view of the latecomers from Lodz. They were clad in the same uniform as ourselves, but whilst some of our people were too big for their suits, they were all skinny to the bone. They must have had first-hand experience in the art of pushing, for although I made several attempts to get near the water pipes, one or two of them always managed to get there first. After they had finished, they were magnanimous enough to let us have a go at the water and I noticed how some of them ate bits of bread. It struck me as rather odd that they should have bread, because they were not with us when we received our ration, but when a number of our people began to complain that they had lost their bread, the mystery was solved.

'I dare say, Dad,' I said, 'that these new people are common thieves.'

'I wouldn't say they were thieves,' replied Dad, 'they are just very hungry. In fact one of our bed-comrades gave me a pretty thorough search and he wouldn't lay off until I kicked him in the chin.' He stopped for a few seconds and concluded, 'You must be very careful. Food is very precious here, but I hope you will not have to steal.'

'I shall never steal!' I exclaimed.

'Let's hope you won't have to,' was all Dad would say.

No, I was quite determined not to steal. As soon as we had our first meal I felt certain I would not want to either. After we returned from the 'bathroom' – as Mr Mousekopf affectionately called it – we were ordered to line up in front of the block and the assistants counted us. Then the Blockälteste counted us and informed us that *Appell* was about to begin. Other barracks, too, had people lining up outside, but as I was in the back I did not see anything properly.

Suddenly our Blockälteste yelled: *'Block sieben, Achtung! Die Augen links!'* ('Block 7, attention! Eyes to the left!') I looked left and stood stiff. A German SS officer came with the Blockälteste and counted us again. That was the *Appell*. When they reached the end of our column, he signed a sheet and went to the next group.

'Augen gerade aus! Rührt euch!' ('Straighten your eyes! At ease!') was the next commandment. Then he informed us that soup would be served soon and afterwards we would have to undergo a series of questions for the 'reference library'. Meanwhile we were to do nothing. It was still very early in the morning and again we heard some music. I gathered up all my courage and asked one of the assistants if he could tell me what it was for.

'That's our band and it plays for the working parties as they march out!' He was quite willing to talk, so I asked a few more questions and he told me that camp D was only a transit place. 'Either you go to work from here or else . . .' 'Or else what?' I inquired. 'You don't need to worry – you'll go to work!' he assured me; but as he went off I had to content myself with that much until our soup arrived. It was not more than 8 a.m., but I had heard that the Germans were similar to the English in some ways, so I supposed that the main meal would be served in the morning, instead of noon as I was used to. During the rest of my stay in Auschwitz, I was to find out that we were as likely to get our soup at eight in the morning as at eight at night. Unless the carriers dropped the heavy barrels. In that case, we did not get any at all.

When, on our first morning in Auschwitz, we were given our soup, it made me feel quite sick. For one thing, there were not enough dishes, so four or six people had to share each one. The spoon with which it was dished out was made from a salmon-tin nailed on to a broomstick. We had no spoons at all. Dad got a large red dish and four tinfuls were poured into it. Mr Mousekopf, Mr Komp and myself were to share it with him. The soup itself was thick and reeked to high heaven. When my turn came to have a 'first go', I very nearly spat it out. The smell itself was nauseating, but the slimy taste of it and the absence of spices was more than I could stand. I just handed it to Dad and told him that the three of them could have my share as well.

'I don't know how you'll live if you don't eat,' was all Dad said. He must have known that nothing on earth could have induced me to touch another drop of that soup. He himself had to force the stuff down and the same went for Mr Mousekopf and Mr Komp. 'It doesn't matter what you eat or how it tastes,' grunted Mr Mousekopf, 'the main thing is that your tummy be filled.'

How right he was! Before eleven o'clock my tummy was playing hell with me. In fact it became so bad that I had to sit down, and when I did get up to get a drink I felt quite giddy. Dad was watching me all the time, but I did not want to complain. After all, Dad had warned me when I refused to eat, and since I had disregarded his warning I had no right to moan. Nevertheless, he came over to me, took out a piece of bread from his shirt, broke it into two and handed me half. 'That's all right. You will eat your soup tomorrow,' and thus my protestations were overcome by logical argument, as well as by the ever-increasing emptiness in the middle regions of my body.

This act of Dad's was only the beginning of a very long series of similar deeds. Before the end of our first week in Auschwitz, the relationship between us became something more than that between father and son: Dad became my best friend as well. During the long hours of heat, we sat on the ground with our backs resting against the wall of the barracks, and we discussed all sorts of subjects. I had no idea that Dad, for instance, knew quite a lot about Michelangelo, Rubens, Van Gogh, and during that first week we talked mostly of art. There was a Dr Adler with us as well; he, too, joined us sometimes and before long I learned an enormous amount about Pre-Raphaelite painting.

The time was about twelve noon when Block 7 had to line up and after a warning – 'If you don't march properly, you will be very sorry!' – we set off through the Gypsy camp and arrived on to a square. Here, our column was ordered to sit down and, five by five, we had to approach five tables set up near the far end. Being near the rear of our column, we got up and went around to explore the place. Gradually the larger half of the Block was roaming about. The people sitting behind the tables did not care so long as they did not have to wait for 'fresh material'.

The square was not very big. Camp C and another camp, which looked empty, made up one half of the surroundings and another large building – or rather the back of a large building – made up the other half. Beside the building stood a tall chimney, shaped like a trapeze.* I decided to explore the place as thoroughly as I could, and seeing that Dad was talking to a 'well-dressed' Pole, I did not bother to tell him.

It struck me as rather odd that there should be no windows at the back, and as I came quite close to the wall, I could feel a radiating heat. Touching the bricks, they felt quite heated up. I was convinced that this was the bakery. Inside my shirt, I still carried my penknife, but being very hungry, I decided to go round to the front of the building where I hoped to exchange the knife for some bread, or possibly even for some rolls.

There were not many people about near the wall and I managed to reach the corner quite unobtrusively. Again, it

* See footnote on page 174.

seemed strange that there were no windows in that wall
either, but the wall itself did not feel especially warm. Bravely,
I walked right up to the front. As I put my head around the
corner, I saw a crowd of children. They stood there all alone,
and hoping that my brothers might be among them, I went
up to them. They had on civilian clothes, but quite ragged, and
the children themselves stood unusually still. It is difficult to
describe just how they looked. They were children in shape
and size, but each of them had the wistful expression of old
men on their faces. They spoke Yiddish and Polish. I asked
them where they came from, but received no reply. Some just
looked at me, others turned their heads away. They must
have been between six and nine. I asked one of the children
if he knew whether there was anyone inside. My question
was addressed in German, and he replied: 'Yes, there are,' in
German as well.

'Where do you come from?' I asked. 'From Theresienstadt,'
he replied. The boy was about seven or eight. His hair was
not cut off and although his suit was ragged, he looked quite
clean and sounded intelligent. Encouraged by his willingness
to talk, I asked more questions and he always replied with
one or two words. Eventually I managed to piece together
that he was the only one from Theresienstadt, the other
children had come from Lodz. His name was Karel and he
did not know where his parents were. They had arrived the
previous evening, but during the disembarkation in the dark
he had lost his parents. An officer had led him to a barracks
where he joined the other children, but there were so many
of them that they did not get any sleep. Food was not given
to them either. Another officer led them to the 'bakery' and
two groups had already gone in. They were the third and last
group. The officer told them they would have a shower there,
and then go back to their parents.

With this information from Karel, I was no longer surprised
by the weary look on the children, but before I could ask

anything more, a man, in uniform, came out. In Yiddish he asked the children to go in. 'You too!' he said to me. It was no use my telling him that I belonged to another group, and that I had to go back to them. 'You come in and have a shower. Order is order!' he persisted.

I hoped it would not take long, and anyway I did not mind having a hot shower. One thing was certain: the building was not a bakery. On the other hand, it did not really look like a shower-house either. It had no windows anywhere except in the front.

I walked in with the other children. We were in a large hall, with wooden benches running around the walls. Facing the front door was another double door. A striking feature of the building was the streamlined effect of the contents. I mean, everything looked quite modern, unlike the rest of the camp. Door handles were polished and except for a heap of clothing in one of the corners, the hall looked disturbingly clean.

The man who asked us in spoke again: 'Take off your clothing and fold it up neatly. Then line up in front of the door.' He stood in front of the double door, but he himself went through a smaller door and returned in less than five minutes with an SS officer.

During those five minutes, besides undressing, I did quite a lot of thinking as well. If that building was a disinfecting block, it certainly did not look like the one we had come through the day before, and the man had said nothing about the other children who, according to Karel, went in before. They had not come out through the back, for we had not seen them. There was no door either. Of course, there might have been a door on the other side but I did not think so. As I was thinking more and more I felt I was working myself up again. Always the same feeling. My heart raced, my whole body shook and had anyone spoken to me, I could not have given a reply. It was quite ridiculous, of course. After all, what mystery could that building have held? Yet there was something sinister about the whole place. Now I know what it was, but at the time I only *felt* that something was not quite as it should have been.

The officer came round and stopped in front of me. I was just undoing my shoelaces, but my hands were trembling. 'How old are you?' he asked me. 'Ni . . . ni . . . nineteen,' I lied (but I was beginning to believe it myself). 'Why are you here?' he inquired further. 'I . . . I was told by that "Herr" that I should come in,' came my reply. 'Your Block?' 'Block 7, in Camp D,' I answered. 'Put your clothes on and *Schiess in Wind*,' ('Buzz off') he ordered.

He went off and I felt relieved. I dressed again, but slowly, because I was curious to see what would happen next. The children lined up in twos and the double door was opened. A strong smell came out of the hall beyond. It was a smell I had never experienced before. Sweetish, yet not sweet. The hall was lit by electricity and beneath the ceiling ran the usual metal pipes, but from where I stood, I could not see much of the interior. The floor, I noticed, was dry.

The children went in, and Karel waved to me as he entered. My dressing, however, was completed and the man who had asked us in made signs at me towards the front door. The meaning was obvious. As I passed him he said something like: 'Are you lucky!'

As I opened the front door, the double door behind me was closed by the officer. Outside, I took a deep breath. I was glad to be out again. It was inexplicable, but I felt very relieved. It was curious, I thought, that no soap was given to the children, and only two people were supervising their showers. When we showered, there had been a whole army of barbers and other assistants swarming around the place. Very curious!

Going back to the square, I went round the other way. The wall on the other side had no windows either. There were piles of clothing and even what seemed to me ashes of burnt clothing. All the time the chimney smoked. Black smoke came gushing out with an occasional shot of red flame. It was not so bad during the sunshine, but at night it looked frightening.

Back on the square everything seemed normal – that is, if the word 'normal' could be applied to anything that happened in Auschwitz. Dad was still talking to the Pole, but he looked quite agitated. When he saw me approaching, he pointed me out to the Pole, probably introducing me. His name was Kapusta (most likely spelt differently).

'Where were you?' asked Dad. 'I thought we were not allowed to leave this square,' he reproached me. 'As a matter of fact, I was in that building,' I replied, pointing at the 'shower block'. 'You were where?' exclaimed Kapusta.

Briefly I told them of my experience and when I finished Kapusta said: 'You must be one of the very few who ever came out of there alive.' It did not make sense. Why should I have not come out alive? Dad's agitation increased. 'If you ever go further than five yards from me, I don't know what I will do with you,' he warned.

Both Dad and Kapusta had a queer expression on their faces. There was something mysterious about that building, and I was very eager to find out what it was, but they were very reluctant to tell me. Dad was irritated, I could see that, so I did not pursue the subject. He and Kapusta were still talking when I sat down, and I heard snatches of their conversation. They were talking about the chlorine smell and Kapusta said something like: '. . . due to overcrowding . . . there is not enough room in the crematorium . . . not quite sure how it is done.'

Curiosity got the better of me. I got up and told Dad that I would not rest until he told me just what was going on. He was clearly annoyed with my obstinacy, but before he could satisfy my curiosity, or reprove me for my obstinacy, one of the men from the tables shouted at us. 'Come along you there! We haven't all day to wait on you!'

Quickly we went up to him. First he questioned Dad. After each question he wrote something on a white form in front of him. Age, occupation, nationality? Why was he brought to Auschwitz?

The last question surprised me greatly. Why, indeed, were we brought to Auschwitz? The man asking us was either trying to make fun of us, or he was plain stupid, I thought. Dad's answer, however, increased my surprise tenfold. 'I was charged with being involved in politics,' he said. It was ridiculous. Dad had nothing to do with politics. Why, then, did he say he had? The man filling in the forms was not surprised in the least. He wrote something down, and asked finally: 'Have you any relatives in the camp?' 'Yes,' Dad replied, 'my cousin. We were arrested on the same charge.' He pointed to me.

Something was fishy. Before I had time to think much about it, the same questions were fired at me. 'Age?' 'Nineteen.' 'Date of birth?' I gave the approximate answer, having calculated it the night before. 'Profession?' 'Carpenter and joiner.' 'Any relatives?' 'Yes, my cousin,' and this time I pointed at Dad.

'You are here for political reasons as well?' he asked. 'Well . . . I suppose so,' I muttered. 'What do you mean "suppose so"? Are you, or aren't you?' 'Yes, I am!' came my reply in a louder tone. After all, politicians always spoke up. And from that moment on, I was in the business as well. Only later on did I come to the conclusion that shouting is not necessarily characteristic of politicians. Probably because the ones I have met were too weak to shout.

Meanwhile, Block 7 lined up again and we were just about the last ones to join. First thing I asked Dad was, why did he lie to the man?

He was quite willing to satisfy my question: 'Look, Hugo, this is no place for us. Kapusta informed me that unless you are here for politics or sabotage, you might stay for months on end. On the other hand, political prisoners are sent away to work as soon as possible. So the choice was obvious. And anyway,' he concluded, 'I am not as innocent as you may think. Perhaps some time I will tell you more about it.'

Both of us stood very quietly in the line, but after a pause, Dad continued to talk. Looking back, I think he talked because he wanted to comfort me, and at the same time he wanted to find justification for his actions.

'Under the present circumstances we are – and will be for some time to come – compelled to alter our moral attitude towards lots of things. I have never lied – deliberately that is – in my life before. I have always tried to do the right thing and my own conscience has governed me. But now this attitude towards "right" and "wrong" will have to change. We are here for no reason at all. You, Hugo, at any rate, had *no time* to commit crimes of any sort. In other words, we are innocent people herded together and persecuted in order to satisfy a mad dreamer's whims. If we stopped doing anything at all about it, this would be a sign of acknowledgement,' here Dad raised his voice, 'and I shall never acknowledge any sort of action for which I deserve treatment such as this.'

Then he pointed at the building facing us. 'You know what this building is? It is a gas chamber. And about twenty-four hours ago, your brothers, and my children, were exterminated in that chamber. Like rats! You, yourself, have been nearer to death a few minutes ago than most men ever get.'

I was shocked! It is very difficult to describe exactly how I felt, but it was far from pleasant. Exactly what the term 'gas chamber' implied, I did not know. But I had heard of gas bombs which were used in the First World War and later in Spain, and I knew that lots of people had died as a result of gas attacks; but I had also heard that there was an international law prohibiting the use of such weapons, and yet there it was! Dad would not tell me a lie. He must have been told by that Pole, Kapusta.

Gradually scenes from the 'shower building' returned to me. No windows, an entrance, but no exit, the thick double doors, ash piles outside, 'Are you lucky!' from the attendant. Yes, it all added up! The place in front of which we stood was a twentieth-century human slaughterhouse. And human beings, old and young, sick and healthy, were led to their end, like a flock of sheep. The picture of naked children going in for their 'shower', and little Karel waving to me, haunted me for a long time afterwards.

All this time Dad stood by my side. He must have known of the battle going on in my mind. I grabbed his arm and held on to it tightly.

'Dad, this is horrible. And the awful thing is that we can do nothing about it.' There were other things I said as well, but for the most part, it was a medley of incoherent sentences. Looking back, I feel almost embarrassed. Having read a great deal of Kipling, and even more Westerns, I have always wanted to be in danger myself. I had images of myself – always cool, brave and never a wrong move – yet when I did find danger, or rather when I actually realized the presence of danger, all courage left me. I had no more will of my own than a caged guinea pig.

Dad was not the only one to 'discover the facts', as Mr Mousekopf called it. Before we returned to Block 7 again, everybody seemed to know about the gas chambers. There were even those who had heard yells from the building, and gradually imagination got the better of us. Speaking for myself, I had the most fantastic visions, and not even my well-wishers could have called me calm.

At bread-time Dad had to remind me to keep some for 'tomorrow', but not trusting myself I gave half of the ration to Dad to keep for me. He wrapped it up together with his own bit in a piece of cloth that resembled closely his shirt material, but as I said before, Dad's shirt was much too big for him. Again, seven were made to share one bed, and the

Blockälteste assured us after *Appell* that we would have no additional companions during the night. Once lying on the bed, I expected to have a very uncomfortable night, but Auschwitz offered great opportunities for the unexpected. I was asleep within a few minutes and the next thing I remember was *'Aufstehen!'*

Washing, *Appell*, soup . . . it was the same as the day before.

Aimlessly wandering about the camp was our only chance to move about. There were little groups of people all over the place. Some were telling jokes, some discussed farming, others the war.

Dad made some friends, and about five of them were discussing the prospects of an armistice. The Russians were advancing, a second front in the west was expected, and according to a Mr Jones, it had already started, but was kept a secret . . . and so we filled our day. There were not many young boys about, which I thought was a shame. Most of the very few were Polish anyway, and conversation with them was by no means an easy task.

On our third day in Auschwitz, I did get acquainted with a boy who was only eighteen months older than myself. His name was Albert, but everybody called him Kolya, on account of his Russian nationality. I met him in the lavatory under rather unusual circumstances. Block 7 had its turn and, of course, no other group was allowed to enter. The place was full anyway. Suddenly Albert – or rather, Kolya – sailed in as if he were being driven by a dozen SS men. He stopped in front of me and begged me to let him have a 'go' because he had diarrhoea. He even handed me a piece of newspaper, the value of which can only be appreciated by those under similar circumstances themselves. I was quite ready to oblige him as I was only playing for time, because of the heat outside. There was not much time left for formal thanking, because no one was allowed to stand about idly and so I had to make a hasty exit. Dad was sitting near Block 7 and I told him of my good fortune, i.e. about the newspaper. 'I felt almost civilized again,' was my conclusion.

Several minutes later, Kolya passed by. I waved to him as if we were old friends and he returned the compliment. In fact he came up to me and shook my hand.

'My name is Albert, but they call me Kolya, and I am very thankful for your kindness. You know,' he went on, 'not many people in this camp would have done the same.' 'Not even for your paper?' I was quite surprised. 'I only offered it to you because you were getting up anyway,' he assured me.

We went on talking for quite some time. I told him my name, and pointed Dad out to him. Then we talked about why we thought we were in Auschwitz. Kolya's father, it seemed, was an officer of considerable importance in the Red Army. Later, I learned that he was one of the brains behind the Russian strategic movement, but Kolya had had no time to evacuate from his school. He thought he was the only one alive; an idea which did not surprise me in the least after I had learned the truth about the real purpose of the 'bakery'.

In fact, I told Kolya about my discovery, but he just shrugged his shoulders. 'I have been in Auschwitz for over a month. You need not tell me of the local arrangements. Believe me, there are worse things than just gassing and burning going on here.'

There was not much time for further discussion because his block had to go indoors, but we made a date for the next day.

Dad was glad to hear that I had met Kolya. He only hoped that he was half as decent as I had described. In the evening we had bread and marmalade and coffee (it was called 'coffee' anyway), and [went] to bed again.

Next day, I met again with Kolya, and Dad continued his talks with his new friends. Mr Mousekopf went on telling jokes to a group of similarly fat gentlemen. On the whole we were beginning to settle down. We had food given to us every day, but no work was required. I realized that it was better this way than to work and have no food, so I did not grumble, but the idleness was rapidly losing its charm. There was an almost tangible atmosphere of boredom before the end of our first seven days.

The only variety was caused by the arrival of fresh transports [of people]. Berehovo transports were unlikely since we had been on the last one, but we were looking for acquaintances just the same.

When any newcomers asked me for information regarding the 'local etiquette' – as one of them called it – I replied with an air of superiority. Asked if the food was edible, I replied, 'You'll get used to it', and tried to sound as experienced as possible.

When we heard *'Brotholen!'* we were no longer last in the queue, because we had discovered that those in front got a bigger spoonful of marmalade than those in the rear. In the wash-block, I too began to push my way through and it surprised me how easy it was. All I had to do was dig my elbow into my neighbour's side and say in a not very gentleman-like tone: 'Hey, you, I was here before', or 'Who do you think you are?' and I would be in front of a water hole. Twice I was even allowed to scratch the soup barrels, and that was paradise itself.

By two or three o'clock in the afternoon I was regularly hungry. Lots of books mention hunger, and I knew that the poor man begged because he was hungry, but the only kind of hunger I knew was when instead of having two rolls for breakfast, I had one, or none at all. The same, I believed, was true of the beggar as well. When he collected enough money, he bought food and ate. There seemed to be hardly any complication. To confess, I was neither acquainted, nor in sympathy, with the hungry. Perhaps because of my ignorance, the realization of the reality of hunger was a gradual process, instead of a sudden one. There were those around me who expressed their fear of starvation on our second day in Auschwitz. They must have known what it was like to count the minutes from noon till about 6 or 7 p.m., when bread was given out.

For the first three days, I was not really worried. Of course, my soup was no longer given away, in spite of feeling sick swallowing the stuff, but the third and fourth times were much easier, and before seven days were out, I could easily have eaten two or even three times as much.

Neither were our meals regular. Those who were at Auschwitz will probably remember times when soup was fetched with – or instead of – the coffee. Some days it was eight, nine or ten o'clock in the morning; very rarely it was at noon, but only once did we get it together with our bread. In other words it was impossible to get used to anything. Because of the irregularity of the soup – the only hot meal of the day – every other function became irregular as well.

After one week in Auschwitz, one did not live from day to day, but merely existed from one meal to another. How I managed the second half of the latter remains a mystery to me. Later on, it was easier to bear being hungry, probably because I became used to it, but in the beginning it was sheer torture.

On the evening of the ninth day, we were sitting outside the barracks (for by then we had permission to stay outside until the lights went on, about half an hour before dark) and the scene was quite pleasant. Yes, 'pleasant' is the right word. We had our bread and a piece of cheese, as well as the usual marmalade; it was no longer hot and there was a mild breeze soothing us. Somebody was singing in the Gypsy camp. I could not distinguish the words, but the accompanying accordion and the male voice singing were ideally harmonized. Nobody seemed to mind his singing. It seemed quite natural that in the midst of death and destruction, we should forget the horror and put ourselves into a calm frame of mind.

Another three days passed uneventfully. There was talk of a transport, but it did not go further than talk. The chief complaint was boredom. Sitting around all day doing nothing began to take its effects. The number of those who ceased partaking in discussions increased greatly; more and more people were wandering about aimlessly, without any expression on their faces.

Kolya and I became close friends. He talked about his father who was the greatest soldier he had known, about his home-town which was the most beautiful town he could imagine, and of his girlfriend who was everything girlfriends ought to be. Sometimes we told stories, making them up as we went along. When Kolya got tired, I took over and we went on spin-ning and weaving as much as our imaginations would permit.

Finally, the talk of transport became a fact. The Blockälteste did not dismiss us after a morning *Appell*, but let us stand there for about thirty minutes, during which time Dad and I had a long consultation. 'No matter what kind of skilled workers they want, we step out,' concluded Dad. He had my full approval.

One of the assistants came along to see if we were standing in proper order, and I asked him for permission to be excused. He let me go, 'for one minute only'. As I went by Kolya's block, I made signs at him – the meaning of which must have been grasped by him, for he followed me soon after to the lavatory.

'Listen, Kolya, there is going to be a transport, and Dad thinks they will take skilled workers only,' I said in a whisper, lest I be found out. 'We are going, whatever they want,' I went on, 'and I thought perhaps you would like to come along with us.' 'As a matter of fact, I thought of going, too,' he agreed.

We returned to our blocks and very soon after a committee, consisting of an Unterscharführer (sergeant) and two civilians accompanied by the Lagerälteste,* halted in front of us.

---

* Camp elder, in charge of the prison population, chosen from common-law criminals.

The Lagerälteste spoke to us: 'A transport of skilled labourers will be selected from among you for a development area.
That means that all those connected with building are needed.
Form a column of five: masons, carpenters, joiners, glaziers,
painters, locksmiths, and those who have knowledge of tree-
felling.'

It was right up our street. Dad really did know about forestry
and I had been thinking so much of myself as a carpenter,
that I was actually beginning to believe it myself.

About half of Block 7 stepped out, and not long afterwards
we were joined by about half of Kolya's block. I was glad to
see Kolya among them. Before leaving Camp D the SS man
addressed us once again: 'If there are any fake *Fachleute*
(skilled men) among you, leave the column now, before it's
too late. The *Schweine-hund* who lies will be found out and
he will be very sorry.'

While he spoke, my face gradually turned purple and though
the sun was not yet at its hottest, drops of perspiration
appeared all over me. I was quite sure that I was not the only
'fake', yet no one left the column. Following his speech, the
SS man and the civilians left.

One and a half hours later we, too, left Camp D without a
single regret. During that time, however, the Blockälteste of
Block 7 became a very different man. He took us into the
Block and ordered his assistants to search us for gold and
other valuables, his verbal request having failed to produce
any results. It was useless to tell him that we had been
searched nineteen times before and that we had completely
changed our clothes at least once, and our pleas were of no
avail. In fact, after the assistants were satisfied that they could
find nothing valuable on us, the Blockälteste brought out a
cane and without much ado, struck Mr Mousekopf right
across the back. 'Now will you tell me where you hid your
gold!'

Poor Mr Mousekopf. I think it was because of his size

and comparative good humour that everybody took him for something more than he actually was. I had no doubt that the Blockälteste picked on him first because he was the least depressed, and had I been in the Blockälteste's shoes, I would have thought that his (i.e. Mr Mousekopf's) joviality was due to some kind of hidden wealth he carried about with him. The Blockälteste, of course, knew nothing of Mr Mousekopf's nature. He had told us that 'back home' he was a farmer, and there were some people with us who seconded this statement, saying that he was the farmer with most land and cattle in his district. There were those who added that he had the nicest two daughters in the land, and so on. Gradually we got to know Mr Mousekopf and his background quite well. He was boisterous, but fundamentally his heart was as soft as butter. He swore a lot, but he could also recite pages of Goethe and the Hungarian poet Adi Endre.

When the Blockälteste struck him, his expression lost all its jollity. It must have been a long time since anybody had struck him. You could have heard a pin drop after the Blockalteste's second demand: 'Where is your gold?' But his requests were futile. Nevertheless he struck Mr Mousekopf once again, as well as several others standing nearby.

'Before you go, you shall all learn a little lesson,' but just what this lesson was going to be about, we never found out, for the Lagerälteste returned and, after a short consultation with our own Blockälteste, ordered us outside again. Shortly afterwards we left Camp D for good.

Again we marched through the Gypsy camp. We were still puzzled by the number of children playing about in the dirt. No one we talked to knew much about them. On one occasion, Dad and I fetched the soup from the kitchen and while waiting outside to be called we talked to some of the Gypsies. They spoke German and called themselves *Reichs-Deutsche*, which means thoroughbred Germans, and told us that they came from Stuttgart. Asked why they were in Auschwitz, they just shrugged their shoulders. But that was all we knew about them.

(Eight months later I was talking to a Pole who had then come straight from Auschwitz and he gave me the following account of the Gypsy camp: 'About a month ago, we were ordered to go to the barracks straight after *Appell* and some time around eight o'clock we heard a lot of screaming from Camp C mingled with rifle reports. We thought at first that the Gypsies were being transported. Their yells went on till very late in the night, but gradually the volume of the noise abated. We could also hear the engine roar of some lorries and I need not add that we were all very much afraid. However, nothing happened to us. When we went out next morning, Camp C was completely deserted. Most of their windows were broken and bits of clothing littered the place. Our Blockälteste remarked: "They have been liquidated. There was too much VD among them." And we never saw a Gypsy again.')

Past the Gypsy camp we entered Camp E and halted in front of Block 3. The Lagerälteste handed us over to Blockälteste 3 and returned to Camp D. Our new 'house-father' – as Mr Mousekopf called them – was a short man and a Pole. He claimed to be a *Volks-Deutscher* (a title given to Polish and other alien traitors) and he made no secret of his political beliefs either. He swore at us with a foreign German accent and informed us that he would 'tolerate no *Schweinerei*' what ever that meant. He disliked (as we soon found) old men and young ones, tall ones as well as short ones, fat men and thin men. Our appearances displeased him; the way we talked irritated him; in short, nothing we did in Block 3 was right in his eyes. He told us all these things before we entered the barracks, but when we did, another shock was added to our misery: there were no beds in Block 3. The only thing we could rest on was the cold cement floor.

Dad, Kolya and myself managed to get a corner and we spent the afternoon sitting there in silence. We were not allowed to sit outside, but no one minded very much because of the heat. We had bread at the usual time, but the portions seemed smaller than previously and only half a spoonful of marmalade was given. The assistant 'house-fathers' were the image of their chief, only more so. *Appell* was not different either – only the personnel had changed. Afterwards we had an hour of fresh air (that is what the chlorine-saturated atmosphere was nicknamed) and we used this time to explore the camp. Most of the inmates were also waiting for transport. Some had been waiting for more than a month, but they were watchmakers. In Block 8, we saw many familiar faces, but as they had to stand in attention for an hour (having misbehaved during *Appell*), we could not talk to them.

Sleep seemed impossible, but it was not. It is true that I felt twice as tired in the morning; nevertheless I slept all night. So, I believe, did the others, too. When we returned from the wash-block, some black coffee awaited us. Soup, the assistants informed, would be given at noon. In Block 8, we found many from Berehovo. Among them was Joseph – better known as Patyu – a cousin of mine. There was great rejoicing when we met him, and right away he told us that a cousin of Dad's was in the next camp. His name was Michael Klein, or rather Dr Klein, and he and Patyu had many talks over the fence. Dr Klein had a law practice in Prague, and after two years in Theresienstadt, finally Auschwitz had claimed him. We went up to the fence right away and, whilst waiting for someone to call him, Patyu told us that he too had volunteered for carpentry and was awaiting transport. An uncle of Dad's – Uncle Alec – was in Block 8, as well, also waiting for transport.

Michael came at last. I had not seen him for some years, but Dad and he had been great friends in their youth. It was a curious scene to watch them stand on either side of the barbed wire and electric fence. Unable to shake hands or pat one another on the shoulder, they just stood there trying to smile, but both probably thinking the same.

'I have some news for you, Géza,' Michael broke the silence. 'I asked Patyu to look out for you, because most transports pass through your camp.' He went on, 'Bella is on the other side of this camp.'

Suddenly Dad became quite animated. Questions like 'How is she?', 'What is she doing?', 'How does she look?' were fired at Michael at top speed, both from Dad and myself.

The answers were the usual ones: 'She's fine. She's waiting for transport, too' and so on. It was agreed that we would try to write a note. With the aid of a stone, we could throw it to Michael and he in turn could get it to Mummy. Then we suggested that Mummy send a reply in the same way. First Michael threw over to us some paper and a pencil. It seemed they were quite well off in his camp. They had permission to bring in their luggage as well as keeping most of the things in them. Friends from Czechoslovakia sent food parcels to them, families were not separated; in short, they were very well off. Michael agreed that they were, but he was afraid that there was a catch in it somewhere.

'From my previous dealings with the SS, I can safely state that unless they wanted something from – or of – us, they would not treat us comparatively like princes.' All we could do was agree.

Meanwhile, the note was completed and duly signed by Dad, myself and Patyu, in the same order. Then Dad stepped right back from the fence and threw the pebble over. For a few seconds no one moved, just in case someone was watching, then Michael approached it and whilst pretending to blow his nose he dropped his handkerchief. The rest was easy. With the handkerchief, he picked up the pebble, and slowly he walked away. For the next half-hour or so we just stood and then sat down, now doing the one, then the other. In front of us stared the grey-green barracks. With those two dirty black windows, they looked like monstrous faces. Beyond those barracks, however, was Mummy! And if objects can be hated,

I hated those barracks for standing between us. I hated the fence for separating us and I hated the world for letting us be so humiliated.

Soon Michael returned. Comparatively soon, that is. He wrapped a bit of paper around a pebble. We all stood back and over it came. Slowly we advanced and I even tried to look as if I was listening to some far-off sound, just in case someone was watching my expression. Then both Dad and I dived at the pebble. The message was clearly in Mummy's handwriting and it ran: 'We are well in spite of looks. Please take good care of yourselves. Let us hope that we shall be together soon. Have you heard anything about the children? Love, Mummy.' Poor Mummy! She probably did not believe the rumours, which we knew to be true!

Michael, on the other side, disappeared. In a few moments, he returned with a bundle which he threw over to us. In it we found a spoon, a safety razor with two blades, and a bit of soap. This was a wonderful gift indeed, for although there was a camp barber in action, Dad's face was full of scars. Soon we were the centre of interest; there were about a dozen men standing around us, all asking Dad to lend it to them for a wash and a shave. Just how he would have settled with his sudden 'friends', we never found out, because the Lagerälteste came along and ordered everybody to go to his barracks. We waved a hasty goodbye to Michael and asked him to talk to Mummy. Patyu said he would come with us to Block 3. 'They won't read out any names if it is a transport, and if it is only a false alarm, then I can always go back to my own block,' he assured Dad, who was worried about him.

The alarm was not a false one. Everybody was already lined up. The assistant counted us. He said something to the Block-älteste, who in turn, consulted his sheet. 'There you go, Patyu,' I whispered, but the Blockälteste just shrugged his shoulders, wrote something on the sheet and went inside. 'Attention!' yelled the assistant, and five minutes later: 'March!'

Through the Gypsy camp again, on to a square. There we waited for at least two hours. The comparison between those two hours and the time we had waited outside the wash-block when we arrived was certainly a sad one. There was no talking or joking. Everyone sat or stood in silent gloom. An occasional 'Damn this waiting!' did very little to cheer us up. Even Mr Mousekopf was silent and no longer looking prosperous. Then we were marched off again. This time the camp we entered had no letter on it and the barracks had no numbers either. We stopped in front of the fifth one on the right-hand side and a man with 'Kapo'* on his arm came out to welcome us. The assistant who accompanied us, and who seemed to be our new 'house-father' counted us, and then we were ordered to sit down in the dust (he called it 'sand') in proper order.

In no way was his little speech original. In the first place, he told us we might stay in his Block for a long time, but provided we behaved properly, he would present no difficulties. Then he was silent for a few seconds, probably in order to impress us. The second half of his speech was only too familiar.

'No doubt many of you still have some valuables on you. Watches, gold, precious stones and dollars. It is no use denying it as I have already *seen* some of you display it. I shall expect you to give it up and some suitable reward will be given for your honesty. I am sure you would not want a search. They are very distasteful in this Block!'

The reward bit was a new variation on an old theme – so to speak – but nothing on earth could have procured results. 'What you haven't got, you can't give away!' to quote Mr Mousekopf, who had had some nasty experiences previously.

Needless to say, the search *was* rather unpleasant. In fact, several people were bruised in the one-sided battle conducted by the Blockälteste and his assistants 'versus' ourselves.

* 'Chief' or 'boss' from Italian *capo*; the prisoner in charge of a work squad.

There were no beds in this barrack either. It did not matter very much though, because we were more or less used to sleeping on cement. Fortune was against us that first night: by the time we arrived inside, all corners were occupied and we had to content ourselves with a patch of ground right in the middle of the floor. It was an unfortunate plot, because everybody had to pass over us (literally) if they wanted to get from one end to the other. Many of them did – for a change in scenery, we supposed.

We did not talk loudly, but in quiet undertones and conversation was at its height for most of the night. Next to us lay a certain Mr Sopar and he, it seemed, was a glazier. Dad and I exchanged glances and quickly I bombarded him with questions about his profession. After all, I thought, glass is as good as wood, and much easier to carry. Mr Sopar was quite glad to have a chat with us and every question I asked was met by another question from him. It was clear that Mr Sopar did not wish to divulge any trade secrets. Instead he told us that he had been an apprentice in Berehovo for two years, and that he knew our street very well. In fact, he thought that he might have put the windows into our house. Then he changed the subject.

'You know,' he said, 'many of the people who are coming on this transport are fakes. I am not pulling your leg. For instance, that man over there,' he pointed towards Mr Mousekopf, 'why, he is a farmer. I know because I did some jobs for him. Of course, you,' meaning Dad and myself, 'you don't seem like the phoney type to me. As I always say, first impressions are the correct ones. When I first saw you, Mr Green,* I said to myself: "He is an honest man!" and was I wrong? No! There is nothing like an honest, hardworking man. I may as well confess,' and here Mr Sopar lowered his tone to a whisper, 'I am a Socialist. I believe that people are good really,

---

* In 1951, at the time of writing, Hugo was spelling his surname as 'Green'; when he received US citizenship in 1956 he reverted it officially to 'Gryn'.

it's just that they are dominated by exploiters. Why even here you find people too proud to talk to the likes of us, but when we get to our destination, I'll show them . . .'

He went on talking and I wanted to kick myself for ever having started him off. All I wanted was to learn something about window-glazing; instead he gave us a political lecture. Several times I tried to interject a remark, but it was all in vain. Meanwhile I must have dozed off, for the next thing I remember was someone tickling me. Well, not exactly tickling, but certainly touching me around the waist. At first, I wanted to shout, but instead I just lay still, waiting for further developments. It could not have been Dad – he was on the other side, or Patyu, or Kolya. Then I realized it was Mr Sopar. Of course, I could not see him – it was much too dark – but I could feel him. I hoped he would not touch my ribs or thighs, because that used to make me laugh. But no, he tried to feel his way into my shirt and pulled it out fraction by fraction. I was tempted to whisper that Dad always kept our bread, but I restrained myself. Then he did touch my ribs and so I had to shake him off. I turned, as if in sleep, and *en route* I kicked in his direction. Judging by his sighs, it must have been a bull's-eye, and he did not bother me again for the rest of the night.

In the morning, I had a better view of him. He was about Dad's size – that is about medium – and he had already started to develop that blank look. He did not look very happy either.

'How did you sleep?' I asked him. 'Oh, all right! I think you were quite restless, my boy. In fact, you nearly kicked me,' came the response. I could not resist: 'I know some people who cannot help this sort of thing. A man I know does the same thing – with his hands.' He did not reply, perhaps just as well. Later on, I told Dad about him. 'Poor man!' was all Dad commented.

We had soup before *Appell* and afterwards we were not allowed to dismiss. Whispers like 'There we go!', 'End of the

Auschwitz holidays!' and 'Fresh hope in sight!' fluttered all over. In fact, there was a sort of unofficial competition as to who could make up the best slogan. Clearly the mood was a good one and so many people could not be wrong.

The sun was quite warm by the time we were marched off, and our 'house-father' must have been quite furious. He came with us as far as the gates and on the way he hit a number of people because they 'did not cover up properly'.

From the nameless camp on to a square. There was a new assistant accompanying us. He gave orders to sit down and wait. So we sat down and waited. We were approximately twelve hundred machines. The only difference was that we could speak and had to be fed, whereas proper mechanical gadgets could do without either.

By the time the sun had risen above our heads, the atmosphere of expectation changed into one of doubt. Uniforms were shed and shirt-sleeves were busy wiping moist brows. From where we sat we could see a couple of people on the roof of a barracks spreading a steaming black liquid. They were naked to the waist, but with no visible sign of malnutrition. Kolya and I decided that they were Poles and definitely old-timers, for only those who had been there a long time could become workers, whilst the others were just 'drones'.

Patyu gave us some information about Auschwitz while we waited. Apparently we were not in Auschwitz at all, but Birkenau. The real thing was about two miles away, and there they lived in stone houses and went out to work every day. Later on we learned that what Patyu had said was quite correct. Actually the place we were in was called 'Vernichtungs-Lager Birkenau' – 'Exterminating Camp Birkenau' – and its original purpose was as a sort of transitory camp – for those who left it at all, that is.

Well, we did not really care whether it was Auschwitz or Birkenau. We only wanted to turn our backs on it as quickly as possible and never see it again, except perhaps on the screen

– if we ever had the good fortune to sit in a cinema again.

A little after noon, a lorry drove up and before it even came to a halt, it was obvious that it contained provisions for our trip. It was loaded with loaves which were not cut up into bits. Two men handed them down and, as we filed past, each one of us received a whole loaf and a packet (weighing about two ounces) of margarine. By the time we were standing in columns of five, spirits had risen considerably. The lorry departed and an SS man yelled 'Attention!', then 'March!' and we were off. Holding on to our loaves, we marched past another SS man who counted us and, as we passed out through the gates, SS men, with rifles levelled at us, took over the job of escorting. From a bird's eye view we must have looked quite fascinating. Columns of striped animals in the middle of a dusty road and grey-green keepers on either side, with things that looked like sticks pointing at us. We must have gone right around the camp, but we did not see many people about. Only an occasional SS man, patrolling with a bloodhound, and some SS women who smiled graciously at every SS man with stripes.

Finally we reached a train of cattle wagons. It must have been on the same line where we had originally disembarked, judging by the various bits of rags and other domestic goods that had been swept out of the wagons, and which now lay littering the lines, as if lamenting for their previous – and probably deceased – owners. Yet the wagons themselves looked tidy and emanated a strong smell of disinfectant. There was a barrel of water in each car as well as a *kürble** – to be employed as a lavatory. It was an odd coincidence, but both the barrel and the container had 'Berehovo' written on them. On our way out of Auschwitz, we were to drink our water from the same vessel as we had coming into Auschwitz. The difference was that when we came into Auschwitz some of

* Wooden drum made from half a barrel.

us had hopes, others fears and forebodings, but leaving, only a few of us still had any hope and we had seen our worst fears become realities.

Fifty prisoners were ordered to each wagon, along with three fully armed SS men. Twenty-five on one side and twenty-five on the other. The middle space was left for the guards. Our sense of justice was far too dulled to comment upon the fact that whilst three people had one third of the wagon, fifty had to share the rest. In our wagon, we had to sit five in a row, pulling our knees up and opening them so that the next five could do the same and literally sit in between the knees of those behind. The luckiest ones had seats either in the back or in front. The former could lean against a wooden wall which did not heave and bash you in the ribs, and the latter hoped to stretch out their legs – and did, too, for a while – an impossible task for anyone sitting behind them. Dad and I had front seats, or rather, I had a front seat next to the barrel, sitting between his knees. There was, of course, a silent understanding between us that we would change seats as soon as we tired of our positions.

There was very little talk in the wagon. Outside it was hot and only occasionally did snatches of voices reach us, carried no doubt by a temperamental wind, which made the sounds incomprehensible. Gradually, the wagon's atmosphere became warmer and warmer, accelerated by the fact that our bodies were touching, a fact which caused a steep rise in tempers besides the rise in temperatures. Very soon we realized that our trip was not going to be a pleasant one. The guards clambered in and began to make themselves at home. Two of them were big, rough-looking men, the third one was slightly built, but his thin face looked cruel. I was convinced that he was capable of committing the most atrocious crimes without batting an eyelid.

There was a silence after they entered. The thin guard was first to move. With an unmistakable movement of his hand, he ordered the people sitting in the front row of the opposite side to move back. They hurriedly obliged and cast accusing glances at one another as if to say: 'Don't you see you are in his way?' Nobody actually looked at him, nobody that is except an equally slightly built Pole. I could see his face, but only the back of the SS man. He looked up and tried to smile with what was meant to convey submission and a report of 'order carried out'. He even spoke, *'Warm, nicht wahr!'** still smiling. The SS man must have looked at him in a strange manner because the smile disappeared from the small Pole's face, and like a nervous bird he glanced left and right, carefully avoiding the countenance of the guard. He must have been thinking: 'I tried my best, but you see, it was not good enough.'

At last the train moved. As it gathered speed, I thought of the last time we had sat in a moving train. It was only a short while ago. There they were – Mummy, Dad, my brothers, friends, relatives – and there was I, a young boy full of life and high hopes. As the clicking of the wheels became monotonous, I thought: 'What are we now? Of all the others, Dad is here alone, but is he the same person he was then? And here am I, but am I what I was? Am I not a stranger to myself, a mere shadow of the hopeful boy, whose only concern at present is whether I should take a bite of my bread now, or whether I should wait a little longer?'

Such thoughts were no good and definitely unhelpful. Instead, I leaned back on Dad, and just listened to the clattering of the wheels. It was rhythmical and soothing, yet it was a hateful sound. 'I hate trains, I hate the clattering, I . . .'

---

* 'Warm, isn't it?'

13

LIEBEROSE

When I awoke again the train was at a standstill. It was still dark, but the night must have already spent its greater part. Only an occasional burst of steam, with an exaggerated harshness, interrupted the stillness of the night. My travelling companions slept – some snoring – and the guards slept too. How easy it would be to escape, I mused. But such thoughts, I told myself, were silly. Why, I did not even know where I was. Probably Germany – but where? The journey from Auschwitz had taken about ten hours. But we had been travelling fast. Maybe it was twelve hours, one could not tell. Maybe we were in Berlin, but it was too quiet for that. Anyway, how could I tell that we had arrived? Perhaps we were just waiting at some signals. There was nothing to do but wait . . . And wait I did, half in this world and half in the boundless orb of the dreamer, until dawn relieved me of my solitary vigil.

Soon everyone was awake – if not widely so, at least rubbing their eyes and yawning long, luxurious yawns. The guards were last to wake. They pushed open one of the doors and the screeching noise of metal contrasted sharply with the still quiet dawn.

'Wherever we are,' said a man next to me, 'we are not in a big town. And that is always a good sign. Perhaps we shall work in farms.' 'Shouldn't think so,' commented another, 'we are a "building commando", not "unskilled labour".'

'Yes, sir . . . we shall build again and don't I just long to be back at work.' It was not necessary to turn round to ascertain that such enthusiasm must come from Mr Sopar.

He had been talking throughout the trip and his chatter was a source of annoyance to everyone in the wagon. Yet I could not help feeling that Mr Sopar talked a lot because he had nothing to say and like most of us he was mortally afraid.

Gradually all traces of night faded and it was possible to see the long, caricatured shadow of the train in the light of the rising sun. Although it was still cool, a warm summer day was indicated and many of us must have wondered if there would be plenty of water and shade. We still did not know where we were. But the guards packed their luggage and straightened out their tunics. Alighting could not be far off.

After a few minutes we heard a lot of shuffling noises and commands from the neighbouring wagon, followed by the crunch of feet on gravel. Then an SS man stuck his face into our wagon and yelled: *'Aufstehen und raus!'* ('Get up and out!'). We stood up and I had to lean on Dad because both my legs were asleep. Then we climbed out of the wagon and I saw that we were just outside a station and I could read the name 'Lieberose' from the distance. The station was in a forest and the only signs of life came from a sawmill adjoining the railway station. 'This is a good omen,' said Dad, 'forests and a sawmill. I am sure now that we shall find jobs and not be entirely ignorant at them.'

Well, of course, it was all right for Dad. What he did not know about wood, I did not deem worth knowing. And during the previous summer I had helped Dad with some calculations and measured quite a lot. The only thing we did not know was whether they would leave us in Lieberose and if so, whether they would want us to work with civilians. For we could see some civilian workers standing on piles of timber, eyeing us without any particular interest. It was the first time I had seen German civilians. You could tell they were Germans, with their small black moustaches and leather caps.

Altogether they looked just like my idea of Germans, except that they were much smaller. It was also the first time that I saw a German look at us. A vacant gaze, it was as free of sympathy and compassion as it was of hatred. Just a terrible, hurting indifference. We could have been barrels of paint being unloaded, or some labour-saving gadgets for their factory.

Again we lined up, five by five. The guards took their places on either side with rifles levelled horizontally, and we were off. Nobody counted or shouted directions, yet we walked in step. In a way, I suppose, we wanted to impress our keepers and future fellow prisoners, if any. We turned on to the main road and saw a column of about fifty prisoners, all dressed in the same attire as ourselves, coming from the opposite direction. They were led by a prisoner who had 'Vorarbeiter – Holzfäller'* written on his sleeve and about eight SS guards on either side of them. We eyed them and they us. They looked very healthy and clean. Better, I thought, than the guards and the leader himself. (I was quite right, for as we found later, they were Norwegians and about them I propose to say some more later.§) After about eight hundred yards, we turned to the right and straight through some barbed wire gates into a camp. We marched up the very short main road on to a square and were told to stand 'at ease'.

So suddenly had we come into the camp that we were too surprised to notice everything at once. But on the whole, the two thousand and four hundred people who stood on the camp square that summer morning were favourably impressed. The camp was small. We stood in the centre of the camp, which was really a forest-clearing. There were trees all over the camp and on three sides it was surrounded by the forest. The fourth side was open (but not without a fence) to the sawmill and a

---

* Foreman – Timber Felling.

§ We never find out what he intended to tell us about the Norwegian prisoners.

huge builders' yard. Opposite us stretched a long green barracks. Half of it was marked 'Lagerälteste' and the other half
had three doors marked 'Tischlerei' (carpentry), 'Schneiderei'
(tailor) and 'Schusterei' (boot-making) respectively. On either
side of us stood six similar green barracks with numbers from
1 to 12. Opposite the office building stood the Hospital. It
was marked 'Revier' and looked quite deserted. At right-angles
to them stood the long kitchen building. We were allowed to
go to the lavatory and found that there were two buildings
provided for sanitary purposes. Both had been divided into
two halves, one consisting of divided cubicles which ran along
the centre of the barrack in two lines with a common back.
The other half consisted of two long pipes with a flat sink
underneath them, spread in the same manner as the cubicles.
There was only one tap and when it was turned on, water
spouted forth from the many holes pierced in the pipes, all
pointing downward. It took a good half hour before we were
all washed and reassembled again on the square. A number
of people in clean striped uniforms stood outside the office.
Each had an armband with the word 'Blockälteste' and a
number.

They made sure that everyone was present, counted us,
recounted us and then we were again permitted to stand 'at
ease'. The group of Blockältestes* had another conference
and the Lagerälteste finally raised his arm, which silenced us
at once.

'Welcome to Lieberose!' he said. His voice was somehow
... German. It was hard and very articulate. One could not
imagine that anyone had ever had to ask him to repeat himself.
He wore a civilian jacket, but with striped trousers and there
was a square of striped cloth in the centre of his back. He
continued: 'You are in a camp where you have many possibili-
ties. You can make a paradise out of it, or you can create hell.

* Should be Blockältesten.

The choice is yours. Order and cleanliness is our motto and let it be yours as well. You will work and you will have good food. But there is no room here for making pigs of yourselves. Now, before I ask Schreiber (the Secretary) to give you some details, I have one more thing to tell you. You will be searched, anyway, but if you have good sense, give up all gold, silver and diamonds to me. You won't regret it.'

He had finished with the usual sentence. It was becoming a cliché with our authorities, yet how miserably wrong they were. The Lagerälteste looked quite hurt when no one stirred after his request and it was not difficult to deduce from his face that he had expected some response. But after ten minutes' waiting, punctuated with an occasional 'You'll be better off if you give up your treasures' and 'Don't annoy the Lagerälteste with stubbornness!' from some Blockälteste, the Secretary started speaking. He was a short man and quite fat, bald and very round-headed. His limbs, as well as his face, reminded me of an assorted bunch of blown-up balloons. By this time, I was quite capable of distinguishing between accents, and the Secretary's was quite plainly Polish.

'You will be detailed to your barracks presently and for the next two days there will be no work for you. First, uniforms will be changed, and numbers given to everyone. You will also have to come, in due course, to the office and give details for reference.' The impression derived from the tone of his speech was, on the whole, favourable. It was [de]void of malice and even sympathetic. Obviously he was chosen for the post because of his efficiency. Later I found that these first impressions were correct.

But now the sorting out had begun. We were formed into groups of two hundred and fifty and marched off to our respective Blocks. Our group was taken to Block 4. The man in charge was quite small, German and his number-strip had a green triangle on it. Standing in front of the barracks on the main camp road, we were again subdivided into six groups. There

were twenty-one of us in the first, and forty-five in the other
five. Then we were told to go into the rooms. The most
striking thing was the cleanliness of the room. After the filth
of Auschwitz and the wagons, the cool and clean atmosphere
of the room was comparable only to an oasis. Inside, a very
liberal quarter of the room was partitioned off and the rest
occupied by bunks of three storeys, a table in the centre and
some five or six chairs. The beds each had a straw mattress
and three blankets, as well as a straw pillow. Actually it was
not straw, but quite fine wood-pulp, promising comfort at
last! The Blockälteste was rushing about in the other rooms
and meanwhile we started to sort ourselves out. It was curious
that about fifteen of our room's inhabitants (known thereafter
as Stube 1) were all under twenty-one. This, we found later,
was not a coincidence. It was agreed that the older ones should
occupy the bottom berths and we began to make up the beds.
The Blockälteste, on his arrival, ordered us to stop.

'There is only one way of making beds in this camp,' he
said, 'and you don't know it.' He called out 'Jezek!' and from
the partitioned part of the room, a boy of about eighteen
emerged. He was thin, but not abnormally so, and one thing
that was noticeable right away was his paleness. His face was
chalk-white, but on closer inspection, the impression was
more of yellow than white. He had very large eyes, which
gave his face a pathetic, but unfriendly, expression.

'Jezek, show the people how to make beds,' the Blockälteste
told him.

Without a word he proceeded to make up one of the beds. All
of us gathered around and watched him smooth the blankets
and arrange the pillow so that the rise from the blankets was
at exactly ninety degrees. Then he tore the blankets off and,
pointing at Patyu, he said: 'Now you build like I.'

His German was very bad, and the accent Polish. Patyu
tried to imitate him and did a good job of it. The Polish boy
frowned a little, but then just shrugged his shoulders and

told us to make our beds according to the lesson just learned.

The rest of the day was not very exacting. The food consisted of a thick soup and three boiled potatoes. They were delivered in twenty-five and fifty litre containers, which we of Stube 1 had to wash and return to the kitchen. The Blockälteste explained that he always left a litre or so at the bottom and therefore it was a privilege for us to clean the bins. Indeed it was. At about six, the rest of the inhabitants returned to camp. They arrived back in batches of thirty to fifty, and as they marched in, they sang. They all made for Blocks 5 and 6, an SS under-officer* counted them and soon they were walking up to the wash-houses. They did not speak to us at all, although at the back our windows opened on to Block 5. One elderly Pole did come to the window, but only to ask if we had any French cigarettes for sale. Though what he was to pay with remained a mystery. Bread was distributed, two hundred grams per person and twenty grams of margarine, as well as some coffee (that is, brown water disguised).

On the whole, we spoke little that day. We were not bad-tempered or quarrelsome, just very tired and indifferent. Secretly, we all hoped that a good night's sleep would bring about some improvement.

We were woken by a bell at six in the morning and from everywhere came shouts of 'Aufstehen!' We made for the washroom to find it already crowded, and as we had only shirts as toilet requisites, the process of washing took little time. The occupants of Blocks 5 and 6 came in a solid block and with newcomers' respect for the seasoned inmate, we gave way.

Breakfast was coffee again, and Jezek – who himself lived in Block 5 but assisted in our barracks – told us that sometimes breakfast was *Haarverflocken*§ or something that sounded

* Probably an SS-Unterscharführer.
§ *Haferflocken*, rolled oats.

like it; and this turned out to be a milk soup with some thrashed-out corn in it. After breakfast it was time for *Appell*.

Every block had an Unterscharführer who counted us while we stood at attention – 'eyes-left' – and caps in hands. Then we relaxed and they signed the paper inside a wooden frame handed to them by the Blockälteste. Then the SS men made their way to the office where the Lagerälteste, an SS man of higher rank, signed the lot. After *Appell* we went inside and the Secretary came round to tell us that it was our Block's turn to go to the office to have our details taken. This caused a lot of hard thinking. What was one to say? It seemed that four hundred of our transport were *Fachleute*, i.e. tradesmen, and the rest ordinary workers. Of the tradesmen, however, more than half had not the slightest idea about their respective trades. In our room, Patyu was the only one who actually once worked for four weeks in a carpenter's workshop. Kolya thought he could do something in the line of building too, but the rest of us had not a chance.

The Blockälteste must have suspected something, because he told a few of us that he would talk to the Vorarbeiters (the men in charge of working parties). For some reason or other he had taken fancy to me. He did not actually say so but, for example, he gave me a soup-bin to clean which had at least two litres of soup left in it. He also began to call me 'Hoffnung', for although my name – strictly speaking – was not 'Grün'* nevertheless he called me that, and added that *'Grün ist für Hoffnung'* (Green stands for hope).

He asked two of us – Nándor and me – to help him with cutting the bread. He was an expert at it. The loaves weighed one kilo each. They were almost black and covered with sawdust. At least that was the impression. There were, moreover, all kinds of strange lumps inside, but they tasted quite

---

* Actually, strictly speaking, this is how Hugo's surname appears on all documentation from that time.

good. When cutting, first he took out a thick slice from the middle, that was one portion, and then cut the two end bits into two. Altogether five portions were given from each loaf. Sometimes one loaf looked bigger than the others, then he cut both a thick and thin slice out of the middle and put the thin one in his cupboard. Sometimes he threw the thin ones to us and these we shared, Nándor eating his right away, while I tucked the pieces in my shirt. Later Dad, Patyu and Kolya were my guests for a late supper.

It was on our second day that we went to the office. The Secretary made us form two single lines, and with the assistance of another Pole, he began to take details. As we were moving slowly, there was plenty of opportunity to observe the contents of the room. It was quite ordinary, and about double the size of the dormitories. There were two tables, a few chairs and some shelves with papers. On the wall facing the door there was, however, a curious board. It was divided into a great many columns. On top of each column was a coloured triangle, and along the side a list of nationalities. German first, then French, Polish, Czech, Russian, Belgian, Dutch, Norwegian, Hungarian, Bulgarian, Romanian, Ukrainian, Slovenian, Italian, Spanish, Finnish, Danish, Luxembourg[ian], Arab, Jewish and Others. The Arab part was intriguing. Against the nationality, and in different columns, were numbers. Altogether there were not more than six hundred. Obviously not counting us. The majority were in the red triangle column. Red was political. The other colours were, and meant: green – criminal; green (upside down) – 'desperate' criminal; black – saboteur; pink – homosexual; red (upside down) – Wehrmacht deserter; red (upside down and in a black frame) – SS deserter; blue – 'Bibelforscher'* (Bible interpreters: apparently conscientious objectors and mostly Dutch).§

---

* or *Zeugen Jehowas*, Jehovah's Witnesses.
§ Hugo has omitted that Jews were assigned yellow triangles.

I realized, as I looked at the board, why my Blockälteste had laughed when I asked him whether his green triangle stood for hope as well. 'I suppose,' he said, 'it was hope at first, but I didn't reckon on the number after the triangle.'

The full title of the camp was: 'K. L. Arbeitslager Lieberose' and it belonged to the Sachsenhausen group of camps. Lieberose, a small village, was some forty kilometres from Cottbus,* and about a hundred and thirty kilometres from Berlin. The camp itself was quite new. Jezek had been there from the beginning.

'When I come here,' he told me, 'it is just a wood. We sleep in cold for two days, then build the blocks, cut wood and put up the fence. And for two months,' he added, 'we wait for people to come.'

But now that the camp was finished (there were still some trees to cut down), the real task of the camp, that is outside work, had commenced. It was to this end that we had come to Lieberose. All work, directly or indirectly, was centred around building. At the time of our arrival the majority were working on forest clearing and in the Bauhof,§ which was adjacent to the camp, there were all kinds of building materials, from bricks and prefabricated wooden barracks, to stores of paint. There was a large scheme afoot, but no one knew what it was exactly.

On the third day of our stay in Lieberose, after the morning *Appell* we were not dismissed, but led again to the square

* According to Andreas Weigelt, the curator of the museum in Lieberose: 'The camp was not situated in Lieberose. Your father arrived in the little village Jamlitz, five kilometres from Lieberose, but in Jamlitz was a bigger railway station and this was called "Staatsbahnof Lieberose". The camp between this railway station and the village Jamlitz was inside an old forest. The sawmill still exists like in 1944' [letter of 17 March 1999]. Jamlitz, where the camp was situated, is thirty-seven kilometres from Cottbus.

§ The Bauhof was an area near the railway where building materials were received and stored.

opposite the office. There were two huge trucks standing there and the Lagerälteste addressed us again from the office steps.

'These trucks have come from Sachsenhausen and have brought clothes for you. Your clothes will have to be returned to Auschwitz. Each one will get a shirt, pants and a suit. The Blockältestes will collect the old clothes, but in your own interest don't keep any of it back.'

One truck contained shirts and pants and the other suits. Distribution was quick and efficient. There was no choosing. Just grab and 'Weiter, weiter!'.* As soon as we returned to Block 4, there was much animated exchanging and running from one room to the other in an effort to find a shirt which, for example, looked like an unfastened strait-jacket once it was put on. But at least the shirts were warm. Blue and collarless with thin white stripes. The pants were long and warm as well. The ones received in Auschwitz were not uniform and certainly not warm. These suits were clean and when we were dressed once more, at first it was not too easy to tell who was who. Only the belts and shoes were still our own. The inhabitants of Blocks 5 and 6 wore wooden shoes and were offering three to four portions of bread for a pair of our leather shoes. And their portions were bigger than ours. For when working, the loaf was cut into only four parts. Some sold, but the majority of us were not too hungry. Mr Mousekopf, who was in Block 4 as well, was one of the first to wear wooden shoes. The new suit fitted him much better than his Auschwitz one.

We still had no work. As we were no longer tired the waiting became boring. 'Why don't we go out to work?' I asked the Secretary, who was a friend of our Blockälteste and would often talk to me. 'Don't worry,' he said, 'you will get your numbers tomorrow, and the day after you will be sorry you ever complained of lack of work.'

* 'Continue, continue!'

Four days after arrival, we received our numbers and were henceforth known only as numbers. They were issued in alphabetical order, Dad's being 80,493, mine 80,494 and Patyu's (whose real name was Joseph Katz, but had changed it to Green, so as to be with us) 80,495.

The triangle on the bits of white cloth was red.* I was thus officially inaugurated as a political prisoner of the German Reich. The title appealed to me greatly. I was only sorry that I had not blown up at least a bridge, to justify the Nazi hospitality.

The numbers had to be sewn on the jackets on the left-hand breast, and on the right trouser leg just above the knee. We looked very clean. In the evening, we also received a small rough towel and a small piece of soap which was to last for a month. We stood up in the troughs that evening and had a really good wash. There was singing and generally an amiable atmosphere.

The following day, after the morning *Appell*, we were grouped into working parties. The largest was Bauhof of some 800 men, then Ullersdorf (a new Arbeits-Kommando), and about a dozen others of some hundred men each. Each group had a Vorarbeiter who were running to and fro, shouting orders and generally trying (successfully) to impress their subordinates.

I stood with the Bauhof group. The Vorarbeiter knew me as he was a friend of Blockälteste 4 as well, and told me to stand in the last row. Then the Blockälteste appeared and whispered to follow him. Dad looked puzzled, but said nothing. The Blockälteste led me to the office building, and bade me to stand outside the door marked 'Tischlerei'. 'Don't worry Hoffnung, your Vorarbeiter is a friend of mine,' he said and went off.

* Patyu says that they wore a red triangle over an upside-down yellow one.

A few minutes later, a dozen people appeared. Four went into the tailor shop, four into the shoemakers' and four came to the carpentry [workshop].

A short and very broad-faced young man came up to me. 'You are from Block 4?' he asked. 'I am,' I replied. 'Gunther told 'em to expect you,' he spoke with a Polish accent. 'Come in and we'll see what you can do. My name is Stefan, but they call me Pilsudski. What do they call you?' 'Hugo Green,' I said. 'Hugo,' he laughed. 'Hugo, co . . . długo. That's good.'

What he said in Polish was a corny rhyme on Hugo, meaning that Hugo spent a long time on the lavatory, and was repeated by every Pole who has learned my name ever since.*

The carpentry [workshop] was a small room, kept clean but not too well-equipped. Of the tools and benches the majority were home-made, though by people who knew their job. Pilsudski was in charge and soon after all the people had marched out of the camp, he and the other three carpenters grabbed some tools and departed. I was told: 'Oil the saws and start cutting wood for some tables and chairs. The design and measurements are on that sheet.' Pilsudski pointed at a piece of paper dangling in a solitary fashion from the wooden wall.

The oiling part was easy. With great enthusiasm I collected seven saws, three large and four small ones. Then I found a bottle of liquid which was dirty enough to be oil, and with a broken-down brush, I began to oil the saws. Essentially, there was nothing to it, I thought. I was made for oiling saws, but after the fifth one was finished, I began to doubt my ability to cut out the wood for tables and chairs. Until that time, my only connection with the art of sawing was that I used to watch a man in our backyard cut up logs and then, with an axe, subdivide the logs and build up a pile of which any

---

* The correct translation is 'why . . . so long?' The reference to the lavatory is not obvious to other Polish speakers.

constructional engineer would have been proud. But our woodsman* never let me do any of the cutting. How – the question loomed in outsized proportion – was I going to cut wood to measure?

At this moment the door was opened and an SS corporal stood in the doorway. I jumped up and, according to previous training, tore off my cap and stood at attention.

'You will bring firewood to the guard room, prisoner, but quickly!' he said.

'What wood should I use?' I asked, and added: 'This is my first day in the carpentry [workshop].'

'Use any wood you like, but quick, man, quick!' and with this, he banged the door behind him.

There was plenty of wood in the room, and a pile behind the barracks, too. I knew, only too well, that this wood was intended for tables and chairs. But orders were orders, and wood had to be cut. I would have been glad of Pilsudski's presence, but he did not say when he would get back. There was only one thing to do: cut up the boards. There was a large margarine carton in one corner and into this I dumped the bits of wood obtained after a process which involved one large and one small saw, an axe and a chisel. This last instrument was sharp beyond all expectations and cut deeply into my left thumb.

Eventually the box was full and, gingerly, I picked it up, opened the door with my bleeding thumb and made for the gate. There was not a soul in sight, except the guards in their mounted boxes and the solitary sentry in the box just outside the gate. The guards' barracks was a few yards from the gate.

'The officer told me to bring this wood,' I said. The guard, an SS man wearing spectacles, looked as if he was expecting

---

* The same woodcutter Hugo had once decided was one of the legendary *lamed vav tsadikim*, the thirty-six righteous men. See Chapter 3, p. 25.

the wood and shouted: 'Erich!',* whereupon another SS man emerged, came to the gate and took the box from me. 'Wait for the box!' ordered the guard. In a few seconds, Erich returned with the empty box, handed it to me and motioned me to leave. The whole scene resembled a pantomime.

Back in the workshop, I did not know what to do. Or rather, I knew I should cut out the measurements, but did not know how to. On the other hand, I could go on chopping wood and push the responsibility on to the corporal, who had not, in fact, said how much he wanted to be cut. The latter idea was more appealing, and for the next two hours I cut up planks and boards until there was hardly any wood left untouched in the room. I made about eight trips to the guard, who looked very surprised after the second lot, but said nothing. No doubt he thought the corporal had ordered it, and to have asked me would have been far beneath his dignity. By the time I had carted out all the wood it was getting on for noon.

I was just on the point of carrying some more boards into the workshop, when Pilsudski and his trio returned. He entered and looked around without saying a word for at least a minute. Then he asked, 'Where is the wood?' I explained to him what had happened. 'But did the Nazi,' he interrupted, 'want all of the wood?' I said I did not know about that, but was not going to take any chances. The Pole had a brainwave. 'Tell me, Hugo, for how long have you worked in carpentry?' I began to stammer, but he asked again. 'Have you ever worked in carpentry before?' Realizing how futile it was to hold out any longer, I said, 'No.' The other three laughed, but Pilsudski went on relentlessly with his cross-examination. 'Why did you say you were a carpenter?'

* Of all the SS guards at Lieberose, only three were ever brought to trial. One, SS Rottenführer Erich Schemel, was given a prison sentence of four and a half years. Perhaps this was the same 'Erich'. Hans Zöller was sentenced to three years, while the camp leader, Wilhelm Kersten, was sentenced to just seven months.

I began to explain how, in Auschwitz, we had been advised to have a trade, and how we hoped that we would not be found out before we had learnt at least a little about our respective trades. I asked Pilsudski not to be too annoyed about the wood and said that at least they would not have to cut any more for a few days.

'Maybe so,' agreed Pilsudski, 'but this was our supply of wood for the whole week, and specifically for furnishing the top barracks. The SS are not supposed to get any wood from here, or from us at all. Had they caught you, you would have had a really bad beating!'

But he was not unkind. The others laughed a lot and I was unsure whether I should join in their mirth or look repentant. At this point a gong diverted our attentions. *'Suppe holen!'** someone shouted outside and I saw two pale Russians come out of the shoe shop and make for the kitchen. Meanwhile, we gathered outside, some eighteen people, all armed with bowls of various sizes and shapes, save me. Pilsudski told me to get on the end of the line, then he disappeared. The two Russians returned, carrying a twenty-five litre container. It was opened by the Secretary who had a litre-sized dishing-out spoon. Actually, it was a tin cleverly fixed on to a broomstick and with it he gave everyone one and a quarter measures. When Pilsudski reappeared, he was carrying a red enamel bowl, not unlike those used in surgeries to contain contaminated cotton wool. In fact, I suspected that it had belonged to the Hospital at one time.

'Now you have your own bowl,' said Pilsudski handing it over to me, 'if anyone asks you how you got it, say you found it in your bed, but forget that I gave it to you!' Why should I forget? I wondered.

The soup was good. It filled half of the bowl, but I scraped it clean with a handleless spoon that was also given to me by Pilsudski.

* Soup-fetching.

14

LIBERATION

This is where my father's account abruptly ends, although he left handwritten notes detailing other incidents he intended to relate. To piece together the missing months from his nightmare as a teenage slave labourer, the following is culled from interviews, radio scripts and other previously unpublished writings:

More and more people kept arriving at Lieberose as that summer wore on into autumn, and winter came on. I think the most pathetic sight was the arrival of Greek Jews who could not cope with the cold weather. By this time we had a very high death rate. I worked out my own equation, which was that on the amount of food that we were given, it was mathematically impossible to do the kind of work that was expected of us and live. Therefore, since there was not a whole lot I could do about increasing the amount of food, I looked for every way I could to not expend more energy than I had to.

Once, when we were on a detail where you had to fill cement bags and then carry them two at a time, I managed to fill four with insulating material, which weighed next to nothing, and I used them to ease my labour. And sometimes you could find a bolt-hole and rest up for a couple of hours in the middle of the day. It was not always easy, or possible, but as you became an experienced prisoner you learned the ropes.

Conserve energy, steal a potato, carefully kill the lice every night, do not eat the daily ration of bread at once, never volunteer for working assignments, cajole inside work in winter, work slowly, never walk near the rifle-butt of the SS guard.

I had no illusions about our captors. I never even wanted to think that they were better than they were. To think that way could be a trap. People tried to curry favour with the guards sometimes to try to survive better, but that was a very dangerous game, because the guards' moods were not consistent. I tried to have as little as possible to do with them. As far as possible you kept your head low, although it was inevitable that from time to time you would attract their attention. If that happened, you could always fall back on the fact that you were not a person, just a number.

The main project of this camp was a place called Ullersdorf, in a very pretty forest, where we were building a resort town for Nazi officers and their families – a bit like Pitom and Ramses, which the children of Israel had to build when they were slaves in Egypt. I do not think any of the buildings were ever completed. All the work assignments had to do with some form of construction, quarrying building materials and building itself. At one point I was a *Läufer*, a runner, which was a good job.

I remember an argument with my uncle Viktor. He wanted to show his people that he was a good worker. I was still a kid, yet I tried to point out to him the error of his ways and I said 'Uncle Viktor, it is not possible, who do you have to impress?' He even tried to tell me, 'You know, you ought to do more and you ought to run faster', and I said 'But why?' It was a different perception of reality. Of course he was already fading. The signs were so predictable: the beginning of the swelling of the ankles, the swelling moving upwards, and the sure knowledge that by the time the swelling reached above your knees, your days were literally numbered.

This was a sign of kidney failure, heart failure; the system was packing up. Viktor also had these swellings under his eyes – water retention. It was an irreversible process. I do not think anybody recovered from them. I remember I always used to watch my father's legs. Please, please, please don't start to swell. Uncle Viktor died and so did many other people.

One of the doctors working in the camp hospital was the father of one of the boys at my school in Debrecen. They were from Cluj* in Transylvania. He was not together with his son, who was actually two or three years older than I was; they were separated at Auschwitz. He took pity on me when I was punished once for stealing a spanner.§ He suggested that I vary my story slightly and say that I was really a medical student, and he would ask for me to come and work with him in the hospital. Sure enough, one day I was asked by one of the administration, 'Were you a medical student?' I said, 'Well, yes.' He said, 'We have you down as a carpenter and joiner.' But by now my stories of carpentry were exploded anyway, and I said, 'Actually, I'm a medical student.'

So I went to work with him during November. The place was dirty, a lot of gangrene. I was an anaesthetist, believe it or not. It was a very simple form of anaesthesia. I poured out some ether on to a piece of cotton wool or gauze and just held it to people's noses. By this time it was bitter cold and at least I was indoors.

In the camps there was 'a regression to primitiveness', that is to say, our interests became restricted to the most immediate and urgent needs. Food and water and sleep. Because there was hardly any food and crowded conditions combined with vermin, plus fourteen hours of work a day, gave little chance for sleep, we were in the main apathetic

---

* Kolozsvár in Hungarian.

§ Hugo was caught out by an unexpected inspection and found to have tucked the stolen spanner into his shoe. He was given twenty-five lashes as a punishment. For him, the worst part of the experience was that, along with the other prisoners, his father was forced to watch the spectacle.

and irritable. Not so much like zombies as tired animals. All thinking was concentrated on a simple and single point: get through today! Survive another day!

There was an important change in the meaning of some key values. Freedom is something you and I consider that we *have*, and if you are imprisoned it is taken away. But in the camps, freedom became what you *were*, and this shaped the attitudes you formed to your situation and your destiny. Apathy could only be overcome by force of spirit. Or you could give in to it and thus disintegrate from within. Irritability and brutalization could only be suppressed through intellectual and emotional effort. If you could not do this, you became less, considerably less, than a civilized human being.

The worst handicap had to do with time. No one knew when the experience would end. It made for a sense of helplessness. Viktor Frankl, a psychiatrist who was himself in the camps, wrote about a fellow-prisoner who dreamt that on 30 March 1945 the war would end and he would be liberated. No real news was possible and when nothing happened, the man developed a high fever on 29 March and died the next day of typhoid. Disillusionment, according to Dr Frankl, brought a quick decline of bodily defences.*

My own experience bears this out: there was always a spate of rumours about food from the Red Cross, of the approach of the Russian army, or the proximity of the Americans, and when events proved them false, morale dropped like a cement bag. Only an inner sensation, that in the end evil would be defeated, gave any kind of certainty.

Our SS guards loved their dogs and music, and in some of the bigger camps inmates were recruited into orchestras, which performed on Sunday afternoons to mark the end of our working week. But these were grotesque concerts, with

---

* *Man's Search for Meaning* (*Ein Psycholog erlebt das Konzentrationslager*, Viktor E. Frankl, Austria 1946.

the shaven-headed musicians in their striped pyjama uniforms on a rickety platform, facing an audience of off-duty
guards and their dogs sitting on benches. Behind them, often
on muddy ground, we sat – exhausted and hungry; and behind
us, high in their turrets, the guards who were on duty, pointing
machine-guns on us. I remember the scene but not many of
the sounds from these concerts.

One of the songs which does haunt me was in Hebrew, a
line from the Thirteen Articles of Faith by Moses Maimonides:
Ani Ma'amin – 'I believe'. 'I believe,' we used to sing, 'with
perfect faith in the coming of the Messiah, and though he
tarry, yet will I believe!' Pushing carts of refuse or carrying
cement bags we sang quietly, almost to ourselves. Once a
Dutch Protestant fellow prisoner asked me what the words
meant. I told him, but I am not sure that he believed me.

Another song was written [in Yiddish] by Hirsch Glick who
was born in Vilna in Lithuania. He was not yet twenty when
he wrote it and he was killed in 1944 when he was barely
twenty-two. It was sung by Jewish partisans in Russian forests,
doomed ghetto fighters in Polish towns, and by so many of
us on long marches from camp to camp on which so few
returned.

> *Zog nit Keynmol az du geyst dem letstn veg*
> *Chotsh himlen blayene farshteln bloye teg*
> *Kumen vet noch undzer oysgebenkte sho*
> *S'vet a poyk ton undzer trotmir zenen do!*

> 'Never say that you now walk the final way
> Because the darkened heavens hide the blue of day
> The time we long for will at last draw near
> And our steps, like drums, will say that we are here.'

In the Warsaw Ghetto, in its relatively early days, there was
a kind of debate going on among the leadership, particularly
the religious leadership of the ghetto, about resistance. There

was a rabbi in Warsaw whose name was Lieberman, who argued: 'Don't be passive in the face of evil.' Well, that was not easy for everyone. But in the same Warsaw ghetto in the spring of 1943, the remnants of that ghetto – about 50,000 of them – revolted against the mighty German army. They already knew and they understood that the choice was really no longer between life and death, but between one kind of death and another kind of death. And so they took on the full might of the German army even though they were ultimately destroyed.

On one occasion in Lieberose, I was party to the killing of a guard. There were a lot of Ukrainian volunteers in the SS and they were even nastier than German Nazis. They really enjoyed torturing and beating up prisoners. But there was one who was particularly dangerous, and particularly violent. He could not have been more than eighteen or nineteen. When his superiors were not looking he had the vicious habit of swinging his rifle above his head and bringing its butt down anywhere at random on a head, a shoulder, a leg – and once that happened to you, you were finished. They were lethal blows. He was a terrible menace and the whole camp was in terror of him.

Once on a work detail, we had to go back in the middle of the day to fetch the soup containers. Two people with wooden staves per container, and we were entitled to two such containers, so four people went back with this one guard. We stopped, he came close to see why and I was one of the people who held him while one of the others used that bloody gun of his. He was beaten to death because we did not want to make a noise and we buried him there. Fortunately he was not wearing his steel helmet. It was just a cloth cap.

The problem was how to disguise it. There was no way to dig a proper grave so we buried him beneath leaves and decided to leave his gun because we could not carry it with us. We debated about what to do with the gun, but we had no screwdriver and did not know how to take it apart.

We were able to sneak back into the work area unobserved

and mingle with the other prisoners and I don't think they missed him until the end of work. We stood outside that evening for hours. They would never tell us why, but obviously we knew, and I was in great fear for many days that possibly one of the others might own up. Then they found his body and tried to reconstruct what had happened. We were quizzed and they took a lot of people out for punishment. They counted one out of ten; they called it in German 'Zehntel', one, two, three, four, five, six, seven, eight, nine, ten. You! It depended on where you stood.

Looking back on it, I think we had both a moral and a physical responsibility to resist, if needs be, with violence. Passive resistance would have been absolutely no use in such a desperate situation. I had heard that if you could get sugar into a combustion engine, it would seize up. So during my Bauhof period, once a week or so we were given some marmalade. I assumed that there had to be some sugar in it, although I suspected that it was all synthetic. I did not eat the marmalade, I collected it. I had a funny little tin. I collected portions and portions of marmalade, carried them on my person and when I could, unobserved, I would open the petrol cap of lorries and pour it all in. Or, when working near railway lines, my favourite occupation was to remove bolts and nuts, hoping that one day a train might break down. It was really a pathetic form of sabotage, but it motivated me a lot.

That year the festival of Chanukah was early – the first week of December. The Jewish prisoners in our barracks – Block 4 – decided that we would celebrate it by lighting a menorah every night. Bits of wood and metal were collected and shaped into lightholders and everyone agreed to save the week's meagre ration of margarine that would be used for fuel. It was my job to take apart an abandoned prison cap and fashion wicks from its threads.

Finally, the first night of Chanukah arrived. Most of Block 4 gathered around the menorah – including some Roman

Catholic Poles, several Protestant Norwegians and the Blockälteste himself – a German count who was implicated in the
attempt on Hitler's life but had somehow had his life spared.
Two portions of margarine were melted down – my wicks in
place – but as we chanted the blessing, praising God who
'performed miracles for our ancestors in those days at this
time', and as the youngest person there, I tried to light the
wick, there was only a bit of spluttering and no flame whatsoever. What the 'scientists' in our midst failed to point out
was that margarine does not burn!

And as we dispersed and made our way to the bunk beds I
turned not so much to my father, but on him, upset at the
fiasco and bemoaning this waste of precious calories.
Patiently, he taught me one of the most lasting lessons of my
life and I believe that he made my survival possible.

'Don't be so angry,' he said to me, 'you know that this
festival celebrates the victory of the spirit over tyranny and
might. You and I have had to go once for over a week without
proper food and another time almost three days without
water, but you cannot live for three minutes without hope!'

By this time, hunger was very great and it was bitterly cold.
Then we had to evacuate Lieberose and go to Sachsenhausen
on foot. When we left Lieberose, we were marched some
distance away, stopped, and then we heard lots of firing and
then smoke. They killed and set on fire everybody who could
not move out.* This march was dreadful. Snow, mud. And

* This Death March began on the morning of 2 February. See footnote on
page 120. They arrived at Sachsenhausen on 10 February. Andreas Weigelt
reports that 'the number of prisoners on 2 February was approximately
3,500. 1200 were killed in Jamlitz, 700 were transported from Jamlitz by
train on 31 January to Sachsenhausen (all of them died or were killed
in Sachsenhausen) and 1600 went on the march. We have no official
documents' [letter of 10 May 1999]. A mass grave with 577 bodies was
found in May 1971 and according to Andreas, the Staatssicherheit – the

when dusk came, turn left or turn right, walk into the nearest field, get down. In the morning, get up, except for those who could not get up, then we would move forward, wait a while, hear the shots and move on.

We went first to Falkensee and then we marched right through Berlin into Sachsenhausen, which is where I worked, most astonishingly, loading forged British banknotes on to lorries. I was at Sachsenhausen for some time; then out again to Mauthausen in Austria, and that journey was by train.* There I was sent on a working detail into a quarry. It was dreadful. In Mauthausen I met some very unusual prisoners, including some Hungarian politicians – the very ones who were party to what had happened to us – eventually they found their way there, too.

On one occasion, instinct saved my life again. We were in this huge tent, packed with people. It was an extraordinarily cold spring, still snowing; it must have been late March or early April. My father and I were together and I panicked in this tent, insisting that we had to creep out. We could not make our way to the entrance, which was at the far end and we were in another corner, so we lifted the canvas, crept under and found our way out. Under a tree there were a few other people who could not fit into the tent. It was chaotic. The only time we were direct victims of a bomb attack was that night. Whether it was an accident or deliberate I do not know. A bomb fell exactly on the corner where we had been sitting in the tent. In fact I was asleep when it happened, although obviously it is a noise that wakes you up.

*

secret service of the GDR – who were responsible for the exhumation, searched the corpses for gold teeth before cremating them. A second mass grave has still to be found.

  * Hugo was in Mauthausen from 29 February to 13 April 1945. [Statement made to *Heim des Landeskomitees für Deportiertenfürsorgs* on 4 July 1945]

For three days during a bizarre and snowy Passover, in April 1945, seventeen thousand of us were force-marched to an even more appalling place called Gunskirchen. This march was even worse than the one to Sachsenhausen because, by this time, practically everyone was sick. There was almost no food at all, and the casualties were horrendous. Less than half completed this march.

Some other people were there already. It was very makeshift and crowded. The weather was very bad and in Gunskirchen itself conditions were terrible.* What food there was, we were told afterwards on fairly good authority, was being poisoned. There was deep mud, fever and stench and many perished from starvation and the typhoid which by then had infected every one of us. People took water out of ditches and caught things like frogs. Whatever was available was devoured. There was even, I think, a certain amount of cannibalism.

That is where on 5 May 1945, just three days before the formal end of the Second World War in Europe, the American troops came and liberated us.§ We had expected it to happen for some days. We knew it could not be far off. We saw plenty of signs of it even on our march and knew that we were being marched from Mauthausen to Gunskirchen to put us further away from the possibility of being liberated.

* There were seven unfinished huts, with 2500 prisoners compressed into each hut, so that the weak were crushed to death at night. There was one twenty-hole latrine. 'The rule of the SS men was to shoot on sight anyone seen relieving himself in any place but the latrine. Many of the persons in the camp had diarrhoea. There were always long lines at the latrine and it was often impossible for many to reach it in time because of hours spent waiting. Naturally, many were shot for they could not wait in line. Their bodies were still lying there in their own filth. The stench was unbelievable.' [Capt. J. D. Pletcher, *The Seventy-first Came to Gunskirchen Lager*, Atlanta 1979]

§ Gunskirchen was actually discovered by American soldiers one day earlier, on 4 May, but Hugo always remembered 5 May 1945 as the date of his liberation.

For the Nazis, the destruction of the Jews had an unchanging function until the very end of the war; it was the only thing about which they never changed their policies. I have never ceased to be amazed by the priority they gave it, even when everything was collapsing. And they knew these marches themselves were very destructive, that people would have – as it were – a natural death by being force-marched fifty, sixty miles without food. They knew that they were losing and it began to enter their minds that they might be held account-able, but dead witnesses cannot give evidence. And I suppose that if we had not been liberated on 5 May, no one would have still been alive. Another week, maybe ten days. It was a close thing.

It was sunny. Around mid-morning we could hear distant gunfire coming closer, the rumbling of tanks. Suddenly our guards, the most sadistic bunch of Ukrainian teenagers who had volunteered for the SS and were still too small for the standard uniforms, and some elderly but no less vicious Aus-trians who were too large for them – literally the dregs of the SS – dropped their guns, stripped off their death's-head insignia, and started to run.

Suddenly there appeared an American tank and that was, as far as I was concerned, the end of the war. On the tanks, the five-pointed star of the United States, and crouching behind them, soldiers who took one look at us and began to throw their food rations in our direction before moving on. Behind them followed infantry soldiers, and both fired at the retreating Germans. By the time this blessed and bloody procession had passed beyond our camp – we sat there, silent, unbelieving, and free.

Some more American soldiers arrived. They came into the camp, clearly shocked by the sight of emaciated people – at that point I weighed about thirty kilos – and the piles of still unburied corpses. Quickly, generously, and as it turned out unwisely, they shared whatever food supplies they had with us. Of the people who were still alive on 5 May, many died in the days that immediately followed. Perhaps because the typhoid and physical weakness had gone too far. And with some, perhaps because of the sudden intake of heavy food after a very long time of under-nourishment.

Behind the barbed wire, you can imagine what we looked like, but for the first time in years, despite so many odds, we were free. My father, by then barely alive, but still conscious, motioned me to sit next to him and together we said the familiar blessing, praising God who sustained us, kept us in life, and brought us to that day. The rest of that day and many of the ones that followed are blurred in my memory, but not the blessed taste of liberty, nor will it ever leave me. To be able to come and go as you please, to think and speak without fear, to decide what you want to eat or wear or read or do . . .

Those who could move about went out of the camp and began foraging for food. There were some farms around there and I caught a chicken. I did not know what to do with it. I had never killed a chicken before and I did not know how to kill this one so I gave it to one of the older people there.

By late afternoon some medics came into the camp too. What must have horrified them was that by this time we had in the camp a very large number of unburied dead and many very sick people. The rest were just sick.

Even though I was ill with typhoid myself, I was still able to move, and I helped to load people on to lorries. We were taken to a place called Hörsching, to what must have been a German Luftwaffe barracks, near Linz, and put into clean beds. My father and I shared a bed, and he died in my arms, about three days after we got there. For him, liberation was just a few days too late. It was horrible. It seemed so unfair. I could never have survived without the support of my father. He was there all the time and I really believed that we had made it.

At that moment, effectively, I gave up. I went berserk and lost consciousness. There is a period about which I remember nothing and I am not sure how long it lasted, either. I was told that as they carried my father out – they were using German orderlies for the work of carrying out the dead – I went for one of them, I wanted to kill him. I was restrained and sedated and I did not see my father's body again. I do not know where he is buried. They must have put him into a mass grave.

I have no memory of dates or sequences of events, only that it was some time in May. I have tried to reconstruct it, what must have happened, and I cannot. I wanted to write it down for my own sake, but there is no precision, so it is very difficult. When I came to, an older ex-prisoner in that ward told me, 'Remember that your *yarzheit** is *daled b'sivan*, the fourth day of Sivan,' but it doesn't figure – that would put it too far in May and my guess is that he just told me so that at least I would have a day. Maybe I was not even told it, but a date stuck, even though all it may be is an indication of the chaotic state of my mind at the time.§

I heard that the American president, Franklin Roosevelt had died sometime earlier, before the end of the war. I remember crying about that because somehow he was perceived by us as being a great friend of the Jewish people. We now know that it was a somewhat unrequited love affair, certainly on his part, but I did not know that at the time and thought it was terrible that he was dead too. So I mourned my father and I mourned President Roosevelt, but I was a free man.

A few days later an SS man, Sergeant Kakadu, was captured

---

* The anniversary of a parent's death, according to the Hebrew lunar calendar, observed by lighting a memorial candle and reciting the Kaddish.

§ In the statement he gave on 4 July 1945, Hugo reported that Géza had died on 16 May, twelve days after their liberation, which correlates correctly with this Hebrew date. Over the years his memory must have compressed the sequence of events that followed his liberation.

by some of the boys. He was one of the guards of old, with us in Mauthausen and in Gunskirchen and extraordinarily brutal. God knows how many people he had killed by hitting them for no reason. He was brought to Hörsching. Suddenly word went round, 'everybody go to the windows'. They dragged him into the quadrangle of the hospital complex we were in and everybody crowded to the windows. He was being strung up. At one point, one or two of the American soldiers tried to stop it but diplomatically withdrew, and they proceeded to execute him right there in the courtyard.

I was a feverish skeleton and it took a long time before I could be cheerful again. But in the end, life took over, and I got better. My hair grew again, my teeth became firm in my gums again, and I wanted to go home, to see if anybody else had survived. If they had, I assumed that they would go home.

It was a strange and never-to-be-forgotten journey back to Berehovo. From Linz, the American army arranged for a group of us to board a ship on the Danube. As things went at that time, I was relatively rich: I was well-dressed, in my rucksack I had three cartons of Lucky Strike cigarettes and as I did not smoke in those days, they were worth a fortune. I had several dozen packs of chewing-gum – an unexpected status symbol – which could be readily bartered for food and drink and the kind authorities even gave me a handful of dollar bills. What more could anyone have wanted?

The boat left – for Budapest we believed – but we only got as far as Wiener Neustadt, still in Austria, but on the Russian side of the border, because the captain believed that there were still some unexploded mines in the river, and refused to go on. We had to get off.

By that time my chest had become infected and swelled like a single breast, full of pus, throbbing and I was running a high fever. I made my way to a Russian army camp, where a Russian doctor took a liking to me – 'nasher' ('one of us') –

because I spoke fluent Russian. He said the boil was not yet ready for lancing and put some stuff on it. The next day, 25 June – my fifteenth birthday – it was ready for the operation. But they had run out of anaesthetic in the hospital, so the doctor rigged up the next best thing, and searched out the two biggest breasted nurses, who flanked me on either side and gripped my wrists – which they could have crushed, they were so strong – and clutched my hands into their massive bosoms.

To a fifteen-year-old this was second only to heaven and quite took over my attention as the doctor sliced open the giant swelling, filling an entire washing-up bowl with the stinking gunge and then put into the ripped flesh a piece of gauze, saturated with brown ointment developed for treating gun wounds, which felt deliciously cool to the burning flesh. The relief once the thing had been lanced was enormous – it was almost symbolic – the ugly pus which came out was like all the badness I had been through leaving me. I know that I saw it as symbolic even then. It was a turning point for me. Within two days the injury was healed and I was ready to continue my journey home.

Life being what it was, three new friends and I waited until dark, 'borrowed' a horse and a cart from a sleeping farmer and headed for the Slovakian capital of Bratislava, where – we were told – there was a regular train service east. Three days later, dusty and hot, we got there. We made our way to the Jewish Community Centre, where I handed in my papers and took a shower. When I got out of the shower I discovered that all of my possessions had been stolen. Everything I had worked so hard to organize was gone.

The community centre workers found some other clothes – some filthy black shorts, an absurd Belgian prisoner-of-war jacket with big brass buttons and a pair of canvas-topped clogs. Scarcely a replacement for the beautiful American army shirt I had arrived with. And no underwear. They returned my liberation certificate and some Czech money and I headed for the railway station.

I caught a night-train to Budapest. I remember that there were hundreds of people waiting for this train – the only train there was – but I managed to find out which siding it was on and climbed aboard before it was rolled to the platform. I got into one of the better carriages – one with windows, for the trains were very beaten-up just after the war – took a seat and, exhausted from the trials of the day, fell asleep. That night was very memorable. When the train pulled into the platform no one got into my carriage although the train was packed. Then I saw why: it was reserved for Russian soldiers. But when they arrived they did not throw me out. They were friendly, and we started to chat. They asked why I looked such a sorry sight and I told them my saga.

In the middle of the night they got up and started to rob the train. Most of the passengers were peasants going to sell their produce – chickens and so forth – on the black market in Budapest. These soldiers fleeced the passengers, returning with blankets filled with bounty – watches, money, the lot. They were kids, not much older than I was, and I think they reckoned the Hungarians owed them something; but when they returned to our compartment, they cut me in for some of their loot, with the result that I arrived in Budapest in the morning wearing a Russian uniform. And I had three full wallets, six or seven watches – including an Omega – three bottles of slivovitz and a loaded gun with some spare ammunition that I later discovered did not fit. The soldiers even helped stuff the toes of a pair of too-large boots with newspaper.

At Budapest, I found that the connecting train to Berehovo was not leaving for several hours. I remembered the address of my mother's aunt, Arunka, and went there early in the morning. I rang the bell. My great-aunt and her daughter came to the door in their dressing-gowns and stared rudely at me, kitted out in my strange collection of Russian army dress. 'What do you want?' they asked. 'It's me. Hugo.' 'Yes. So?'

I only wanted to know who was alive, whether they had heard from my mother. They did not even ask me in and only retorted with banalities like: 'Your mother doesn't live in Budapest', and 'We had a hard time here ourselves, you know' – they had lived in the Budapest Ghetto through the war years. I pointed out that I had money and wanted nothing. 'Good, so you'll be able to get home.' I was filthy. 'So you'll be able to wash at the railway station,' they said when I told them I would be catching the afternoon train.

Devastated, I left, wanting to sob, but I was fifteen going on seventy and did not show a thing. Then I made my way back to the train station and waited for the train back to Berehovo.

15

20:20 HINDSIGHT

In the mid-1970s, Hugo was shocked to see some of the Holocaust denial literature that had then begun to proliferate. Invited to appear on BBC TV's Light of Experience in January 1978, he spoke publicly for the first time about the Holocaust: 'I have a confession to make. After many years of relative silence, I am now conscious of a witness complex in myself. There have been some despicable and obscene attempts to play down the Jewish Holocaust as a fabrication perpetrated by the Jews themselves, and I have a growing urge to speak for and on behalf of those who no longer can. I subscribe to what has become my version of the eleventh commandment: Thou shall not grant Hitler a posthumous victory. Thou shalt survive.* Recently I have felt a growing pressure to tell my story of survival. Tonight is my opportunity to share it with you . . .'

He dedicated an entire year of public speaking engagements to themes on the Holocaust, and for the rest of his life, whenever anyone asked, he gave an honest and considered reply, as if he were a witness giving evidence at a trial. These are some of his reflections, with the benefit – as he used to say – of 20:20 hindsight. They are drawn from a number of sources, including radio and television broadcasts, articles and lecture notes.

---

* Adapted from a phrase first coined by philosopher Emil Fackenheim.

When we arrived in Auschwitz, it was a bright, sunny day and a series of jet streams appeared in the sky. They may have been experimental V2 bombs, but I had not seen such a sight before, and for a while I believed that God Himself would now intervene. In the days that followed the transformation from schoolboy into prisoner was both swift and slow. I was certainly not as conscious of it then as I am now, but an internal rearrangement was taking place.

Externally we were entirely at the mercy of the guards. Not only were we surrounded day and night with electrified wire, but we were permanently in the sight of rifles or machine-guns. It was also clear that these arrangements were entirely bereft of normal human feelings and reactions and we had become nothing but numbers. I was 80,494. The difficult job was not to become that in our own eyes. I realized that I would have to develop certain qualities if I was to survive emotionally and spiritually, not to mention physically. Feeling had to become, and did become, an entirely inner condition. Dignity meant I had to maintain self-respect and to see that the elegant, well-fed guards were merely mechanical parts of a death machine. And to see in the *Muselmänner,** as our captors took to calling us when we began to look emaciated, a redeeming humanity. Hope was to believe that evil would be destroyed, even though it looked invincible, with no evidence whatsoever of any forces of good.

And there was faith. That God knew what was happening. That he let it happen and that it had a purpose. Most of the time this was difficult. Too difficult.

I knew then, and know now, that my survival had nothing to do with being different or better or more deserving. And one of my burdens, indeed an irrational sense of guilt ever since, has been precisely that I do not know why I survived. In all sorts of ways much of what I have tried to do and tried

* Muslims.

to be ever since has been to give some sense and meaning to that survival.

Being in slave labour camps after Auschwitz gave me a measure of breathing space. I had periods of reflection, especially about guilt – and one early realization was that I was not guilty. I knew that I was innocent and that, contrary to appearances, it was our gaolers who were the guilty ones. It was a conviction that I never lost, even though everything around us was designed to convince us otherwise. The armed guards, the dogs, our complete powerlessness, our reduction to numbers and the actual behaviour of many fellow prisoners – cringing, servile, defeatist. Yet my knowledge, I believe, saved my sanity. On the other hand, there was a dreadful feeling, probably common to many people in prison, that in one important respect I was already dead. My father and I were together, but the rest of my family I knew had perished, and therefore there was no one anywhere outside this situation who could remember me.

One experience gave me lasting understanding of what it means to be abandoned. We were slave labourers in Lieberose. I was fourteen years old, but already a seasoned prisoner. We had to be up before dawn and work until dusk six and a half days – rain or shine, hot or cold. Only on Sunday afternoons did we have a few hours of rest.

On one of these Sunday afternoons there was a surprise announcement: everyone could send a postcard – anywhere in the world – courtesy of the Red Cross! Quickly, and with much excitement, long lines formed around some trestle tables and soon I was given a blank card together with one of those indelible pencils that you had to lick before use.

The prospect of contact with the outside world was exciting. That world, beyond the electrified barbed-wire fence, which was so near and yet so far. I found a quiet spot behind the infirmary – began to lick my pencil – and thought over the painful question: to whom was I to write? All my family were gone. Those much older than me – grandparents, uncles, aunts – had already perished at Auschwitz and certainly all those who were younger than me. Nor did I know if my mother or anyone else in the family was still alive – much less where they might be. There was certainly no one left of family and friends in Berehovo and while I had an idea that we had relatives in America and Palestine, I had no idea of their addresses or even of their full names.

Gradually, the realization came that as far as I could see there was no one – anywhere in the world – to whom it mattered whether I was alive or not. After a while I returned to the trestle table and handed back the pencil and the blank card. And so did hundreds of others. We were silent and dispirited and our feeling of being abandoned was complete. The only thing I had to show for this experience was a purple stain on my tongue and around my lips which took many days to wear off.

It was a fairly common experience to find the lifeless body of one or more people hanging in the latrine-washroom first thing in the morning. At first I was horrified and angry at these suicides. But after the postcard episode, I began to understand better why they chose this grotesque setting for their final act of desperation. As the days grew shorter and the nights longer and the number of suicides increased, I was aware of my disapproval giving way to a kind of admiration and respect.

Two contradictory emotions governed much of my inner life. That I was innocent and that I was abandoned. They came to a head a few weeks later on Yom Kippur, the Day of Atonement. A day we had spent in the synagogue as far back as I could remember. We knew the date. On that day in 1944, I was at my place of work. Like many others, I fasted and cleared a little hiding place for myself amongst stacks of insulation boards. I spent most of the usual working day there, not even emerging for the thin soup given to us at midday. I tried to remember as many of the prayers as I could and recited them, even singing the *Kol Nidre*, asking for God's forgiveness for promises made and not kept. But eventually I dissolved in crying. I must have sobbed for hours. Never before or since have I cried with such intensity and then I seemed to be granted a curious inner peace. Something of it is still with me. I believe God was also crying. And I understood a bit of the revelation that is implicit in Auschwitz. It is about man and his idols. God, the God of Abraham, could not abandon me, only I could abandon God.

I would like you to understand that in that builder's yard on that Day of Atonement, I found God. But not the God I had childishly clung to until those jet streams dissolved over Auschwitz. People sometimes ask me 'Where was God in Auschwitz?' I believe that God was there Himself – violated and blasphemed. The real question is 'Where was man in Auschwitz?'

On 9 November 1938, when Kristallnacht – 'the night of broken glass' – got going, virtually every synagogue through-out Nazi Germany had its windows and doors smashed, its holy scrolls and books piled into bonfires. Crowds of school-children and their parents and grandparents, teachers and youth leaders, police and postmen stood in circles and shouted their *Heil*'s and sang their Horst Wessel songs. Behind them the night sky was lit up by the torched synagogues, Jewish shops looted and homes vandalized. By dawn, 91 Jews had been killed and the very next day over 35,000 Jews were arrested, sent to concentration camps – at Dachau, Buchen-wald, and Sachsenhausen – to be my own Alma Mater six years later. Within days hundreds died of torture, 244 in Buchenwald alone, and hundreds more committed suicide.

All this in the heart of Western civilization and there was no outrage. While handfuls of Jews protested, there were no mass demonstrations in Paris or Brussels or London or

Washington. Did they know? I often wonder if when you start to burn books and scrolls and holy places, it becomes thinkable and emotionally and politically feasible to burn men, women and children as well, because you are in fact setting fire to civilization and you are creating spiritual anarchy.

We tend to speak about the *Shoah* in terms of the victims – we know who they were – and the perpetrators – and we know who they were as well. But there was a third party to it, and increasingly I believe that all this became possible because of that third party, and they were the people who we call these days 'bystanders'. The people in my town, and in all the other cities and villages in Europe: the non-Jewish men and women who were not directly threatened or involved and who let it happen! Who did not protest, or interrupt, or show any significant anger. They were, it seemed to me then and still now, nice enough, ordinary people, but their moral sense had become blunted. Perhaps only for a time, but long enough to let wickedness have and rule the day.

Kristallnacht was aimed at and focused on Jews, and for six million of Europe's Jews, it was the beginning of the end, but it did not end there. Political and cultural dissidents followed, as did homosexuals and Seventh Day Adventists. In the name of racial purity, they rounded up Gypsies and annihilated them; Slavs were classed as *Untermenschen* and when we in the camps were at death's door, they called us *Muselmann*, or Muslim. No one is safe when religious or ethnic prejudice is tolerated, when racism is rife and when decent, well-meaning people keep quiet because it is prudent.

Thousands of people must have seen us marching. They saw what was happening, they saw what we looked like, yet I cannot recall one kind word, or encouragement, or somebody throwing an apple at us, or a potato, or a piece of bread. One often hears the claim that no one knew what was going on, but I categorically refute that. You could not live in that country and not know what was going on. Nobody actually came off the sidewalks and hit us, but I sensed a deep complicity with it. I really do not understand how could they not have reacted. It is a puzzling thing. Perhaps they saw us as the enemy.

While the *Shoah* marks the virtual destruction of Jewish life in Europe, it is certainly for Christians a disaster: it is the ultimate betrayal of the values for which Christianity stands. And for the academic institutions of Europe, the judiciary, industry, business, trade unions, educators. Because all parts of society colluded in one way or another. There was a natural inclination to sweep things under the carpet, but in the end, unless you confront these very dark and destructive bits in your history, and consciously try to make amends, and to mend the nastiness that is in you, it is likely to have a kind of underground life and crop up at all sorts of unexpected and inconvenient moments.

We must begin earnestly and without much more hesitation to understand what happened at Auschwitz, Warsaw, Dachau. Our generation will never come to terms with this and yet we must clear the way so that the wounds may gradually heal. We have to do protracted battle with our experiences and with our memories, to make sense of them if we can; to impress our fellow men with our terrible knowledge, lest we or our children or our children's children be doomed to suffer the agonies of its recurrence.

Just as creation itself is an ongoing process, so – I believe – is revelation. Here and there is a fresh glimpse of God and if you subject human history to a spiritual scrutiny, there are revelations about the state of our morality as well. There *was* revelation at Auschwitz – of a dreadful and devastating sort. Of what happens when a principle of evil is harnessed to up-to-date technology, and in an atmosphere that is denuded of morality.

In the intervening years, I have often thought how Auschwitz-Birkenau was the denial and the perversion of all the Ten Commandments, which stand for what we have come to call the Judaeo-Christian spiritual tradition and morality – and one of the pillars of Western civilization. In that Nazi empire, with its direct links between the pomp of Berlin and Berchtesgaden (where so many of Europe's leaders came to be entertained by Hitler and to applaud his plans and programme) and the unspeakable terror of the camps of Auschwitz-Birkenau and Bergen-Belsen, it was clear that:

I God was replaced by a Führer and his minions who claimed for themselves the power of life and death.

II They fashioned countless idols of silver and gold and filled their world with the sight of swastikas, the sound of *Heil Hitler!* and the smell of burning corpses.

III They swore falsely and made lies an instrument of state policy.

IV They created camps of slavery in which the hours of light were spent in forced labour and the darkness filled with loneliness and relentless hunger. In some of the camps I inhabited, the few workless hours were set aside for ritual punishment beatings.

V Children were made to watch the humiliation and debasement of their parents – and parents had children torn from their arms. Families were desecrated.

VI Murder was at the heart of that culture, and killers were promoted and honoured.

VII There was a reward for the betrayal of relationships and sexual abuse was rife.

VIII Stealing and looting were sanctioned on every level of Nazidom right down to gold teeth and fillings extracted from corpses.

IX Truth was the first and permanent casualty of the system.

X Covetousness, envy and unchecked greed became part

of the way of life. Neither person, nor property were respected. The spoilers' appetite for spoils knew no limits.

And when the gates of Auschwitz were opened and the world was able to take in and to react to what the heirs to the traditions of Luther and Goethe, of Mozart, Beethoven and Wagner, could perpetrate, and the pain of the remnant of my people – nurtured in Torah and Talmud and the people of Heine and Freud and Einstein and Martin Buber – both the image of God and the image of men and women were desecrated and besmirched.

One of the very few sustaining thoughts that I had when I was a prisoner was that one day the world would see what was done there. The systematic, indeed 'scientific' murder of innocent men, women and children. To whom it was done – in the Birkenau part of Auschwitz – to Jews from all parts of Europe, who for centuries did their best to cling to an ancient faith and never understood why anyone should want to revile them. They raised families, built caring communities and worked and prayed daily to complete the building of God's Kingdom on Earth. And not only to Jews, but to the equally innocent Gypsies – especially of Germany – and Russian prisoners of war. And in the nearby Auschwitz 1 camp – resisters of Nazism from throughout occupied Europe.

Who did it? Evil men and women who looked so much like ordinary men and women. Many of them were well-educated, some had even taken the Hippocratic Oath of healing, all of them in elegant uniforms. Well-fed and, I imagine, devoted to their parents and children, and who – day in and day out, week after week and month after month – stood at the head of selection lines, personally and directly prodded and pushed people into gas chambers; measured and poured cyanide pellets; fuelled the crematoria, kept meticulous records and filed proud reports.

This was my thought: that one day these people who made murder a virtue and the death of innocents a cause for celebration, that they would be exposed and made accountable and brought before some bars of civilized justice. Yes – and be punished for it!

There is also a sadness that will not go away. I keep seeing my brother and grandparents in the selection line in Auschwitz, and so many aunts and uncles and cousins and friends and neighbours – indeed most of the Jewish community of my hometown – slowly, unknowingly walking to their deaths. I think of all the love and laughter and learning that was extinguished with their lives – and often wonder how it was that I survived. Perhaps to give just this kind of testimony. I think of the homes they might have built, the illnesses they might have cured, the decencies that could have been performed, and how civilization could have been strengthened. There is a bit in me that would like to be anaesthetized and have all the memory of Auschwitz wiped out. But that cannot be, because so much of what I am was forged there and so much that could have been perished there.

When I think about the summer of 1945, when through a chance I cannot fathom, I was free and still in life, and filled with so many uncertainties, there was one certainty for me: that when the world saw and understood what unspeakable atrocities had been committed in the name of racism born of long-festering prejudice, intolerance and the deafening silence of decent bystanders – why, I was sure that never again would there be antisemitism, or race-hatreds of any kind and that nothing would ever again erode the Divine image imprinted in every human being and the dignity of individual men and women. The sad truth is that tyranny and race-hatred did not end when the Second World War ended, as we then hoped and believed but the vision for peace did not die.

People often say that time is a great healer. I am not sure

about that. What I think time does do for you, is that it gives you a perspective. On my [visit to Berehovo] I could not help but think that although Jews there were involved in the community over such a long time and although, particularly in the Czech period, they really had full legal equality – Jews owned land and worked in businesses and professions – the fact is that while Jews and non-Jews depended on each other for many of the essentials in life, and we lived in the same society, we were not really part of the same community. There was hardly any visiting, sharing, or gossiping.

I realize now that of Berehovo's three big and beautiful churches, I had never been inside any of them, and the chances are that none of the Christians ever set foot in any of our synagogues. And when the chips were down, I do not know of a single instance of a Jew [from Berehovo] being saved or hidden by a non-Jew. That I spend much of my time working for better understanding between religious groups, is partly because I know that you can only be safe and secure in a society that practises tolerance, cherishes harmony and can celebrate difference.

To people like me Israel is very special. It is the Jewish monument to the spirit of man who wants to live and not die, to build and not to destroy. It is the place where Jews exercise sovereignty. It turns out that it is still vulnerable, but it has got tremendous determination to do well. I believe that ultimately the test of any morality is what you do when you have power. For a very long time Jews – as Jews – were actually powerless, but now there is some Jewish power and it is going to be a very testing time to see what happens. I like to think that eventually history will come to judge us as having dealt responsibly and morally with the bit of power that we have. Israel has an awful responsibility on its shoulders. It must redeem land, which they have done in spectacular fashion. They must redeem people, which they are doing and who become, in an amazingly short time, productive, creative,

responsible members of society. But there is also an expectation for Israel to redeem history. And that is very difficult.

In the Book of Exodus, when the Children of Israel left Egypt
after a long period of degradation and suffering, the Passover
Service was instituted with the injunction that 'of that day
you shall tell your children'. Well, we who are older are trying
to say something to you who are younger and it is this: that
you are now comfortable in your home and not condemned
to being slave labourers. And you can read any book that you
like and not one ordered by a propaganda minister. That you
can worship where and how you like. Which is to say that
you have freedom to think your own thoughts and to live
your own life. But there are still so many prisons. Of poverty
and of ignorance, of loneliness and being abandoned, of political tyrannies and religious fanaticism, bars around people
made of racism, wounds inflicted by the barbs of intolerance
and bigotry – all of them betrayals of humanity. Human
rights are either the rights of all men or else they become a
meaningless façade for a bankrupt conscience. Civil liberties
are an empty slogan unless they guarantee every citizen freedom of opportunity to work where his talents best suit him,
to live wherever he may choose and to enjoy an equal partnership in the brotherhood of man.

Those who survive a tragedy such as the Holocaust cannot
keep silent, but must do everything in their power to testify
to the fact that life is the gift of God, and that it is sacred. I
recreated a family. I have devoted my energy to the building
up of my people. I also became and remain a kind of ethical
nuisance. Wherever there is oppression or hunger or brutalization, regardless of colour or creed, I consider it is morally
my territory and their cause is my cause. Bigots, racists and
fanatics are my personal enemies and I intend to do battle
with them until they become civilized, decent people, if needs
be for the rest of my life.

Time is short and the task is urgent. Evil is real. So is good. There is a choice. And we are not so much chosen as choosers. Life is holy. All life. Mine and yours. And that of those who came before us and the life of those after us.

Rabbi Hugo Gabriel Gryn, CBE
25 June 1930–18 August 1996

Appendix

WITNESS ACCOUNT

Major Cameron Coffman, Fort Thomas, Ky., Public Relations Officer of the 71st Division, visited Gunskirchen Lager on the afternoon of 4 May 1945, shortly after its liberation by American troops. The news release he wrote about Gunskirchen, which was published in several United States papers, is printed below in full:

With the 71st Division of the Third Army in Austria, May 4, 1945: Nazism at its worst was unfolded in stark reality before Doughboys of the 71st Infantry Division today when they stumbled upon a carefully concealed concentration camp six kilometers north of Lambach, Austria, which held 18,000 persons who were not true 'Aryan' or whose political opinions were contrary to Hitler's 'New Order'.

My days of reading about Hun atrocities were over. I visited that camp today. The living and dead evidence of horror and brutality beyond one's imagination was there, lying and crawling and shuffling, in stinking, ankle-deep mud and human excrement. The sight and smell made your stomach do funny things like an egg-beater churning within. It was impossible to count the dead, but 200 emaciated corpses would be a very conservative estimate. For the most part they had died during the past two days, but there were many other rotting bodies inside the barracks beside living human beings who were too weak to move.

It is practically impossible to describe in decent or printable words the state of degradation in which the German guards had permitted the camp to fall. Located in a dense patch of pine trees, well-hidden from the main highway as well as from the air, the site was well-suited for the slimy, vermin-infested living conditions that existed there. To call the camp a pig sty would be doing injustice to a self-respecting pig. The sight was appalling, and the odor that reached you a hundred yards or so from the camp site was nauseating.

Traveling into the camp along a narrow wagon road was an experience in dodging the multitude of dazed men, women, and children fleeing from the horrors of this living hell. The natural impulse of these people after the Americans arrived was one of hysteria – a desire to escape – to leave that place forever behind them. The road was clogged with hundreds, but many did not get far. Dozens died before they had gone but a few hundred yards from their 'hell-hole' prison, Americans soldiers cussed violently in disgust as their trucks roared past the grotesque figures in the ditches and shuffling feebly along the road.

As we entered the first building the sight that met our startled gaze was enough to bring forth a censorable exclamation from a sergeant who had seen the bloodiest fighting this war has offered. He spat disgustedly on the filthy dirt floor and left the building which was originally built for 300 but now housed approximately 3,000. Row upon row of living skeletons, jammed so closely together that it was impossible for some to turn over, even if they could have generated enough strength to do so, met our eyes. Those too weak to move deficated [sic] where they lay. The place was crawling with lice. A pair of feet, black in death, protruded from underneath a tattered blanket just six inches from a haggard old Jew who was resting on his elbow and feebly attempting to wave to us.

A little girl, doubled with the gnawing pains of starvation, cried pitifully for help. A dead man rotted beside her. An English-speaking Jew from Ohio hummed, 'The Yanks Are Coming', then broke out crying. A Jewish Rabbi tripped over a dead body as he scurried toward me with strength he must have been saving for the arrival of the American forces. He kissed the back of my gloved hand and clutched my sleeve with a talon-like grip as he lifted his face toward heaven. I could not understand what he said, but it was a prayer. I did not have to understand his spoken word.

Few of those remaining in the building could stand on their feet. The earth was dank and a chilled wind cut the smell of death and filth. Small fires of straw added to the revolting odors that filled the air. One man crawled over several prostrate bodies and patted the toe of my muddy combat boot in child-like manner.

Everywhere we turned the pathetic cry of 'wasser' (water) met our ears. An English-speaking Czechoslovakian woman told us that they had received no food or water for five days. The appearances of the starving horde more than verified her statement. A lieutenant stooped to feed one creature a bit of chocolate. The man died in his arms. That lieutenant, formerly an officer in the Czech Army, fingered his pistol nervously as he eyed a group of German soldiers forcibly digging a grave outside. I also pumped a cartridge in my automatic. As I left him there were tears streaming down his face. His mother was last reported in a concentration camp 'somewhere in Germany'.

Before our arrival conditions had been so crowded that all could not lie down to sleep at one time. Those with strength enough to stand took turns sleeping. The dead were buried in mass graves behind the so-called barracks, but the death rate became so high that unburied piles of dead remained with the living. Many of these unfortunates were using the corpses as pillows. I counted 27 in one heap in a dark pine grove in the camp area. It was not a pretty sight.

An unforgettable drama was enacted when a sergeant of our group of five raced out of one building, his face flaming with rage. The sergeant, a Jewish boy of Polish descent, had found three of his relatives lying in the filth of that barracks. They are sleeping tonight between white sheets for the first time in three years in one of the better homes in Lambach. Their diet of a daily cup of anemic soup has suddenly changed to eggs, milk, and bread. A Yank with an M-1 rifle casually drops in at regular intervals to see how they are faring.

Military government and medical personnel of the 71st Division were busy at work before we left the camp two hours later attempting to bring relief to the chaos of suffering the fleeing Germans had left behind.

Extended supply lines made the food situation a major problem until ingenious doughboys discovered a German supply train nearby. Captain William R. Swope, Lexington, Ky., assisted by an excited Austrian girl brakeman, drove the train onto a siding near the camp. Physical force was necessary for order when the first food lines were organized as it was the first these hunger-sated persons had seen in many days.

A scene on the return trip to Lambach was a fitting climax to the horror we had left. Two 'fugitives from hell' were ravenously tearing the entrails from a long-dead horse and gulping huge bites. Another sergeant, whose mother and father disappeared into a Nazi concentration camp three long years, ago, turned his head and in a tear-choked voice remarked: 'And Hitler wanted to rule the world.'

Quoted works

Berehovo-Beregszász Zsidósága Képekben, Tel Aviv-Netanya, 1989.

Herman Dicker, *Piety and Perseverance: Jews from the Carpathian Mountains*, Sepher-Hermon Press Inc., 1981.

Emil L. Fackenheim, *Jewish Return Into History: Reflections in the Age of Auschwitz and the New Jerusalem*, Schocken, 1978.

Viktor E. Frankl, *Man's Search for Meaning (Ein Psycholog erlebt das Konzentrationslager)*, Austria, 1946.

Anton Gill, *The Journey Back From Hell*, Grafton, 1988.

Foreword to *The Diary of Anne Frank*, Macmillan, 1995 (© Rabbi Hugo Gryn).

Melanie Phillips, *Observer*, 25 August 1996.

Livia Rothkirchen, *Deep-Rooted Yet Alien: Some Aspects of the History of the Jews in Subcarpathian Ruthenia*, Yad Vashem Studies Vol XII, Jerusalem, 1977.

The Seventy-first Came to Gunskirchen Lager, Atlanta, 1979.